Produced by Softwood Books, Suffolk, UK
Office 2, Wharfside House, Prentice Road, Suffolk, IP14 1RD

Text © Peter Barter, 2024
All rights reserved.
Without limiting the rights under copyright reserved above, no part of this publication may be reproduced, stored, or introduced into a retrieval system, or transmitted, in any form or by any means (electronic, mechanical, photocopying, recording or otherwise) without the prior written permission of both the copyright owners and the publisher of this book.

First Edition

Paperback ISBN: 978-1-0369-0209-4

www.softwoodbooks.com

HAVE YOU GOT A MINUTE?

Peter Barter

CONTENTS

Introduction	
1. Early Years	10
2. Holbrook	31
3. H.M.S Ganges (University of Shotley!)	53
4. To Wales and Beyond	69
5. H.M.S Bulwark - almost a world cruise	73
6. H.M.S. Dryad and H.M.S. Victory	85
7. Leading Seaman to Sub Lieutenant	89
8. H.M.S. Houghton, Woodbridge Haven, and Exmouth	99
9. A Lifelong Partnership	108
10. On Flying	116
11. The Transition from Flying, through Teaching	126
12. From Teaching to Bristol	136
13. On Dental Practice	146
14. Dentistry for Dogs!	158
15. The Harley Street Experience	162
16. The Move to Tattingstone	166
17. On Sailing	173
18. Cornish rebellion	186
19. Australia	196
20. A new Practice in Norfolk	206
21. Yacht deliveries	214
22. Our French Son	219
23. In search of the Irish in me	222
24. Spain and the Spanish Experience	225
25. On Art and painting	236
26. The Shotley Peninsular	243
27. The making of an unusual film	249
28. On Busking	254
Epilogue	261
29. Dentistry	266
30. Kidney Dialysis	269
31. Dahlias	273

INTRODUCTION

Every story should have a beginning, a middle and an end.

This story has a beginning, a huge and unwieldy middle but as yet, no end.

The object of this exercise was to complete the book before the end arrived, but since I'm not the owner of a functioning crystal ball, I am unable to predict when that might be.

This piece of writing is brought about, largely by regret.

My grandfather had not enjoyed good health after being gassed in the First World War. My mother had travelled extensively in the years between the wars and had worked for Mr and Mrs Winston Churchill and was at Glamis Castle when Lady Bowes-Lyon, (soon to become the Queen), came back from honeymoon. (We still have the fox-fur stole that Lady Bowes-Lyon gave to my mother as a leaving present). My Mum had worked amongst some amazing people (including the lady for whom 'Alice through the Looking Glass' had been written) but her experiences have never been written down. My father spent much of the war on convoy duty; the Atlantic Convoys, followed by the Russian Convoys up to Murmansk and then to Malta. He finished the war in the Pacific before the Japanese surrender. None of these experiences were recorded and he never spoke of them.

The sad thing is that other than these facts, I know very little of my parents' lives, nor that of my grandparents and I deeply regret not asking them to write it down. Of course, it is now too late. Had I taken the trouble to write down the tales of their lives, it would make fantastic reading.

Their lives were full of hardship, struggle, and determination to survive, often against all the odds. I never heard them complain — they were all very accepting of their lot and simply got on with life and did the best they could with the hand that they had been dealt.

My life, by comparison, has been easy and is much less noteworthy, but when my grandchildren reach the age at which I am now, life for them will be so different to what it is today, and to what it was when I left school nearly 65 years ago. I am therefore recording my little tale, so that, in years to come, should my grandchildren's children be sufficiently interested, they can have a look and try and imagine what life was like for their great-grandfather and his family,

My life has been formed and shaped by making the most of the opportunities that have come my way. They say that luck plays a big part in the life that one lives, and for me that is very true, for I consider that I have had more than my fair share. But having said that, it's often said that one creates one's own luck and I suppose that can explain how the opportunities that have presented themselves have been turned into positive experiences. I am aware that I've been very lucky, not only in the path along which I have travelled but in those who have walked beside me.

My travelling companions have been many and varied, and along the way I have made numerous friends from all walks of life and across many borders, and many of those friendships have survived for over 60 years. The family, however, is the most consistent companion – either in the form of my Grandparents, my Mum and Dad, Uncle Jack, then dear brother Leonard whose companionship has been beyond value. Pat, my beloved wife of now 53 years has been a constant source of support and love, without which much of what I write about would not have happened.

Then there are our children Sarah and Nick, who have at some time or other been steadfast and supportive on that particular stretch of the journey where they have held my hand - and continue to do so. Now I am accompanied and supported by my wonderful grandchildren

But as I slow down and the ones behind overtake me, I hope that the path my grandchildren will travel will be full of opportunity as it has been for me, or will it be strewn with difficulty and struggle? Zach (Bean), Lorca, Emily and Lucia and now Caspian, are a daily source of enormous joy, wonder and surprises with their interests, activity and progress along life's path. Their lives will be so different from mine and their achievements will be more noteworthy too, so hopefully, in years to come, they will write their own story and somewhere down the line, and in another world, I'll be able to compare.

Who knows what the future holds?

1
EARLY YEARS

I do not have a great recollection of my early years, but I think that not unusual, since not many of us have memories of life before the age of three or four. These were war years (I was born in 1940) so my earliest memories are of Suffolk in wartime England.

North Suffolk was a bit like an American colony, surrounded by airfields on which the American Air Force were the dominant presence. We were used to the constant drone of aircraft either taking off for sorties over the continent or returning to base after bombing raids over Germany, Holland and the Low Countries. Occasionally the sky was filled with aircraft who were not friendly, as this area was often targeted by bombers decorated with the German swastika. On one occasion, my grandfather, at the end of his garden with me in the pram was the target for a trigger- happy German. Fortunately, the bloke behind the gun was a very poor shot, or my granddad took appropriate evasive action and both the pram, and its occupant, and its minder, were unharmed and lived to tell the tale.

On another occasion, a bomb was dropped on the centre of Eye – just a hundred yards from where we lived. This must have been an attempt by the aircrew concerned to either get rid of their load before heading for home or they mistook Eye for somewhere of strategic importance. Those who know the area, and Eye in particular, will understand how ridiculous the latter suggestion is. Whatever the reason, the offending aircraft was too low, the fuse did not arm, and the bomb bounced from Broad Street through the front window and into the main shop of Nunns, the Tailors and Outfitters. It didn't explode, thankfully, and so was quickly disarmed and removed, the damage was repaired, and life soon returned to normal for the inhabitants of Eye.

Had the aircraft been a bit higher, so that the fuse could arm, the outcome may well have been disastrously different.

Later in the war, the area was the target for V2 flying bombs and I do remember their characteristic high-pitched whine as they lost height prior to hitting the target. At that time, we lived in rented accommodation in Castle Street -a two bedroomed cottage with a small garden, at the bottom of which stood an Anderson shelter. I believe that I am correct in saying that these shelters were distributed to every household for protection during an air raid. I remember having to run to the shelter or, if too late and the engine noise suggested the aircraft was quite close, plan 'B' was invoked, and we had to hide under the table in the kitchen. We all had gas masks too which we learned to put on with great efficiency. I lived with my mother and brother Leonard. Leonard was eighteen months older than me. He had been born in Portsmouth where Mum and Dad lived prior to the outbreak of the war. Dad was in the Navy and at that time, a Gunnery Instructor based at H.M.S. Excellent on 'Whale Island' as the Naval Gunnery School was called.

Mum and Dad after their wedding in Eye Church

As soon as war was declared Mum decided that she ought to relocate to Eye where my grandparents lived, as it was likely that Dad would be away at sea for most of the foreseeable future and Portsmouth was a strategically important target – and this is how things turned out. Dad spent all the war years at sea, mostly in small escort vessels on the Atlantic Convoys, followed by the Russian convoys, then the Malta convoys. After that he joined the aircraft carrier Colossus and finished the war in the Pacific fighting the Japanese. During this period when wartime Britain was at a low point, many children from London were evacuated to the countryside as the perceived threat of air attacks and bombing raids was becoming reality. Cousin Bruce, who lived in Croydon, was sent up to stay with us in Eye. Bruce's Dad (my father's brother) had been killed whilst serving as the Gunnery Officer of HMS Exmouth. Exmouth was blown up by a mine off the East Coast of Scotland and all hands were lost.

When the war ended H.M.S. Colossus came home from the Far East via South Africa and Dad thought that he would put some green bananas in his trunk and these would be nicely ripe by the time he arrived in England. This was the first glimpse that Leonard and I had had of our father, and I still remember him arriving home from South Africa with those bananas (and, if I remember correctly, a pineapple). I would have been six when I was presented with this strange fruit and invited to eat it. I must have appeared a most ungrateful wretch as I didn't find it attractive, and I certainly didn't want to eat it. As soon as the coast was clear, I discretely threw it into the stream at the bottom of my grandfather's meadow. Hopefully my father never discovered the true destination of that banana which he had so carefully transported from Cape Town. My Dad was only home for a short while before he had to return to his ship. This was 1947 and when he was promoted to Lieutenant Commander (a rare occasion for someone who started off as a sailor) he was then was sent out to Pakistan to help train the newly formed Pakistan Navy. He would have liked my mother to go as well, and take us kids, but she thought that it would be better for us to stay in England rather than go to an emerging Muslim country where schooling might be problematic. We were settled in school here and Mum thought that this was the best for us two boys. She was probably right, as we had a very happy childhood, despite the war and its' aftermath and rationing, and despite not having a father around.

Leonard, Skimp and me after a fishing expedition (with pike) caught with home-made rod.

Bruce, Leonard and me with Skimp and Mum at Meadowside

When Dad next came home, I was almost 10 and Leonard had just started secondary school and was not particularly happy. Dad had been appointed as the First Lieutenant of HMS Woolwich, the Depot Ship of the Reserve Fleet off Harwich. There were many ships laid up here, after being made redundant at the end of hostilities and the Ship's Company of HMS Woolwich were responsible for the maintenance of this 'mothballed fleet'. Dad knew about Holbrook and The Royal Hospital School, which was just a few miles up the Stour from Harwich, and he obviously thought that this might be the answer to the difficulties that Leonard was having at Eye Modern School, and to this end arranged for Leonard to start at RHS as a Boarder. I followed him as soon as I was eleven. As we were both away at boarding school we never really got to have a deep relationship with our father, and sadly didn't really get to know him. I cannot remember him ever visiting us at Holbrook despite the fact that, during our early years at RHS, he was stationed down the road at Harwich.

The war years were tough for everybody, and my Mum was no

exception, being a single parent with two young boys to bring up. But it wasn't as tough for her as it was for many others, as she had her parents close by. My grandparents lived in Eye, at 'Meadowside' and had lived there for many years.

Grandparents and 'Meadowside'

They had a very large garden - over an acre of land- and it was with them that I spent most of my childhood. I would visit them every day after school and at the weekends Leonard and I were expected to do the 'jobs' before being let off to play. Those 'jobs' were many and varied.

Cleaning out the chickens, digging the garden, unloading muck and tidying up the muck heap, weeding and hoeing, pruning the apple trees and gathering apples, cleaning out the heater for the greenhouse, getting the coal in, chopping sticks for the fire, pumping water from the well to water the plants in the greenhouse, painting the greenhouses in the summer and replacing broken panes of glass were just a few of the things that we were expected to do, depending on the time of year. Hedge cutting was a summer activity and there were plenty of hedges to practice on.

We didn't complain, as we had been brought up in the tradition that everyone made a contribution to the jobs that had to be done, especially when growing your own food during rationing years. By the time I was 15, I was certainly capable of doing any job around the house or in the garden and what is more, I enjoyed doing it.

The long hawthorn hedge that ran the full length of the property alongside of the road became my responsibility and I had to keep it trimmed and the ditch inside clean and tidy. I used to take great pride in clipping this hedge so that the top was perfectly level and the sides straight. It usually took a day to complete and once the cleaning up had been done and I remember standing back and admiring my handiwork and correcting any deficiencies that I had overlooked.

Granddad had been in the 'Buffs' during the Great War and was gassed in the trenches and was invalided out of the army in 1918. His exposure to gas had a long-term effect on his breathing and his heart, which restricted his ability to do heavy manual work, but he was able to cope with growing flowers and plants in his garden or greenhouse, and this gave him a small income to supplement his war pension. He also kept geese, chickens and ducks, so we were never short of eggs and every so often we had the luxury of a Roast Chicken for Sunday lunch. My grandfather looked after his livestock with great care and affection and when the time came for them to be slaughtered, he could never bring himself to do it. He had to pay a man to come in and kill the goose for Christmas or whenever the occasion arose.

There were no fridges or freezers in those days so various methods were employed to enable produce to be stored so that they could be used in the winter months. Runner beans were salted, eggs were placed in isinglass, plums and other soft fruit was stored in 'kilner' jars and jam and chutney filled the shelves. My grandmother was an expert wine maker so there was usually rhubarb wine in the pantry, maturing in an old oak barrel.

Although we spent much of our time at Meadowside, we actually lived in a small, rented cottage in Castle Street, next door to Tipple's Shoe Shop and Mr Tipple was our landlord. During the war we moved from that little cottage to 'Albion House' in Lambseth Street. This was also rented, but unlike the last cottage, our new landlady was Mrs Bishop who owned a General Store (the main one) in the centre of Eye.

Mrs Bishop had a large garden and loved flowers and relied heavily on grandad to supply her with all her bedding plants, tomato and vegetable plants as well as to do all her pruning and tend her garden occasionally. Grandad pruned the roses and fruit trees for many people in the town who had large gardens, and invariably took me along to help him clear up afterwards. Mrs Bishop was very fond of my grandfather and because of this, she let my mum rent Albion House for a very modest sum. It was lovely house with a nice, secluded garden and before we moved in, we went to look over it. There was ripe pear on one of the window ledges and I can still remember that smell and the joy at knowing that we had a pear tree in the garden. Albion House was closer to Meadowside than our previous cottage, so to get to 'Nan and Dad's' it was just a couple of minutes run up the road, and that is where we spent much of our time. Our childhood was a very happy one. 'Albion House' was a comfortable house (although not by modern standards!). There was no bathroom nor central heating and the outside toilet was through the coal shed. We bathed on Saturday nights in a big tin bath which mum had to fill with hot water from kettles and saucepans heated over the paraffin stove or from the 'copper' in the corner of the kitchen which was heated by a coal fire underneath it. My grandparents had a paraffin stove too and they did all their cooking on that. Despite its simplicity, this cooking method was quite efficient, and paraffin was relatively cheap and readily available from 'Beales' the ironmongers whose 'lad', Billy would deliver it on his bike. Billy was a man in his early twenties, and he was a keen gardener, who had an allotment as well as a big garden. Every year the Eye Show was eagerly anticipated by all the allotment holding and green fingered locals as this is where they could demonstrate their skills in vegetable and flower growing and perhaps win a prize or even a cup, in the various sections of the Show. Competition was keen. Winning the Cup for best Exhibitor carried great credence as skill in growing was much admired. Billy was a keen competitor and would often appear at my grandfather's gate to ask if he could borrow a plant or two from granddad's greenhouse to supplement his entries in the flower show. Many a prize had been taken and a cup won because of the secret inclusion of a specimen from the greenhouse at Meadowside! As children we also looked forward to the Eye Show. We were encouraged to enter vegetables that we had grown and wildflowers that we had picked, and, on several occasions, we were lucky enough to collect the odd prize of one or two shillings.

The Eye Show was eagerly anticipated for another reason. Uncle Jack lived in Felixstowe where he had a hairdressing business, and he used to come over to Eye about three times each year to see his parents and sister. The bus arrived at 11o'clock and we would always get very excited as soon as we got up at the prospect of seeing Uncle Jack later that morning. If the Bank Holiday was on a Monday, he would sometimes come the day before and spend the night at Meadowside and in that time he would help granddad with the heavy jobs, like renewing a gate post or replacing the chicken fence. After church on Sunday morning (which we had to attend as we were servers) we would run home and then to Meadowside and if we could smell pipe smoke as we ran up the path, we knew that Uncle Jack was there, and this added to our excitement.

Uncle Jack was a small man - perhaps no more than five feet tall. He was bald, he was quiet and only spoke when he had something to say, whereas his wife, Doris was quite the opposite. She spoke continuously and much of that was drivel. We as a family were 'quiet people'. My grandparents were not demonstrative and nor was my mother; voices were rarely raised and certainly nobody ever lost their temper, and during long winter evenings there were even longer periods of silence. But when Auntie Doris came it was quite different for there was no silence when she was in full flow, and everybody breathed a sigh of relief when they returned to Felixstowe.

The feeling was reciprocated I'm sure, for Doris only came occasionally - the odd Christmas and August Bank Holiday. When Leonard and I were small, Doris would bring their son John, who was a few years older than us. I sadly cannot remember much about John due to his very infrequent visits. But we did look forward to seeing Uncle Jack and I have often tried to find the reason for that.

Mum leaving Felixstowe after spending the day with Jack & Doris. (Doris in Pink)

If he had brought us gifts on each visit or if he was an entertaining personality that might have explained why he was so popular. But he didn't bring us gifts nor was he a great extrovert. He was small, quiet and undemonstrative but he was very wise. He didn't say a lot but when he did, it was worth listening to. He also had a great sense of humour and his 'one liners' were very amusing. He also had a reputation as a fearless fighter. He was small and the inevitable target for the school bullies. If they tried it on with Jack, they soon regretted it, as he fought many a much bigger boy and won the fight.

I suppose the treat that we always looked forward to, more than anything else, was really nothing more than an adventurous walk in the afternoon.

It was tradition in our family to go for a walk after Sunday lunch, like so many other families in Suffolk. There were many interesting footpaths in the countryside around Eye, and, as children, we walked them all. I suppose they averaged about five miles in length or more, but sometimes they felt a lot longer. I remember frequently being dead tired and wishing that we were back home. There is nothing like a good long walk to bring out a range of feelings and emotions even in a young child. The excitement at the start of the walk and when you discover interesting things - a pheasant sitting on eggs or running away with her chicks; a newborn calf or a moorhen's nest; the discovery of pigeon's nest with eggs in it or the frustration of not being able to find the nest belonging to the skylark that you have just put up. As the legs began to show signs of having had enough, the desperate tiredness that had been present for the last couple of miles would suddenly lift and thought of tea would again lift the flagging spirits.

When Uncle Jack visited, we really looked forward to going for a walk with him. He left Mum, Nan and Granddad at home and just took Leonard, me and the dog. Sally was a wire-haired terrier, a lovely placid creature who was my grandfather's constant companion. She lived to a ripe old age and was then replaced by 'Skimp', a Cairn Terrier. Skimp was always up for a walk and I've tramped many a mile with that little dog and when Jack came over, skimp too got excited as he knew that a long walk was in the offing. Invariably the destination was 'Waterloo Wood'.

Waterloo Wood was the most exciting place to walk (probably because we only entered it with Uncle Jack) and we knew when we set off that we were in for a really enjoyable afternoon. This ancient woodland was about two miles away surrounded by the fields belonging to Major Ridley. The river Dove, which we fished for roach, dace and pike, ran through the wood and the wood itself was virgin territory. The undergrowth enveloped us (as small children it seemed much worse than it was) and we frequently startled a pheasant sitting on a nest of thirteen or fourteen eggs or disturbed a moor hen from her nest. The mysterious darkness of that primitive forest was hugely attractive for small boys, and we were in heaven when Uncle jack took us through the wood on one his 'Sunday walks'.

At the far end of the wood the undergrowth began to clear as the soil became sandy and it was in this part of the wood that we searched for, and found, remnants of two American aircraft that collided in fog during the war. Most of the wreckage had been taken away but often we found bits of the fuselage or parts of instruments that we carried home as trophies. Even now, Waterloo Wood still holds that fascination and promise of excitement which it did in the times when Uncle Jack would take us for a walk.

Uncle Jack also used to take us fishing - in fact it was he who showed us the rudiments of the sport and it was with him that I caught my first Pike. I took it home to show my mother and grandparents and I was very proud of that success. Having written that, I now realise why we always looked forward to Uncle Jack's visits with such joyful anticipation - it was because he did things with us that my father should have done (but couldn't because he was away) and that my granddad couldn't do because of his ill health. We were always sorry see Jack go back to Felixstowe and would walk with him to the bus stop so that we could have the last few minutes of his visit with him. His visits were very precious and never disappointed.

Sometimes he came to visit us on his bike. He had an ex-paratrooper folding bike and he would pedal the thirty or so miles to Eye in a couple of hours. Years later, as a teenager, I spent the odd weekend with Jack and Doris in Felixstowe. When I became of age (to drink a pint) it was Uncle Jack who introduced me to the pleasure that could be derived from such activity!

Leonard and I were lucky in our childhood. There were no threats to us living in the countryside. Road traffic was infrequent, we lived in a rural area with square mile upon square mile in which to roam. As long as we respected the farmer's crops and buildings and did no damage, nobody challenged us. The rivers were always a great place to explore and a tributary of the Dove which ran along the bottom of granddad's meadow was a great place to play. We explored it, dammed it, bridged it and placed ropes to swing across it. The possibilities were endless and whole days were spent away from home just enjoying the freedom that the countryside offered and allowed. In spring I spent many hours, after school and at weekends birds nesting and collecting eggs. Of course, this is now banned, and rightly so, but then, it was an accepted part of growing up in the country and I had a beautiful collection of a huge variety of bird's eggs which I had found, blown (removing the yolk via a small hole in opposite ends), then mounted in a box on cotton wool and labelled. The skill and fun was to find the nest followed by the excitement of identifying the owner. We didn't vandalise the nests but took just one egg for the collection and only if we didn't have one like it.

Another item that was a source of great fun was a catapult. The fork was made of hazel wood as that was strong and the forks were regular. Elastic could be bought from the Ironmongers, and, with a little practice the resulting weapon could be used to great effect.

It is surprising how accurate a catapult can be after a little use. Shop bought ones, made with aluminium forks, were better of course but they cost money and that was in short supply. I became a very proficient shot with this primitive weapon.

As we got older, we had our bicycles and when considered proficient in riding our bikes, we were allowed to cycle to Diss. The attraction there was the cinema during the winter months and in the summer, the open-air swimming pool. Children's programmes were shown in the Cinema on a Saturday morning and that usually consisted of a cartoon, a short serial, followed by a children's feature film, often a Western. We were allowed to go only after we had done the jobs, so it was often an early start, clean out he chickens and clear out the greenhouse boiler and lay it ready for the afternoon lighting. Once the jobs had been done, it was off to Diss on our bikes with sixpence in our pockets for the cinema. Great times!

During the time we lived at Albion House, Leonard, who wasn't getting on terribly well at school, was sent away to stay with a friend of Mums in Bromley. It was argued, I believe, that Bromley school was better than the local school in Eye and if he had a few terms in Bromley, he'd stand a better chance of passing the 'Eleven -plus' (the required standard for getting into the Grammar School). Auntie Audrey was a frequent visitor to Eye where her Aunt Lily lived in Buckshorn Lane. Audrey's husband Charles had an Electrical business to run so didn't come that often and looking back, I expect that they only came during the school holidays. They had two children, Michael who was a year or so older than Leonard, and Barry who was probably my age. During the war years I suspect that Bromley was a less attractive place to live than Eye, so they spent a lot of time in Suffolk. We saw a lot of them especially at the various functions that the American Airmen laid on for the local children - Christmas parties and the like. I cannot say that they were close friends so when Leonard left to go and stay with them it was a miserable time for him. Miserable is probably an understatement as he hasn't spoken much about it, but I do know that he was very unhappy in that environment, and I don't think his education necessarily improved either. When he returned home, he then took the 11Plus exam and failed, demonstrating quite clearly that his time In Bromley hadn't improved matters. He was destined for a career at Eye Secondary Modern School. For him, that too was pretty unpleasant. He was small, just like granddad and Uncle Jack, and was undemonstrative and very quiet by nature and his glasses made him an automatic target for the bullies. At that time my father had returned from Pakistan and he and mum thought it might be a good idea to send Leonard to Holbrook. Leonard duly took the exam, passed, and soon became a boarder at The Royal Hospital School, Holbrook. Being the eldest, he was, I suppose, a bit of a 'Pathfinder'. He's the one who had to 'break the ice' and because of that, had the toughest of times. He never complained.

Whilst Leonard was in Bromley and then at Holbrook, I had the life of an only child, and I missed my brother terribly and I suppose that period of separation created the bond to my brother that has been a constant in the whole of my life. I was always very pleased when Leonard came back home for holidays because I was very lonely without him.

The Baileys lived opposite us in Lambseth Street. Reg Bailey, the father, was an egg dealer and game merchant and because of this had been excused military service during the war. He had capitalised on his good fortune and exploited the black market to the maximum advantage. At the back of their house was a warehouse, always full of rabbits, pheasants, hares, partridges and anything else that might make a few pounds when sold to either the Americans or whoever wanted to supplement their meat ration with something from Reg Bailey's warehouse and could afford to pay. Reg and Vera had three children - Alma the oldest daughter, Jackie, probably three years younger and Peter two years younger than Jackie. Peter was the problem. He was spoilt, ill disciplined, wilful and furthermore had a good command of the vocabulary of bad language that was in common use by his father. The Baileys were affluent but did not have the respect of the community, which is normally enjoyed by affluent families, because his affluence was derived from the black market during the war when many men were in the forces and away from home. Most people resented that affluence especially as he was a loud-mouthed man whose language left much to be desired. As I write this, this type of behaviour is more common now and is tolerated, but at that time, some sixty years ago, it was not.

But the Baileys had a car. Cars were a novelty at that time and their Austin 1800 was a top of the range machine. It was quite able to accommodate Reg and Vera as well as their three children and me, on frequent trips out to Diss Cinema or to the beach on a summer afternoon. I was often invited to join them on these days out not from any desire to give me an enjoyable experience, but simply that I would be company for Peter, and thereby, hopefully, would encourage him to be better behaved than he would have been without my presence. He was a spoilt brat over which they didn't have much control, and they hoped that my presence would distract him and keep him from being a trouble to them. I don't think this plan enjoyed the success that had been hoped, but his behaviour appeared to be modified especially when threatened that unless he did behave, I would not be allowed to come again. As a consequence of this enforced and unlikely friendship, I was exposed to the cinema and to many trips to the coast and other interesting places that would otherwise not have been available to me.

We didn't have a car, and the only trips to Southwold or Felixstowe that we enjoyed as a family were the annual Sunday School outings by bus. We would wait outside Mr Green's General store in Lowgate Street, at 8.30 in the morning, dressed in shorts and sandals and raincoat and carrying the treasured bucket and spade. These were home made by granddad - the bucket was an old paint tin, itself painted a bright colours for the occasion and with a wire handle if none had been present on the original. The spade too, was fashioned by my grandfather and mum carried the bag with sandwiches and drinks, spare clothes and that knitted bathing costume that I changed into as soon as we got to the beach. My poor mother suffered throughout her life from acute travel sickness which took hold of her whether in a car, a bus or train. So she knew, well before the bus arrived, that she was going to have a miserable day. She would be sick on the way there and sick on the way back. Most people would, by virtue of this affliction, exclude this form of travel from their holiday agenda. But mum was not prepared to spoil our day, and she put up with this wretched condition just so that we could enjoy the annual day out to the seaside.

Grandad made many of our toys too. He was quite a good carpenter and as money was short, Christmas presents were usually made by him. During a recent discussion on the radio about the money some parents spent on toys for their children, the presenter asked his listeners to phone in and tell him about their favourite toys, which they had received as children. This made me ponder on my childhood and without doubt, my favourite toy was an acorn 'pop-gun' made by my grandfather out of a piece of Alder. The Alder was used because up the centre of the 'branch' (that the pop gun was cut from) was a column of soft, foam-like material which could easily be removed. This left a hollow tube (the 'barrel' of the gun) into which a plunger could be inserted in that space. An acorn was pushed into one end and the plunger inserted in the other and quickly pushed the length of the 'barrel'. The air inside was compressed to a point at which the acorn could no longer hold it and the acorn projectile was then ejected at great speed. A wonderful toy!

The Sunday School featured prominently in our lives. In fact, Sunday was always a busy day. The first job was to attend High Mass at St Peter and St Paul, the Parish Church of Eye, where Canon Rae conducted the morning Service. We were servers so we had to take part in the theatricals of High Mass and being in charge of the Incense was a much sought-after position. Mum's friend, Mrs Leader, organised the Sunday School at the Baptist Chapel and we had to attend that in the afternoon and that was sometimes followed by another service in the Baptist Chapel in the evening.

Father Rae, the Vicar of Eye Church, was a wonderful man and I enjoyed the performance of being a server or swinging the incense boat. Much of the service was said in Latin and it was well known of the friendship between Father Rae and the Pope. As soon as the Easter day services were over, Canon Rae would pack his bags and head off to Rome for a fortnights holiday. I was very fond of him and would always visit him when on holiday from Holbrook.

At Mum's request he gave me elocution lessons to attempt to rid me of my Suffolk accent which was thought to be a handicap for a future career.

I would have to stand at one end of the nave in the church and read or recite passages of Kipling whilst he stood at the other end shouting instructions as to how to improve my diction.

The Chapel Sunday school was overseen by Mr Green who offered weekly prizes to the individual who could discover the origin of the weekly text. At home, I had a reference book called a 'Cruden's Concordance' or some such name and which was a dictionary of all the major Biblical texts. I collected many prizes and was feted as a diligent student although all I had done was to look up the text in the book that I had at home. At the back of the Sunday school were some sheds that offered excellent protection from prying eyes. This was the perfect location to have a go at smoking one of those black and gold cigarettes that my father had brought home from Russia. I now know them to be Black Sobranie and I duly took one from the silver box on the sideboard and a box of matches when we went off to Sunday school. Unfortunately, I didn't have an opportunity to light it up that afternoon, but when Sunday School was over, we went, as usual to Meadowside for Sunday tea. A short cut took us across the neighbouring meadow to the gate to granddad's property where we set about lighting up. My grandmother, always on the look-out for bad behaviour and misdemeanours by her grandsons, came out to see why we hadn't appeared when she thought that we should have been home by now.

We hadn't accounted for her incredible eyesight. From a hundred yards away, she immediately knew what we were up to, and the usual punishment was metered out. A couple of Christmases previously, we had each been given a toy rubber dagger as a present. There isn't much you can do with a rubber dagger, so it was soon discarded for more interesting and useful toys. Sadly, the rubber dagger wasn't put in the bin, it was taken into ownership by my grandmother and kept on a ledge just inside the sitting room door. This was a very handy and easily accessible place to keep a weapon especially when the grandson's behaviour got out of hand or unacceptable. A quick slap across the legs or any other exposed part of the body delivered a vicious sting that was never forgotten. Prior to the rubber dagger being used as an instrument for enforcing discipline, my grandmother had always kept a 'switch' in the same place. The 'switch' was a thin but very flexible piece of willow or ash or any species of wood that would provide sufficient flexibility to ensure that the recipient was is no doubt as to the reason behind its delivery.

We lived in fear of the rubber dagger as we did of our grandmother.

Ours was a matriarchal family - even my mother lived in grandmother's shadow, and many is the time when I had been told to be quiet or specifically to 'stop showing off' when I was just doing what most children are expected to do in today's society.

My grandmother had had a very hard life - she had been through two world wars and the depression during which she had a husband who was a war casualty. They lived in Peldon in Essex and the only work that she could get was as a seamstress.

Her particular forte was making shirts. She was given the material by the company she worked for which she then took home and constructed as many shirts as possible using a prescribed pattern. The completed articles were ironed with a flat iron, heated either on the fire or on a paraffin stove, wrapped up, placed in a redundant pram for ease of transport, then walked the ten miles or so to Colchester to head office. On one occasion they were not accepted because the ironing was not up to standard and my granny had to wheel them all the way back home, repeat the ironing and go back to Colchester before she could collect her meagre wages.

As Granddad got better, he was able to take up paid work and that took him, via several stops to Creeting St Mary where my mum was born and then to Stowmarket and finally to Eye. Granddad had secured a job working for Notcutts in Woodbridge and he was sent by the firm to lay out and construct a bowling green in the garden of a house in Church Street and whilst he carried out this work, he was allowed to live in the flat attached to the house. It is strange that I should now live in the house opposite the one that brought them to Eye, and I have seen the place where the bowling green once sat.

The local school was as good or as bad as any other post war primary school in rural England. The emphasis was upon discipline and working towards the 'Eleven plus'. I think there were 28 in my class, eighteen girls and ten boys. I was a chubby child whose nickname was 'porky' and because I couldn't run fast enough to get out of their way, I was frequently the target of the bullies. Strangely enough, the girls were as good at bullying as the boys and one family in particular, the Bloomfields, were quite adept at waylaying the smaller kids and giving them a good beating as a form of minor entertainment after school. Bullying is very much part of school life, so you had to put up with it. There was no point in threatening that 'my dad will come to your house' as my dad was miles away at sea, and they knew it.

Mr Bourne was a good headmaster, but he ruled the school with a rod of iron. Well, not exactly, because his preferred method was the use of his 'Malacca cane'. This conjures up an exotic instrument, but it was far from that. It was a short thick cane of about two feet in length and one-inch diameter. When wielded accurately it could inflict a memorable wound upon the recipient and I had experienced it on several occasions. One evening as we left the classroom to go home, I had obviously been responsible for some activity or had been involved in some incident that Mr Bourne didn't approve of. As he liked his caning to be witnessed by at least the class members, if not the whole school, and as this incident had occurred as we were all going home, Mr Bourne announced that I would be caned first thing in the morning. When caning is spontaneous one doesn't have time to think about it or worry, but when you have overnight to prepare, it takes on another dimension. When I got home,, I told my mum that I was going to be caned in the morning, so she spent all the evening sewing several layers of thick serge into the backside of my shorts.

When I bent over the next morning to receive my punishment in front of the whole school my bum must have looked huge. Mr Bourne was well used to seeing my bum prior to receiving the cane so it's a great wonder that he didn't comment on how it had developed overnight. He didn't comment, and I took his punishment with far less pain then normal, due entirely to my mother's brilliant needlework.

It was all worth it for I passed the Eleven plus and that enabled me to get into Holbrook to join Leonard shortly after my eleventh birthday.

Mum had always thought, rather mistakenly I'm afraid to say, that I had a musical talent which she felt it her duty to encourage. Maybe she felt that I had inherited my grandmother's musical ability but in another form. Nan had a wonderful singing voice, and she frequently entertained a full house at the 'Reading Room' (long since demolished) accompanied by George Edwards, a fine tenor. George was the butcher who was well-known to local music lovers for his splendid voice.

Mother took a cleaning job at the White Lion Hotel, to fund piano lessons for me, so that I could eventually play the old upright piano that sat forlornly in our front room. I started off with a teacher in Magdalen Street and duly turned up every Saturday morning for an hour's tuition. Every Saturday was the same. My lesson coincided with this lady's lunch preparation and every Saturday she had roast beef or lamb. I would sit at her piano and play as directed whilst she stood at my shoulder with her sleeves rolled up and the joint of raw meat in the hand. When I made a mistake, which was a frequent occurrence, she would hold the meat in one hand whilst picking up a ruler in the other and then proceeded to hit me across the knuckles with it. The smell of the uncooked meat is firmly engrained in my memory together with the effect of the ruler on my knuckles. I didn't make much musical progress and was duly switched to another teacher who lived a couple of miles away in Cranley. Miss Woods was the daughter of the miller who once ran Cranley Mill, and she was much kinder than the other one. The downside was that I had to bike to Miss Wood's and that involved going up Cranley Hill.

As hills go, Cranley is nothing more than a gentle slope, but when one is used only to the flat topography of Suffolk, Cranley is huge. So, come rain or shine, with head wind or not, every week I dutifully pedalled to see Miss Woods for piano lessons. To be fair she did get me through a couple of exams and my mum was well pleased but in reality, the progress that I made was pitiful and that was due entirely to my own lack of musical talent. Sadly (for my mum's sake) the piano lessons continued well into my time at Holbrook but despite all the money and time that was spent on my musical education it was all in vain. Perhaps that is too pessimistic for the basic education in music did enable me, many years later, to assist my grandchildren in getting their musical careers in motion.

During my last years at Eye Primary School my dad came home from Pakistan and was appointed First Lieutenant of the Reserve Fleet at Harwich. His base ship was HMS Woolwich to start with until that was replaced by HMS Tyne. The Reserve Fleet consisted of a collection of redundant destroyers and frigates that had been mothballed as there was no further operational requirement for them in Post War Britain. As long as peace was maintained then these fine old ships would eventually be destined for the scrap yard but whilst in the reserve fleet, although they were mothballed, they had to be kept in readiness for any future conflict.

HMS Woolwich was secured between two mooring buoys in the middle of the River Stour between Harwich and Parkstone Quay and it was to the latter that all motorboats to and from the Woolwich went. Stores and mail were brought on board by boat and the off-duty officers and men were taken ashore to Parkstone Quay by the same method.

It had always been assumed that when old enough, I would join the Navy, and this was frequently reinforced by my grandmother so Dad thought it a good idea if I spent a few days in the Woolwich to see if I could cope with navy life.

I was only 10 and didn't really know my father as he had been absent during the war and in Pakistan for three years after that. Anyway, I was taken on board and a suit was made for me and I was given a hammock in the seaman's mess and a Petty Officer by the name of Cowan was detailed off to look after me. He showed me around the ship then took me up the mast as far as the 'crow's nest' and generally took great care of me. I was shown the 'lower boom' where all boats are tied up to when not in use and instructed in the way to climb a rope ladder when descending into the boat and then coming back on board. Later than evening I was having a cup of tea in the mess deck when a sailor, who obviously didn't like the idea of an 'officer's kid' being there, flicked a cigarette end in my direction. Unfortunately, his aim was better than he had expected, and the fag end hit me in the neck and then fell inside of the 'white front' or tunic and by the time I had extricated it, it had burned me. He was most apologetic and probably was wetting himself in readiness for the wrath of the First Lieutenant, my dad, when he found out about it. I didn't tell my father as I knew there would be trouble and in any case the burn was not visible, so I soon forgot about it.

The next day was a Saturday, and I spent most of it aboard one of the MFVs that were used to transport stores and sailors to and from the ship to Parkstone Quay. An MFV (motor fishing vessel) is a slow, bulky and unattractive sea-boat but one which is a delight to drive, especially for a ten-year old. I was in my element and the coxswain was only too happy to let me drive it. Spending the week living as a sailor was an unforgettable experience for me.

2
HOLBROOK

I joined Holbrook in April 1951, a month or so after my eleventh birthday and, like all the other new boys or 'nozzers' arrived at the school three days before the start of the term.

This was so that by the time the school term started, and all the other pupils returned, we had been kitted out with our school uniforms and everything that we required for life in a boarding school. We knew where we would be accommodated, where the classrooms were and what to do and where to go whatever the situation or school requirement. We were all given the school standard haircut as well as basic instruction in marching. Holbrook was a school with very strong naval traditions and whenever a group of boys were required to get from one part of the school to another, they did so in an orderly group (three abreast) and marched to the destination. On getting up in the morning at 7am, everybody had a shower – nude (shower room with 30 spaces), then got dressed, made your bed (ensuring it was identical to those around and to the proscribed bed making formula with 'hospital type corners'). It was then time to 'fall in' in the muster yard (three deep and ten along) and after a few military sounding orders from the PO boy - the prefect- the group marched to the dining hall for breakfast. After breakfast, we returned to the house, where we were allocated jobs which had to be completed within the following 30 minutes or so. These jobs were basically 'housekeeping', and may have included, for example - polish the floor of the day room (wax polish); clean the brass work in the shower room (toilets and taps); sweep the muster yard; clean the windows etc etc. Once the jobs had been done, you went to the toilet, collected your books or PE gear, then 'fell in' again before marching off to Chapel.

Each morning we had a short service in the chapel - a couple of hymns, a prayer or two, a quick sermon from the Chaplain or a talk by a senior member of staff and then it was off to class. The route from the chapel to the classrooms was between the gym and the swimming baths. The smell of socks and sweat from the gym was only marginally less intimidating than the smell of chlorine from the pool. It wasn't the smells per se, it was what emotion that they engendered in the mind. In both cases it was fear, for neither the swimming pool nor the gym were happy places as far as I was concerned. They were run by ex-Naval PTIs (Physical Training Instructors) whose only qualification was an interest in sadism as applied to small boys.

I was very lucky when I went to Holbrook for not only did I have my dear brother Leonard there to guide me through, but our cousin Bruce had joined a couple of terms before me as well. When I think back, I realise how fortunate I was - Leonard had not had the advantage of an elder brother being there to protect him and being small, and wearing glasses, he didn't have a happy time.

Holbrook was truly comprehensive. Each year was divided into 5 or 6 groups, depending upon the numbers in that year. the top group was the Upper Stream (ie 4U) and the rest of the year was graded from A to D (or E if there was a big intake). This applied throughout the school except for the first year. The top class in year 1 was 1A and the class teacher for this privileged lot was 'Nobby' Lumsden, the deputy headmaster and maths teacher. Nobbys office was conveniently placed adjacent to the classroom, with an access door from the back of the class. Our desks were arranged in rows of 6 and there were 5 roe sat in alphabetical order from the front left (or right as seen by the teacher). As my name started with B, I was at the front and nearest to the teacher's desk. From the moment we were shown our seats on that first day, I felt very vulnerable and exposed, which indeed I was. Maths was to be my first lesson in my new school with Nobby Lumsden taking it. He was a small man with aggression to match, and from what little we had seen of him so far, we couldn't count on his humour or his empathy. Because it was so different in every respect from the cosiness of Eye National School, I could sense a mental block coming on.

The subject was fractions - that was Ok as I thought that I could cope with that – at least the addition and subtraction of fractions, but that wasn't all. The task in front of us was to convert fractions to decimals.

My mind went blank. It had seized up at precisely the same time as Nobby Lumsden looked at me and asked me what was, in all probability, a very simple question.

My brain was in lock-down. There was no way that I could provide the answer. To be fair to Mr Lumsden, he gave me all of a minute to answer. I didn't, and I couldn't.

The classroom was silent.

The more I thought about it, the hotter I became. I could sense no activity within my brain.

Mr Lumsden was not a patient man, not around the subject of elementary mathematics anyway. He had given up the idea of expecting an answer and his irritation with this new boy was evident in his face. As suspected, humour or empathy, sympathy or kindness was not prominent in his character.

He announced in a most matter-of-fact way, that he was going to walk into his office (via the door at the back of the classroom) get the cane, and, furthermore, if I hadn't come up with the answer by the time he got back, he was going to apply the said cane, three times, to my backside.

My heart rate must have trebled as he set off purposefully for his office door. Each one of his steps towards the door to his office echoed ominously , accentuated by the blakeys that he had on the soles or heels of his shoes. (Blakeys are bits of metal placed on the heels or sloes to take the wear and prolong the life of the shoes).

Fortunately for me, in the row behind was a small and very young mathematical genius. Not only had he got the answer, but he was also prepared to share it with me surreptitiously so that by the time Mr Lumsden returned brandishing the cane, I had an answer for him which I delivered hoping that the true source of the information would not be revealed, and that answer was correct. I was spared the cane although it now sat in a menacing way on the desk an arms-length from my seat.

It's funny how that first ten minutes of my very first lesson at The Royal Hospital School, Holbrook, is as clear today as it was sixty-eight years ago. It has been deeply etched into my memory.

If that lesson did anything for me, it made me want never to be unprepared again, if it could possibly be avoided. The seeds of a work ethic were sown at that moment and in that classroom. From that day on I was determined to work hard and avoid, if possible, any further embarrassment in front of my peers or a teacher that was due to lack of preparation which might then lead to more embarrassment or physical injury.

My life has been about being prepared!

I was allocated to Anson House along with Bruce and Leonard. The house was in two halves of 30 boys in the Junior half and the same number in the senior side. The housemaster, Cyril Fletcher lived in a flat between the two halves with his wife. There was also a House matron who was responsible for the welfare of all the boys. She looked after the linen, the supervision of clean clothes and repairs thereof and she held a surgery in the morning and evenings to deal with any medical problem that any of the boys had. She was a kindly face and sympathetic ear in what was otherwise a severe and harsh environment. In the depths of winter, when the unforgiving east wind would blow along the corridors and around the naked legs of the small boys as they marched between houses and dining hall or between classrooms. Chapped legs were what brought most boys to matron's door. Our shorts were made of serge and the edges were quite traumatic to the somewhat delicate skin of the inside of an adolescent leg. We all suffered, and the only remedy was a large dollop of thick castor oil cream applied to the distressed area by 'Tugboat Annie', the matron, after the evening shower.

I got on very well with Mr Fletcher but after I had been there two years he retired (or moved to another school). His replacement was a Mr Norman Worswick whose wife and daughter joined him in the house-masters flat. I didn't get on too well with Mr Worswick although to this day I do now know what I had done to upset him. Suffice to say that for the rest of my time at Holbrook I kept as far away from him as I possibly could and that seemed to suit both parties.

The school day consisted of four lessons in the morning with a fifteen-minute break. This break time was known as 'Stand Easy' when we were allowed on to the parade ground, where there were toilets, and where we queued up in house groups for a slice of currant bread. It was usually warm, straight from the oven and delicious. The first ones to appear on the scene collected the tray of bread from the kitchen and claimed the crusts from the end of the loaf. If you were lucky and the slicer had just skimmed the extremity of the loaf, the first slice to be made was the thick crusty bit and that was much sought after.

Thus fortified we returned to the classroom for another two sessions before going to our boarding house where we put our school- books in our lockers and once cleaned up we were ready for the mid -day meal. We marched to the dining hall and went to the house table and sat down to eat.

The tables were quite long; long enough to accommodate 30 boys. Food was brought out from the kitchen in large trays transported on trolleys and placed at the head of the table where the senior boys portioned it on to plates which were then passed down to the most junior boys at the far end. The size of the portion on the plate was in the control of the senior boy at the top of the table. Those at the far end who received their food first could only look longingly at the top end and dream of one day being in that exalted position where they could control the portion size!

Monday and Wednesday afternoons were spent in class whilst Tuesday Thursday and Saturday were spent on other activities which included time on the sports field, in the gym or in the swimming pool. During the summer we played cricket, did athletics or swimming. I was fortunate in that I showed an interest in sailing so learnt to sail in one of the three school boats. Because of that I was able to reduce my time on the cricket pitch and enjoy the relative freedom of the river in a dinghy. One of the masters had a MFV type boat. His name was Mr Sharpe and what he did at the school I really cannot remember. Anyway, he had this beautiful boat which was really too big for him to handle on his own, so he was always very pleased when Mr Worswick allowed me to crew for him. He was a natural teacher and took great pleasure in imparting some of his immense knowledge to my keen and absorbent brain. I learnt a lot from him and the foundation for the love that I have had for sailing and all things nautical was laid in Holbrook Creek with Mr Sharpe.

During the Autumn term we played soccer or rugby, and boxing was compulsory. Each boy was initially matched by weight to another boy in his house. I was quite big boned and heavy with it, and I was frequently paired with a much bigger opponent. Sometimes it all went wrong and on one occasion I had to box my brother. Each fight was of three rounds, each round of three minutes duration. I hated it. Three minutes seems a lifetime when you are being pummelled. I was the same weight as Reg Varnes, who even at that age had the physique of a body builder and who, when he left school, became a PTI, so it was an accepted fact that at the start of each Boxing session, I would go into the ring and have the sh... knocked out of me by Reg Varnes. The one time I fought Leonard, the PTI in charge became quite angry and threatened to punish us both unless we made a bigger effort to box.

Mr Worswick with a few from Anson House. Me on the left, Bruce front row on the right.

I elected to play rugby and eventually got a place in the school team at Under 14 and Under 15 level.

This was a great personal achievement as this meant that alternate Saturdays we would have away fixtures at other schools. If the opponents' school was a long way off (Gresham's, near Holt, springs to mind) an early start was necessary which meant skipping the last lesson and picking up a packed lunch for the bus journey. I played in the scrum, either second row or wing forward (as the position was known in those days), anywhere except the front row.

The spring term didn't include boxing, but we had the added delight of cross country.

There was no such thing as a short course.

One course was just longer than the other and sending the class on cross country was often an easy option for the PTIs who would use any excuse to get us away from the gym so that they could nip into the office for a fag.

East Anglian winters have never been enjoyable and all my winters at Holbrook were cold and miserable. One day, with a couple of inches of snow on the flagstones of the terrace, the PTI sent us off on cross country in shorts and skimpy singlet, socks and plimsolls. When we returned, he had us wait in the cold until everyone was back, then together we all had to do press ups on the terrace and in the snow until the lesson was over. Many of the class were in tears before the end, much to the amusement of the PTI. He may have had a Masters in Sadism.

Bad weather was never an excuse for not taking part in a sporting activity. We turned out irrespective of gales, monsoons and snow. I think it was taken, by the staff, as an admission of weakness on their part if they agreed to cancel a sporting activity. It was the same in the swimming pool and, as a consequence the stench of chlorine is something that I cannot forget for it is etched in my memory in the 'unpleasant' file.

When new recruits had their first swim, nobody appeared interested in whether we could actually swim or not. The question was never asked.

Instead of making that obvious enquiry, we were all lined up, in the nude, (for that was normal procedure) at the base of the diving board. It wasn't the top board, but to most of us it was terrifyingly high. Although I thought that I could swim, (after all I had been to Lowestoft three times and I felt quite confident as I demonstrated to movements of 'swimming' within sight of my mother sitting on the beach), my stomach took many serious turns for the worst when, on this, our first visit to the pool, we were lined up at the foot of the 3 m diving board and told to jump in.

PTIs with 'boy catchers' - long poles with a metal hoop at the end - stood around the deep end to fish out the unfortunate little fellows who really couldn't swim. Those who required fishing out were automatically selected for the 'non-swimmer' classes. Those that made it to the side unaided were accredited with the dubious honour of being a 'swimmer'. I was in this lot, although I might have preferred it if I could have been in the 'non-swimmers' for a while. At the same end as the diving boards was a water slide. It looked more horrifying than it was. After a while it was fun to use but that didn't apply to the other apparatus that graced the Olympic sized pool.

Between the diving boards at the deep end, and the other, shallow, end where the non-swimmers huddled, was a device that consisted of two platforms, suspended 14 feet above the water with wobbly steps that accessed them from the side of the pool. Between these platforms, suspended from the roof, were two trapezes - something that most of us had never seen before, (unless of course we had been lucky enough to attend the circus).

We soon learnt what this circus apparatus was doing in the swimming pool and equally quickly discovered that the trapezes were not there for our amusement, nor for our pleasure, but just another variation of the sadistic activities that the PTIs could bring to bear on us little boys.

A PTI stood on each platform whilst the naked and terrified individuals, queued up to mount, in turn, the wobbling steps up to the first platform. On arrival at the platform, the boy took hold of whatever was available to steady himself (usually one of the wire stays that stabilised the platform) whilst the PTI hooked the nearest trapeze with a pole and brought it within a long arm's length of the platform. On the other platform the other PTI, his partner in sadistic activity, did something similar.

The idea was that the PTI on this platform would command the boy to lean/jump out and catch the trapeze bar whereupon he (the boy) would swing out in the direction of the other platform. As he started on his swing, the PTI on the other platform would let his trapeze go, so that at the furthest point of both arcs of swing, at the midpoint between the two platforms, when the trapezes were at their closest, the boy would let go of his trapeze and grasp the other one, and, transferring his weight and body to the second trapeze, would let go of the first one and swing to the second platform and in to the arms of the smiling, second PTI.

The smiling PTI, whose job it was to catch the boy and haul him on to the platform, frequently demonstrated another level of sadistic interest. The poor innocent boy, believing that he had enough momentum to get to the platform with a little assistance from the PTI, often found that he was 'just not quite close enough' for the PTI to catch him and his only way out was downwards.

As you can imagine, there were many opportunities for error or accident and each one would be rewarded by the need to return to the first platform and have another go.

If you missed the first connection, (on platform one) you fell in and at such an angle it hurt and the trapeze returned empty to the first platform; if, at the mid-point of the swing, you missed your hold on the other trapeze or the timing wasn't right, the same thing happened, and you plummeted downwards. If, on arrival at the second platform you failed to be held by the PTI then your destination was the same. We soon learnt that it was wise to try and get it all done properly the first time for if the PTIs had plenty of time, a failure to arrive at the second platform meant that you had to have another go. We soon learned that it was less unpleasant in the long run if we could get to the other platform without getting wet, but at most times, when the odds were heavily against you, this was very difficult to achieve.

There were times of course when, with the best will in the world, and due most probably to the high level of fear that lurked in our heads as we entered the swimming pool, things didn't go according to plan.

And this occurred frequently on the trapeze, especially when we sensed that the PTI was in a bad mood.

The boy on the first platform would try extra hard to catch his trapeze and start his journey but when he had caught the incoming trapeze with his free hand, instead of letting go with the other one, he retains his grip on the first one.

He is thus suspended between the two – one hand has a hold of the trapeze whilst the other has a firm grip of the platform on which he is standing.

There are several ways in which this situation gets resolved. Usually the irate PTI on the other platform uses his pole to bring his trapeze back and when the noise level in the pool has dropped and he has the attention of the terrified boy who is holding the other one, the PTI instructs (demands) the boy release his hold on the platform and as the trapeze plus boy start their journey across the water, the PTI releases his trapeze intending (hoping) that it will be caught by the airborne boy.

Both trapezes are stationary; both PTIs are fuming, and the shouting starts. He, the unfortunate one, is suspended in all his glorious nakedness between two trapezes which are now pulling his arms out of his sockets.

It seems an eternity, but eventually he has to fall.

It is not the fall that is the problem, it's facing the wrath of the PTIs when getting out of the pool.

One PTI, whose nickname was 'Ichabod' carried a strip of rubber in his belt. This piece of rubber (affectionately known as 'Betsy'), was once the operational end of a large industrial 'squeegee', used for clearing surface water from the pool edge and when put to use to inflict pain on the bare bottom of a small boy, was very and painfully effective.

If Ichabod was in charge when such an incident as described above, occurred, one knew what to expect. The whole trapeze experience did little to encourage the use of the pool and often enhanced and amplified the fear of water in the many boys who had little confidence in their ability. Thus, the love of the swimming pool in general; of the trapeze in particular was eradicated from the thoughts of most eleven and twelve-year old at Holbrook, especially if they were short in stature. Imagine, if you will, being a short, eleven-year-old who had just learned to swim, being told to take up his position on the trapeze platform with the PTI waiting for him on the other one. Firstly, and most importantly, the terrified eleven-year-old knew, from the start, that there was never any chance of him making a success of this manoeuvre simply because he was too short to reach the first trapeze. Of course, the whole experience made them suspicious of the benevolence of a smiling PTI. They were probably scarred for life, and that is why the RHS swimming pool, originally intended as a source for recreation, was an instrument of fear in many of the boys who had to use it.

Each evening, we had homework.

This was set for us during the day, and we had to go back to the classroom after tea for two hours to complete the homework. The classroom block was patrolled by the duty master who prowled around ensuring that we didn't talk or mess around. Once the homework period was over, we returned to our houses to spend the rest of the evening preparing for the following day. Completing any unfinished homework, swatting up for a test or exam the next day were the usual activities, but if you were lucky enough to have no other pressing commitment, you could go and play on the playing field if it was light enough. We had no television although we did have access to a radio, and we had a table tennis and a snooker table if we had the time to use them.

We did however, have a cinema.

On alternate Saturday evenings, during the autumn and spring terms, a film was shown in the assembly hall and attendance was compulsory. The hall was poorly heated so when it was cold, there was a serious competition to sit as far away from the doors as possible, but even in the centre of the hall the temperature hovered at best a few degrees above freezing.

Because of the popularity of the cinema, the threat of detention during the week before was at its most acute, so generally the behaviour of everybody was improved until the film had been shown.

The punishment regime at Holbrook was tough. Badge boys (prefects) were allowed to administer the 'nimble' (a gym shoe) and the housemasters and Headmaster, the cane. At a lower level there was detention or stoppage of some privileges like shore leave on a Sunday afternoon. Some teachers had their own pet punishments and on one occasion I had a taste of Mr Markham's preferred deterrent to indiscipline.

As I remember, Mr Markham, the metalwork master, was on duty when I was late for a class. As a punishment I had to come to the metalwork block every morning during break (thereby missing out on the much-loved slice of currant bread) until I had completed the assigned task.

He presented me with a steel block, four inches long, an inch wide and four inches deep. With a scribe, he placed a line along the four -inch face to a depth of about a quarter of an inch. He also gave me a hammer and a cold chisel. I was told that as soon as I had reduced the height of the block to the line so marked, I could return to enjoy the mid- morning break.

It wasn't easy, especially after the first day the chisel's edge became blunt and this deteriorated daily. I think it took about a week and I was glad when I had completed the task. Some years later I met Mr Markham (when I was then a member of staff) and reminded him of that time. He said he couldn't remember it. I did!

We had no half term break, so each term was roughly a twelve -week block of purgatory. The best day of the week was Sunday, not least because we had a lie in till 8 o'clock and for some reason the food was more palatable at the weekend. We had a roast dinner on a Sunday which was always something to look forward to unless you were at the lower end of the dining room table when it probably wasn't as nice as what was served to the top.

After breakfast on a Sunday we had to get ready for Divisions which were held on the Parade Ground come rain or shine. Only in the most severe of meteorological conditions were Divisions cancelled and then they were held in the corridors to the school blocks.

We had to wear our No1 suits with highly polished shoes, pressed collars, silks and white fronts (the naval ratings uniform). The school band would play well rehearsed, and over exposed tunes, and we would have to form up on the parade ground where each house would be inspected by a designated master. Once that was over, we marched around the parade ground in sequence and as we passed the saluting base we would give an 'Eyes Right' and the Petty Officer boy in charge would salute the Inspecting Officer on the Dais whilst our faces were turned towards him. Once past, the order would be given for 'Eyes Front' when we would return to looking ahead and thinking only of getting off the parade ground and what was for lunch.

After Divisions, there was Church. We had a super Chaplain who was sympathetic to our predicament and preached short sermons. We dreaded visiting clergy for they seemed to take advantage of the captive audience and drone on for hours. But our Chaplain, Padre Newman, was good. He was young, approachable, had a great sense of humour and was liked by everybody. He was a sportsman too. He took Confirmation classes for the second year, and I enjoyed those, and when I was confirmed, I had my granddad, mum, and Father Rae from Eye all in the congregation to witness my Confirmation by the Bishop of St Edmundsbury.

Neville Bartlett, the geography teacher was the organist. The organ in our Chapel was a most beautiful instrument and was acknowledged to be one of the best organs in the country. People would come from all over the country to play it. Neville Bartlett, a dour old bugger at the best of times except when he sat at the organ stool. He could fire that instrument up so that to sit and listen to him would cause one's soul to be elevated to another plane. At least, that is how I felt about listening to it being played.

After church we went back to the house and changed into our everyday uniforms, unless we had other things planned and we had another chapel service in the evening on a Sunday.

Leonard (standing)
Bruce (on the left) and me – probably on a Sunday afternoon

In the summer term, Sunday afternoons could be spent on the

playing fields (there were about 35 acres so no shortage of space), or we could go swimming if the house master on duty had booked a slot for our house and furthermore was prepared to supervise us and act as lifeguard. Sometimes, depending upon the tides, we could go sailing or, if we didn't feel like any of that we could stay in the house and read.

I was the proud possessor of a small radio which was tuned by turning a condenser and the signal, when actually received was incredibly weak. Despite this, I spent many a Sunday afternoon on the playing field with my radio attached to the barbed wire fence hoping that this would encourage a stronger signal which in turn would allow me to listen to the transmissions of 'Radio Luxemburg'.

We were allowed out with our parents or relatives if they came up on a Sunday and occasionally, we could go into Holbrook on our own. Mum would come over on a Sunday about once a term and take us out to tea in Stutton. It was a difficult for her as she didn't have a car and the buses to and from Eye were not very frequent. It was always good to see her for she brought loads of buns, cakes and other lovely things which we kept closely guarded in our lockers until the last crumbs had been eaten. Bruce's mum, Auntie Hazel used to come up from Croydon too. Bruce's dad had been lost at sea whilst serving in HMS Exmouth (as a result of a blunder between the Admiralty and Coastal defences). HMS Exmouth was heading North up the East coast and was blown up by a British mine which she had not been made aware of. There were no survivors.

Auntie Hazel had a tough time bringing Bruce up alone, as living in south London throughout the war had its own problems. I think Bruce also had a tough time at Holbrook. He too was small of stature and very gentle and undemonstrative by nature. He wasn't particularly good at sport but was a great trier. Bruce struggled a bit with academics too, principally because of being Dyslexic. This was unheard of at this time, and he was just considered slow, or thick or not trying hard enough. It was only later, when he went to train as a teacher that he received a diagnosis. Knowing now of his disability, I think Bruce worked incredibly hard and achieved a very standard through his own perseverance and determination. It must have been very hard for him.

He spent most of his time in the 'B' stream, but always working towards getting up to the 'A' stream but all was well eventually as he became a teacher and retired as a Headmaster of a large primary school in Southend. He was keen on the outdoor life and spent some of his free time as a member of the Mountain Rescue service in Snowdonia and the Lake District. No doubt Holbrook had been a good grounding for that sort of activity and the comprehensive system of education certainly benefited children like Bruce. Unbeknown to us, Bruce kept all the letters he had received from his mum whilst at Holbrook, and she had kept all the ones that she had received from Bruce. These letters now form a very important archive at RHS for they show very accurately what went on in a pupil's mind during his time at RHS. Bruce was very unhappy, and his Mum wrote to the then Headmaster informing him that she was going to take Bruce away from Holbrook. He wrote back to her saying that HE would decide what was best for Bruce, not her, and Bruce would remain a pupil at RHS!

In truth and in many respects, it was good for us all. No matter what class a child was allocated to on their arrival, if that was not a true reflection of their ability and this was endorsed by a good mark in the end of year exams, they would start their next academic year in a higher stream. It was truly comprehensive. I think Leonard started out in the 'A' stream but by the time he left he was in the upper stream and collected a handful of 'O' levels'

The school had originated as a charity school for sons of sailors and was based in Greenwich but in 1934 the site upon which it now stands was bequeathed by a Mr Reade to Greenwich Hospital for the purpose of building a school. Since my time there, it has been added to and developed and now ranks amongst the best schools in the country. The location of the school, overlooking 35 acres of playing field adjacent to the river Stour, are complimented by academic and sporting facilities which are second to none. It is now a co-educational fee- paying school and a member of The Headmasters Conference, but previously it was a charity school for sailor's sons. The 'military' side of school life was taken care of by the Senior Naval Officer - in my time a Major from the Royal Marines, Major Buckley. He was the epitome of a Royal Marine

- smart, athletic, proud of his Corps, a stickler for discipline and a meticulous planner. He was responsible for maintaining the ceremonial side of the school, and for ensuring that we all behaved in a manner that resembled a fully trained and disciplined ships company. There was no relaxation of the strict code of behaviour and at all times, and in all weathers, he expected us to conduct ourselves in a smart and seamanlike way.

On the parade ground, on the side facing the river Stour, there was a fully rigged mast of maybe one hundred feet tall and at the base of which was a concrete structure called 'the ship' inside of which was the shooting range. Fortunately, by the time I had arrived at the school, the mast was deemed too dangerous to climb but we all received instruction and practice on the firing range.

We learnt how to shoot competitively with .22 rifles, and I found that to be a most enjoyable way of spending an afternoon. The rifle range was run by an ex-Petty Officer of the Gunnery Branch and his other duties included the drilling and practising of the ceremonial guard. The Guard consisted of about 30 boys selected for their bearing and marching skills who could also demonstrate the ability to carry a .303 Lee Enfield rifle in a variety of interesting positions, whilst dressed smartly in No1 uniform with white belt and gaiters. The guard paraded at divisions on a Sunday and at other times when ceremonial duties required it. To be part of the guard was a great honour and there was much competition to be selected. I was fortunate in that I had a long spell as a member of the guard and enjoyed the fun of rehearsing and preparing for the big occasions.

As the end of term approached, the excitement of the forthcoming holidays began to build so there wasn't much work done in the final days of term. At the end of the summer term, we had had end of year exams, and our reports had been made out and sent to our parents. If we had done badly, it was probable that we would be put down a stream for the next year. Fortunately for me that was never an issue. Although I was the youngest in the class, I was usually in the top three of the class. If I wasn't top, I would be very disappointed, so I tried to make a bigger effort next time.

When the day came to go home, buses were hired to take everyone to the nearest railway station at Bentley. There isn't a station there now, but then, it was a small stopping point on the Ipswich to London line and on the day we broke up for our holidays, a special train was chartered to take the majority of the school to Liverpool Street from where they went their different journeys to their homes. For the first year I was at school, we lived in Eye, so I missed out on the train trip as I went home on the bus. Then my father was transferred from the Reserve Fleet in Harwich, to become the Wardroom Mess Secretary at the Royal Naval Air Station, Culdrose in Helston Cornwall and we lived in a 'married quarter' near the base.

Although a special train was chartered for the majority of the boys, those who lived in far-away places were allowed to leave school a day before the rest because of the travelling time to their home address. Thus, boys whose parents lived in Scotland, Ireland, North Wales or Cornwall, got away from school a day early. the downside of course was that we had to leave home a lot earlier than the rest at the end of the holiday to ensure that we were back at school in time.

Holidays in Cornwall were fantastic. Dad's job included overall responsibility for the Air Station farm which included a herd of breeding sows and a unit where the pigs were fattened before sending them off to market or the slaughterhouse. There were several acres of arable land on which they grew potatoes or other root vegetable. Swill was collected daily from the Air Station kitchens and mixed with pig meal to produce a very inexpensive food for the animals whilst disposing of all the unwanted food and waste from the base.

By virtue of this 'agricultural' part of his job, Dad had met several local farmers and became quite friendly with Sidney Knowles, who lived with his wife Marion and their two daughters Patricia and Mary in Manaccan on the Lizard Peninsular. On our first holiday, when Dad had just taken up his posting, and before he had been allocated a married quarter, we spent the entire holiday at 'Choon Farm' with 'Uncle Sidney and Auntie Marion' as they became known to us. That was the beginning of a long and enjoyable friendship which continued for many years and Sidney and Marion were God Parents at the Christening of my daughter Sarah fifteen years later.

Uncle Sidney believed in working hard and playing hard. Although we were only 11 and 12, we were expected to contribute to daily life on the farm. We learned how to milk the cows and feed the pigs and had to help with getting the cows in from the field and putting them back out after milking. With Patricia and Mary who were the same age as us, we would go to the beach at Kennack sands, or Cadswith, Mullion or Sennen Cove or pick cockles at St Anthony, or take a boat up Frenchman's Creek and fish for mackerel, or ride the carthorse, Albert up and down the lane by the farm. At the weekend the barn would be cleaned, and Dad would set up his 8mm film projector and screen. With bales of hay to sit on, many villagers from Manaccan would come and watch a film that Dad would hire and all would have a thoroughly enjoyable evening. Dad would often show some of the films that he had taken when in Pakistan or he would hire Tom and Jerry Cartoons, or the old silent movies and the audience would love it. They were happy days.

When our next holiday was due, Mum and Dad had moved into a married quarter, so we didn't spend so much time with Uncle Sidney as we had done, although we saw them quite a bit.

The next summer we were that much older and were expected to earn some pocket money. Our first job was potato picking on the Air Station farm - I believe we got paid ten shillings a day which was really quite good money.

Dad was friendly with the local vet, Norman Dinsdale and he kindly took me out on his rounds which were very interesting as we visited many different farms where he attended to the sick and dying animals. Another of Dad's friends was a very keen sailor and he took me to crew in many races during the holidays. Wherever there was a regatta I would be taken there as there was bound to be someone who needed a crew. Fortunately for me, what knowledge I had acquired at Holbrook stood me in good stead and ensured that I didn't make a fool of myself amongst these Cornish kids who lived on the water, and all had their own boats. I sailed a lot and met many people.

On one of the last holidays we had in Cornwall - I think it was when Leonard was about to leave Holbrook, Dad got us job weeding anemones. These were grown in fields, and we had to weed them by hand.

It was pretty daunting task, starting one end of the field, working two or three rows at a time until you had reached the far end of the field when you turn around, and started again on the next three rows. The farm was at Constantine, near Helston and at that time, RNAS Culdrose was a very busy airfield. It was home to many of the Navy's jet aircraft and was the training base for Observers (aircraft navigators).

Our anemone field was immediately beneath the flight path for aircraft returning to Culdrose, so I watched many planes come in to land from this vantage point. From that time the seeds were sown that led me, many years later to try and make a career as a naval pilot and the memory of that time is deeply embedded in my brain - both the aircraft coming in to land and the endless rows of anemones which needed weeding.

The deal was that we were paid ten shillings a day; we brought our own lunch, but the farmer's wife provided the pudding. This was invariably tinned peaches and clotted cream but in the middle of the day it was very well received.

At the end of the holiday, the train journey back to school was always a sad time as neither of us were very enthusiastic about returning to Holbrook. The closer we got to the school the less we talked and the more miserable we became. This wasn't entirely the fault of the school or the fact that our housemaster was Norman Worswick, but to a large extent was due to the amazing time that we had enjoyed in Cornwall, which neither of us wanted to leave.

When I came up to the fifth form (and I was the youngest in the class), there was much pressure from my Mum and Granddad for me to stay at school and take my 'A' levels and then perhaps go to university and study medicine. The argument for this course of action was reinforced by the fact that I was usually either top or second at the end of term or end of year exams. This appeared to indicate, to some people at least, that I could have a good future if I was to use my brain for a bit longer in school. Unfortunately, I was not happy at school. As each new term started and the bus bringing us from Ipswich to Holbrook came to the village of Freston, as it turned right to Holbrook at the top of the hill, at the junction by the water tower we got our first glimpse of the school spire. Oh how that memory is ingrained in my brain for with the sight of the school tower, my heart sank to a depth of depression that I will never forget for it meant the beginning of another twelve weeks of misery with no relief. Although I was made a 'Petty Officer Boy' (a prefect) it made little difference to how I felt about the school and my mind was fixated on how I could leave with as little hassle as possible.

Historically, the school was geared up to producing sailors. The classrooms: the curriculum, the Naval Routine, the tradition of the school was intended to encourage boys to join the Royal Navy. Until recently, everyone HAD to join the Navy, either as a boy seaman or through the Artificer Apprentice route, or through Dartmouth. Now of course boys were free to pursue whatever career they liked but because of the historic and traditional link between the school and the Navy, I felt that to go down this route would have the least opposition, especially as, when I was very young it was always assumed (for what reason I still don't know) that I would follow in my father's footsteps. I was brought up to believe that I 'would follow your father and go into the navy'. My grandmother was largely responsible for this, and she used this in a derogatory fashion whenever I did something that was not to her liking. 'You are just like your father' she would say and that was never considered to be complimentary.

After I had taken my O levels, the careers master tried to persuade me to stay on at school, which is what my mum wanted too. Mr Worswick, the housemaster thought that I was perfectly suited to a career in the Merchant Navy and to that end I had to take the entrance exam for HMS Worcester, the cadet training ship for Merchant Navy, which I passed. But I was not very enthusiastic about that either although looking back it might have been a very interesting career as post war, there were many famous shipping lines covering every port of the British Empire. However, Major Buckley sent for me, and I told him of my desire to leave and that I did not wish to stay at school to take the entrance to Dartmouth once I had taken my A levels. His advice to me was that should I go to Dartmouth, I would be a small fish in a big pond. If, however, I decided to join HMS Ganges, as a boy seaman, I would be a large fish in a small pond. Although he got the metaphors wrong

(Ganges had more recruits than Dartmouth and Ganges was a bigger pond!) I knew what he meant.

At the next opportunity I went to the recruiting office in Ipswich and signed on as a Boy Seaman and I was due to join HMS Ganges on 6th September 1955. My mother and grandparents were bitterly disappointed, but I promised them that I would get to Dartmouth but by a different route. I'm happy to say that that was a promise that I was able to keep.

An Afterthought!

Now that three of our grandchildren have been to Holbrook (Bean has gone on to York University and Lorca and Lucia are still there and doing well), I can now look at the school and see how it has evolved into one of the finest in the country and our grandchildren have benefitted hugely from the generous Bursaries that Greenwich Hospital provide for sons/grandsons of seafarers. The normal fee would be in the region of £28,000 per year per child, so to have three children there for a total of 16 academic years brings the total to an eye-watering £448,000, all because I spent 12 years in the Navy! That was time well spent!

Emily (on the left) with Bean (the big one) and Lorca and Lucia at RHS.

Sadly, there is a downside to Boarding School and we now have had some experience of this, both through my own time at RHS and with Lorca. All it takes is one bully or one abuser to turn the whole experience on its head and I wonder what the percentage of pupils is who go through the Holbrook (or Boarding) experience anywhere without some emotional or mental scars. Many of us just bury it and move on but for some it must have a profound and lasting effect that essentially, leaves scars for life.

3
H.M.S.Ganges. (University of Shotley!)

In 1955, H.M.S. Ganges was a training establishment for the Royal Navy, specialising in the training of Boys for the Seaman and Communications branches.

It was situated on a promontory at the confluence of the rivers Stour and Orwell in Suffolk. There were 1000 recruits there at any one time, all aged between 15 and 16. The school leaving age was 15 and for most of the boys a career in the Royal Navy was the first choice on leaving school.

For some however, (the more criminally inclined), this was a 'second chance' - an alternative to Borstal or a corrective training institution and the decision to come to Ganges was usually supported and encouraged by their parents, the local constabulary or Magistrates or possibly all three. Under those circumstances, this was an opportunity for the fifteen -year old, to 'go straight'.

On 6th September, 1955 a special train had been laid on from Liverpool Street station for all those arriving from London and further a-field but as I was a 'local' I took the No14 bus to Ipswich and from there the one for Shotley. I was met by a duty Petty Officer who directed me to the 'Annexe' - a satellite of the Ganges site devoted to the training of the new recruits. It was situated on the opposite side of the road to the main site and well hidden from inquisitive passers-by. It had accommodation for maybe 200 new recruits and a parade ground to match. The mess decks where we slept had a similar layout to the ones in the main establishment and of course the parade ground was where we were all 'broken in' to the art and craft of military marching and rifle drill.

On arrival we were allocated our accommodation and the first evening was taken up with getting to know the layout of the Annexe, getting acquainted with our mess mates and understanding how life would never be the same again.

We were treated quite well during those first few hours in order to minimise the number of boys who decided not to stay, and it wasn't until the following day that the pressure started to be applied. Each mess deck was under the supervision of an 'Instructor Boy', someone who had completed his training but instead of being sent to sea or to another Naval Establishment for specialist training, was employed in the 'Annexe' to help with a recruitment of 'New Jacks'.

In overall charge of each mess were two Non-Commissioned Officers - either a Petty Officer or a Chief Petty Officer and the Instructor Boy was responsible to them. Competition was fierce between the instructor boys who wanted their mess deck to have the smartest and best disciplined recruits, and it was from that layer of the command chain that we got the most grief. As I was to find out over a year later, when I became an Instructor Boy, the first night was the most difficult to control. The thirty or so recruits had been travelling all day; many had not experienced much in the way of discipline of any sort before, and the excitement factor was high as this was a completely new experience for them as for many, this was their first time away from home. Many just wanted to make the most of the new experience and it was very late when we all got to sleep.

The ear shattering bugle call, announcing 'Reveille' burst through the Tannoy system at what seemed a most disrespectful hour, brought our slumbers to an end. Standing in the doorway to the mess, the presence of the ill-tempered Petty Officer confirmed that from now on, we could forget your cushy life with mummy and daddy, for this was something different.

We were now all subject to naval discipline and the sooner we got used to it, the better it would be for everybody.

We were issued with our kit - everything from toothbrush to bootlaces, shirts, underwear, uniform and cap. Our civilian clothes were parcelled up, addressed, and sent to our mum at home.

There was no going back.

This was in the days before the Human Rights Act and I suppose had we thought about it, we would have come quickly (and accurately) to the conclusion that we had no rights.

At the time it was issued, every item of clothing was stamped with our name in black ink or white paint, depending upon the colour of the item, and in a specific position determined by the nature of that item. Shirts were stamped in black at the tail and over the left-hand pocket, socks were stamped in white with the name running vertically upwards from the ankle, and trousers in black on the waistband and so on. Everything had the right place to be stamped and even handkerchiefs were included.

We were also issued with a 'housewife'.

To the uninitiated, a 'housewife' is a type of 'wallet' in which is stored buttons, sewing wool, needles, thimble, white tape and other small items that may be required during the servicing or repair of our kit. It was an essential and very important part of our kit.

That afternoon the reason for all this precision stamping was made clear. Firstly, every item of clothing had to be folded in a certain way and to a certain size before being placed in our lockers and every item had to occupy a specific position.

Every locker, when it was done correctly, would be identical, with each item in the correct place, and folded to the correct size (to the dimensions of the Seamanship Manual) with the name of the owner of that item visible to the inspecting officer!

Once this had been explained to us, we were all given several skeins of red silk thread, and we were then shown how to chain stitch. After a short practice on a piece of rag, we were instructed to sew our name, over the white stamp, on the 'housewife'.

Their mirth was somewhat diminished when, taking their completed item to the petty officer for inspection, they were told that it was not up to standard, and the sewing had to be unpicked and done again. It had to be completed to a high standard and anything below that would not do. Once that first task was completed, just when we thought that that was it, we were given more bad news.

Every item of clothing that we had been issued with was to have our name embroided in red silk; each item had to inspected and passed by the duty Petty Officer before the next one was started, and then the really bad news, this all had to done in our own time, and all completed the week before we moved over to the main establishment – just one month from now!

It is in an unfair world that we live in and even the names with which we were born contribute to that unfairness. In my group alone, the difference in name length was considerable - J. Smy was the lucky one, but M.P. Hollingsworth wished he could change his name by deed poll for to achieve the name-sewing task that had been set, for him it would take four times the effort.

No allowance was made for the difference in work involved and I was quietly content that my embroidery task was manageable.

The weekly kit inspection played an important part in our daily lives. Not only was this a reminder of how behind we were in our embroidery, but we had to master the art of folding the individual items in the proscribed way, and the standard of cleanliness of each item was checked. Certain periods during the week were allocated to washing (as in laundry) when we had to strip off to sports shorts and, with a deep enamel sink each, and a length of 'pusser's hard', we set about doing our washing.

Pusser's Hard was the standard issue bar of brownish yellow soap, about 8inches long and 3inches wide by the same thickness. The water was quite hard and so it took a great deal of effort and application to work up a lather. It was only later, when we had graduated to the main establishment that we were allowed to make use of washing powder, such as Daz or Omo or any of the wonderful new washing aids that were becoming available. During our New Entry Training we had to make do with Pusser's Hard as that came under the heading of 'character building' and to add insult to injury, every item of clothing, once washed, had to be 'passed' (inspected) by the duty instructor before it could be hung on our allotted rails in the huge drying cabinet.

Some boys, to whom the washing of clothes was a completely new and often alien, experience, had to have many attempts before the item was allowed into the drying cabinet. We quickly learned that collars and cuffs were the areas most closely inspected, so these got the greatest attention in the wash and quite quickly this aspect of life for a new recruit became less traumatic as we improved our washing skills.

Life wasn't easy for many of the new boys, but I was lucky. Having spent the last four years at Holbrook, for me, Ganges was a piece of cake, but for many of the others it took a lot of getting used to. Many of the boys were homesick as well but as there was nobody around with a sympathetic ear, that soon faded, and they buried the thoughts of home and got on with life.

Our first month in the Royal Navy passed very quickly. It mostly involved getting used to Naval discipline, understanding parade ground and rifle drill and learning to march. Our days were filled with Naval Stuff, and in between we watched films and had lectures on anything and everything that had a relevance to life at sea. We also developed domestic skills, and became proficient at cleaning, polishing, washing and ironing our clothes and developing self-sufficiency. Sewing our names in our kit was a form of entertainment since there was very little spare time and even less to do, so our embroidery task was top priority, and everyone completed theirs in good time. I do remember some of us feeling sorry for and helping-out Hollingsworth so that by the time we had finished our initial training, everyone had their names safely sewn in their clothes!

Before we could say that we had completed our introduction to life in the Royal Navy, there was just one thing we had to do. We had to climb the Ganges mast and we were introduced to this activity early on in our first month.

This monument to the days of sailing ships was something that every Ganges boy remembers and remembers well.

It was 176 feet tall with a large metal safety net around the base and from a climbing point of view it was split into three sections. The first section of about 70 feet led up to a stout platform. The second section of about 60 feet led from the platform to the 'half-moon' and the top section was the bare mast which terminated in the lightning conductor on the 'Button'. Ratlines were like rope ladders fixed between highly tensioned stout wires and it was up these ratlines that we had to scramble. The first section of well-spaced footholds terminated at the platform in 'the devil's elbow' - a name that was to describe the configuration of the ratlines that we were expected to climb. The stout platform which supported the rigging for the second section could have been accessed via two large apertures at the point where the ratlines were attached to the mast - but not by us.

The ratlines had another small section which led around the overhang of the first platform. Upon reaching the platform, at the top of the first section, we had to climb the outside of the platform before we could get a foothold on the ratlines of the second section. For this six or eight-foot passage, we were climbing a rope ladder at forty-five degrees to the vertical, but we were on the underside! Once over the rim of the elbow, we had a clear run up the next section as far as the half-moon.

The half-moon was as far as we were expected to go. Anyone foolish enough to want to go to the top - the Button - from this point, had to shin up the bare pole and there weren't many who were keen or brave enough to do that. I certainly wasn't.

The half -moon was the point at which you reached the end of the ratlines on your side and then had to start the descent on the other side. At this point, almost 100 feet above the safety net, there wasn't a lot of room to spare. The rigging terminated at a point where there was a metal platform with two holes in it. One for the 'up' side and one for 'down'. the procedure was that when you reached the end of the climb, (at the top of the ratlines) you hauled yourself through the hole and, with arms around the mast to keep you there against the wind, you shuffled round to the other hole on the opposite side and started climbing down. When you got to the devil's elbow, you had to negotiate this beast in reverse, until you were on the lower section and from then on it was easy.

I cannot remember much about that first time up the mast, probably because, like everyone else, I was rather scared. Mast climbing always seemed to be arranged early in the morning when it was just getting light and often very cold.

As we stood at the bottom of this enormous structure which we were about to climb looking up as the top faded into the distance, the picture that registered in our brains would be etched in our minds for ever. I don't remember anyone refusing to go up the mast neither do I remember anyone asking if we didn't like heights. I cannot imagine this being allowed in society today - Health and Safety would certainly have a different take on it now and I'm sure the Human Rights Act could be quoted in defence of refusal to take part in this out-of-date ritual. Some lawyers would make a case out of this being 'abuse'.

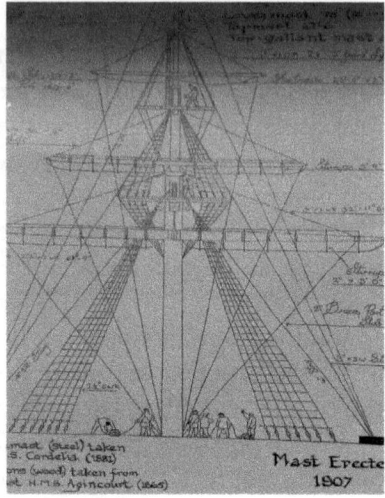

Mast Erected
1907

Early one morning, some months later, when I had several trips over the mast under my belt, I walked past my friend who was about to set foot on the lower rigging. It was a cold and frosty morning and in passing I said quietly to him 'Good luck - rather you than me'.

Unfortunately, his instructor heard me and called me back

'It's your lucky day Barter, I am going to teach you not to talk to my class unless invited' I want you to go to the half-moon and ensure that all my class get through safely'.

So, I had to go to the top platform and help each boy through. But there's only room for one! As each boy came through the hole, I had to move around the mast so that he could access the hole on the other side. That morning I did over twenty rotations of the mast until everyone was through and then I climbed down to be met by the instructor who thought the whole episode very funny. I didn't enjoy the joke, but I never made such a comment again.

At the end of this first month we were despatched to the main establishment to start our proper training. This was a big moment for us all. We were no longer 'The Nozzers' but were about to start our training in the Main establishment. I was sent to Blake 7 mess and our instructors were Petty Officer Parham and Chief Petty Officer Brotherton. From the outset, it was clear that CPO Brotherton was not to be messed with. He appeared to lack even a basic sense of humour and would tolerate nothing unless it was your very best. It was also pretty clear that there was to be no honeymoon period to get used to being in the main establishment. From day one he expected us to behave correctly and furthermore be better at everything than anybody else. He was always impeccably dressed, and everything had to be done by the book. He was greatly respected by all the other instructors, and he was determined that the class for which he was responsible would be the best in the whole establishment.

Each week there were kit inspections, and mess inspections either by the Divisional Officer or by the Commander of Ganges, or, once a term by the captain. There were seamanship competitions, sailing competitions, gun-drill competitions, field-gun, shooting, rowing and sporting competitions. The competitive spirit was in every aspect of life in Ganges and Bill Brotherton wanted us to be the best and if we didn't acquit ourselves as he had expected then he didn't hide his feelings.

On the day we arrived in Blake 7 mess, I was appointed as a Petty Officer Boy alongside another boy called Hughes, and we were in charge of Blake 7 and would be held responsible if any of our charges stepped out of line. I still don't know how I came to be selected as the 'Badge Boy' for Blake 7 but I suspect it might have been something to do with the fact that I was the only one with a few GCSEs.

I didn't enjoy this position as we had a pretty mixed bag in our mess including a few hard nuts from Glasgow, Sunderland, Liverpool and Newcastle as well as a tough specimen from Norfolk. There were some good lads too, so we were a very mixed bunch, and I suppose the decent boys helped me to bring the rough members into line. It was not a time that I remember fondly. CPO Brotherton would not accept excuses for failure, and we had to be the best at everything and Hughes and I, as leaders, had to be better than everyone else.

The training was very intensive and involved our participation in one activity or other from 7am to 7pm every day. Included in the curriculum was schoolwork - the usual basics of English, maths, science, geography, naval history and navigation; seamanship (which included knots and splices, rule of the road for vessels at sea and a multitude of other seaman like activities), semaphore and Morse codes, and gunnery, including the drill involved in a ship borne gun turret which was very physical too and often involved, as a punishment, the running round the gun battery with a 15" shell across ones shoulders!

Every afternoon and on Saturdays too, we were involved in a sporting activity which might be swimming, gymnastics, sailing, rowing (called 'pulling' as the boats involved were 32foot cutters (not sculls!), field gun training, tug of war training, or even parade ground drill if we were not up to scratch. We even had time to play rugby or football but only if there were no other activities with a nautical flavour.

We had periods allocated to washing our clothes with the inevitable inspection before putting them into an industrial sized centrifuge - spin drier and then hanging them on the drying racks. Once dried, we had to iron them and once again, each ironed item had to be inspected by the duty instructor and the weekly kit inspections occupied a disproportionate amount of free time, but it was of such importance that we dare not risk an adverse comment from the inspecting officer.

Between the accommodation blocks and the river there was a flight of three steps, each flight consisting of maybe twenty steps. It was a long way down and a long way up although, looking at them now, they are not as big as my fifteen-year-old self remembers them! These steps were called 'Faith, Hope and Charity' and probably for very good reason.

During the evening, and until such times that peace and quiet reigned, the duty instructor would patrol the accommodation area and come down hard on any mess that was misbehaving. One dark and wet Sunday evening, Blake 7 were a bit lively and wouldn't settle down. Lights were out and we should have been asleep, but we weren't.

The duty Instructor, (I believe it was our own Percy Parham,) without so much as a warning, came into the mess, put the lights on and in a tone that was distinctly unfriendly, ordered us to put our boots on and our oilskins, grab our respirators (gas masks, which were issued to every new recruit) and 'fall in' outside.

'Fall in' is a military term for lining up in a squad, three deep, ready for marching or 'doubling' (running). We had never experienced this nocturnal activity before and wondered why we were still in our pyjamas, with boots and no socks and with oilskins and gas masks. Oilskins were similar to very heavy-duty PVC used as a protection against very severe wet weather, a bit like old fashioned fisherman's waterproofs. We didn't have long to wait.

Percy instructed me to march the class in the direction of the river and as soon as we arrived at the top of Faith Hope and Charity, he ordered me to stop the class and instructed everyone to put their gas masks on. It was raining and very cold. As everyone who has ever worn a gas mask knows, the first thing that happens is that they fog up and you cannot see where you are going. Eventually when everything warms up the fog clears a bit but never completely. As soon as we were all properly kitted out, Percy decided to explain why we were here, as if we didn't know. He then ordered that we should 'double' down the steps to the bottom, about turn and then double up them. And this would continue until he felt that we had expended all the energy that was obviously preventing us from sleeping, at which time we could return to our beds in the hope that we would then sleep peacefully until the following morning.

I cannot remember how many times we traversed this set of steps but by the time Percy had decided to get us back to the hut, we were exhausted and with an air of contrition surrounding us all, we got back into bed without a whisper.

'Faith, Hope and Charity'

Sunday afternoons were free for recreational purposes. One could go to Ipswich on the bus by special request although there wasn't a great deal to do there. In those days, no shops were open on a Sunday, and there certainly wasn't any cinemas or other amusements. There was a ferry across the river to Harwich and from Harwich you could take another ferry to Felixstowe.

Harwich was also a miserable place on a Sunday so there was no incentive to return once you had made a visit. My Uncle Jack and Auntie Doris lived in Felixstowe, so I sometimes went there to see them. It was a bit of a hike and took up much of the Sunday afternoon to get to their house from Shotley. The two ferry trips – Shotley to Harwich then Harwich to Felixstowe- took over an hour then I had a twenty-minute bus ride from the ferry terminal to the centre of the town from where I could walk to their house. I had an hour or so with them and then I had to start the return journey, so I didn't do that very often.

Payday was a fortnightly ritual that was eagerly awaited. When we first arrived at HMS Ganges, we were given a 'ships book number' and we were also given an Official Number. The former was for use within Ganges; the other one followed you throughout your service. On Payday, we all mustered and lined up in order of 'Ships Book Number'. As we came to the front of the queue there was a table, behind which sat the Supply Officer who oversaw the payments, a Petty Officer to witness it and a leading rating to pass the money over. As the previous boy marched away, having received his pay, the next one would take a pace forward, call out his name and ships book number at the same time as removing his cap and placing it in front of the paying officer who would place the princely sum of five shillings on to it. A smart left turn was followed by marching away at the same time as replacing the cap.

(Five shillings in today's money is 25p but it would buy an awful lot more than that would buy today). The remainder of ones pay - I cannot remember how much that was- was sent to our mum by way of an 'allotment'. She would have the 'allotment book' and each week would go to the post office where the book was stamped, and the money paid to her. My mother took this money and placed it in a deposit account in my name, which she kept for me until I had finished my training. She also used to put money into the account for birthdays and Christmas so after a year or so it had built up to a reasonable amount.

On Sunday evening, the Chaplain took to the airwaves. We had a tannoy system (a Public Address System) throughout the establishment which was controlled by the main Regulating Office, and it was used to inform everybody of things that were considered important in the general administration of daily routine. For example, reveille, or the bugle call to get us up, was broadcast over the tannoy, as was 'pipe down' or time to go to sleep.

Anyway, for an hour every Sunday evening the Chaplain would organise a 'record request' programme where any boy could request a record be played for his friend in another mess (or in his own mess if he wanted to). There was no phone system, so in order to get a request in front of the DJ Chaplain, you had to walk from your mess to the Regulating Office and hand him the details on a piece of paper.

The only problem was that there was a very limited library of records and as I remember it couldn't have been more than ten. We got very bored by the Yodelling of Frank Ifield, or 'Cool Water' sung by Frankie Lane or 'Big Bad John'. Whenever I hear one of these tunes, my mind immediately goes back to a Sunday evening at Ganges.

During the yearlong course, there were two periods when each class was taken out of the instructional routine and occupied with mundane tasks. This was called 'work ship' which basically meant that you contributed to the overall running and maintenance of HMS Ganges. You could spend the two weeks sweeping up leaves, painting kerb stones, working in the mess hall washing dishes or a whole range of other activities. My first 'work ship' was working in the kitchen of Erwarton Hall, the official residence on the Captain of Ganges who was by then, Captain Michael LeFanu. I still remember it for I had flu throughout the period, and I felt really ill. My illness was not allowed to get in the way of my work and from 7am to 7pm I did all the kitchen duties (other than help with the cooking).

The Le Fanus entertained a lot so there were always mountains of washing up and cleaning, besides polishing the silver and brassware to be done. I was quite happy to work in the kitchen as I would have felt far worse if I had been in an outside working party.

My second 'work ship' some months later was quite different. I was the Captain's 'Runner'. this meant that I had to wear my best No1 uniform all day and spend the entire day with Captain LeFanu, accompanying him on official visits and running any errands that he might require.

He was an amazing man and although he was at the peak of his career and I was the lowest form of life, he treated me extremely well and that period was one which started off a friendship that lasted for many years. At the end of that two-week period he took the trouble to write to my father saying that he felt that I had a good future in the R.N.

Some weeks later, one Saturday afternoon, over the tannoy came a call for me to report to the guardroom. I immediately wondered what I had done wrong, but I need not have worried. There I found Captain and Mrs LeFanu. Captain LeFanu told me to go and change into my best uniform and report back to the guardhouse in fifteen minutes. On my return he told me that he and Mrs LeFanu were going to drive out to Eye for the afternoon. Three miles short of the town, Captain LeFanu got out of the car (to walk the rest of the way to Eye) and his wife took me home, dropping me off at the front door. 'Tell your mother, 'Said Mrs LeFanu, 'that Captain and Mrs LeFanu will be calling in for a cup of tea in an hours-time'.

I went in, to the great surprise of my mum, who put the kettle on, got the best China out and waited for her very important guests. After tea I was duly taken back to Shotley having had a surprise home visit.

We finished our training in the August and at the passing out parade I collected an embarrassing number of prizes – best student; navigation prize; seamanship prize; School prize (for the best at schoolwork throughout the year) and several others, all of which were presented to me by Captain LeFanu. I had an armful of books, many of which I had kept until fairly recently, but sadly I now have none in my possession.

I quite enjoyed my time at Shotley. Having been to Holbrook, I found the routine quite acceptable and the variety of activities we were able to enjoy was amazing. I sailed a lot (skippered 32-

foot cutters on many occasions) and sailed dinghies for Ganges against other establishments. I learned to shoot (and then did this at competition level afterwards), I played rugby, I learnt how to cut hair (the boy barber's course!), was in the field gun crew, and took part in many and various activities from winning the Silver Bosun's call; to winning the heaving Line Competition to learning how to dance in the Gym on Sunday afternoons. I lived life to the full and although Ganges had a reputation of being one of the hardest and toughest training establishments, I must confess that I didn't find it so and enjoyed it.

At the end of my training instead of going with all my contemporaries to the next stage of specialist training, I was appointed as an instructor boy to help with the new recruits in the annexe. Of the prizes that I had picked up during our final term including the 'Advanced Class on Entry' prize which was essentially for schoolwork; the Seamanship Prize, and a prize for best in Navigation, all of which probably contributed towards me being selected as an Instructor Boy.

This was for a four-month spell and at the end of it I was pleased to leave.

I don't remember too much of that period, so it was a great surprise when I had an email, out of the blue, last year from someone who was in the Annexe and in my class when I was an instructor boy. He was most complimentary about how I had treated him whilst he was a new recruit, but I found it a bit embarrassing because I couldn't remember him!

The most vivid memory that I still retain of my time as an instructor boy regards the mast and the ritual of climbing it. The 'new jack' period in the Annex lasted four weeks and, on many occasions, it was necessary to take one's charges over to the Main Establishment for any one of a number of reasons. Whatever the need, to take them across the road to the Main Establishment, it was a matter of high importance that our charges looked very smart, were well disciplined and behaved well, if for no other reason than to minimise the verbal abuse that was hurled in their direction from the 'old timers' who had graduated from the Annex, probably as early as a month ago!

The mast trip always took place after breakfast. During the

summer months this was quite pleasant, but during the wintertime not only was it dark but often very cold and ice in the ratlines was quite common. The unpleasantness of this activity was the one that etched the deepest memory into the psyche of every 'Ganges Boy' and whenever one meets a fellow graduate of 'The University of Shotley' one of the first subjects to be brought up is 'The Mast!'.

Myself with Tony and Ivor after fifty years

At the end of my course, when I stayed behind as an 'Instructor Boy' the rest of my class went off to their chosen specialisations for further training and it was three months later that I got to do the same thing. I was sent to HMS Harrier in the wilds of Carmarthenshire, for specialist training as a Radar Plotter. That was the next chapter in my Naval Career.

4
To Wales and beyond

Time at Ganges went very quickly. I enjoyed the year in Shotley as it was no hardship to me, having been well prepared by four years at RHS. We did a lot of sailing – every weekend was spent on the water and as a Qualified Coxswain I was expected to take a crew out at every opportunity, in either 27' whalers or 32' cutters. The ebb tide at Shotley is pretty fierce and it was quite easy to forget about this and be swept past the pier out to sea when you should be on your way to supper. You only did this once as it was a long row back against the tide whilst the crew got hungrier and more hostile.

I sailed for HMS Ganges against HMS St. Vincent in Portsmouth harbour. On one occasion I got very close to the Royal Yacht which was moored alongside the Dockyard wall. The apparently uncontrolled route of the sailing dinghy which appeared to be heading for the gleaming paintwork of H.M. Yacht Britannia caused a number of those on board to get all steamed up in case I damaged that precious paintwork. Thankfully I knew what I was doing, although it might not have appeared like that to the observers, the precious paintwork remained unscathed.

The Radar Training Establishment to which I had been sent was HMS Harrier in Pembrokeshire, a short bus ride from Haverfordwest, and I trained to become a Radar Plotter 3rd Class. Harrier was a very isolated establishment and apart from the Saturday dances there was not much to go into Haverfordwest for. As it was a Naval establishment the routine was the same as every other Naval barracks in the country. We had Divisions every Sunday which involved an inspection when everyone was expected to be very smart and shiny.

One week the camp barber failed to appear from his shop in

Pembroke Dock, so this presented the staff with quite a crisis. A call went out for anyone who could fill the void.

Who could cut hair? Well, I could! As I had completed the 'Boy Barbers Course' at Ganges, I quickly volunteered and was given the full run of a shop and a timetable when I could have it open. With all tools supplied, I was allowed to charge sixpence a haircut or beard trim. Immediately I had a full customer list, and it was a very lucrative time. I was sad when the proper barber got better and was able to return to work.

I was also keen on shooting, as I had been in the Ganges team and that continued whilst at Harrier. This was a great skive as the officer in charge - one of the schoolmasters- was very enthusiastic and we frequently went off to take part in competitions at Trevoll in Devon and to Bisley.

This was, of course, before the days of ear defenders, or any other sort of protection and invariably the firing point was constructed of timber and corrugated iron sheets. This meant that after every firing, the deafness that we experienced took some hours to recover. We accepted this as normal without realising that each time we used these firing points, damage was taking place to our ear drums. Now my hearing is quite bad and that is partly due to the shooting practice without any ear protection.

As a trainee I had other jobs as well, for we, at the bottom of the food chain, were the undisputed source of cheap labour. One of my jobs was to keep the offices of Commander (Air) clean and tidy. If he was working late, or if he came in early when I was still cleaning his office, our paths would cross, and he was soon aware of my enthusiasm to fly. I was so fortunate to have been in that position with such a kind and understanding Officer. He was a great chap and at every opportunity would call me and ask if I would like to accompany him on his next flight and of course I took advantage of this wonderful opportunity. At that time, he was flying the Sea Venom, a single engine two-seater night fighter (the Naval version of the Vampire). I had many trips in the left-hand seat with him and couldn't wait for the next call to accompany him to St David's for a quick flight. I was a very lucky chap.

The Sea Venom with hook down.

On one occasion I didn't admit that I had a cold, and my ears were blocked. Any admission to that effect would have kept me on the ground and soon after I understood why. That decision by me, not to tell anyone about my cold, turned out to be a huge mistake and one which had a long lasting and devastating effect on my future career.

The Venom has an unpressurised cockpit and descending from thirty thousand feet with blocked Eustachian tubes was an incredibly painful experience and which resulted in perforating both my eardrums. This in turn meant that my hearing was going to deteriorate even more due to the scarring from the perforations, and it would ultimately preclude me from flying jets in the future. But at the time I wasn't aware of the seriousness of the situation and continued to fly whenever I could.

Time in HMS Harrier passed quickly. The training course of nine months was soon over, and spare time was filled by cutting hair, competition shooting, going flying, going to the dances in Haverfordwest or spending sunny weekend afternoons on Dale Beach. I was 17 years old, and life was great.

A friend from school, Reg Varnes was also in Harrier at the same time. He had been in Anson House at RHS with me and was a bit of a sports fanatic. He wasn't very tall but was almost as wide as he was high, and he was also a bit of a body builder. He and I had history in the Holbrook Boxing Ring, but we laughed a lot about those times. And we were great friends.

He also had a car. A sports car with a soft top which lifted him to the top of the social ladder (with me alongside)and together we explored the flesh pots of Milford Haven. That summer, Reg entered the competition for 'Mr Milford Haven' and won it! That got him lots of girlfriends! I was happy to be his helper!

As soon as the course was completed the Admiralty lost no time in finding ships for us and I was no exception. I didn't even have time to go home for the weekend before I was expected to join my first ship. The day after the course the course was over, I was told to pack my kit, (in my Naval Kit bag), was given a travel warrant (free rail ticket) and with a list of things to do called 'The Drafting Routine', made my get-away from HMS Harrier in the direction of the big wide world.

I was instructed to join HMS Bulwark in Portsmouth as a Radar Operator and my career as an Ordinary Seaman in the Royal Navy had begun.

5
H.M.S. Bulwark – almost a world cruise

I joined HMS Bulwark in Portsmouth Dockyard after an overnight rail journey from Haverfordwest. The January sky was clear and cold as the dawn broke over Portsmouth Harbour and, with kitbag over my shoulder, I walked from Portsmouth Harbour Station to the Dockyard. The darkness of the early morning was broken by the stabs of blue light from the welding torches being used by the Dockyard mateys as they carried out repairs to the ships.

This was a new, unfamiliar world for me, as it is for everyone who joins a ship for the first time. A ship the size of Bulwark – a fully operational Aircraft carrier – is a huge military machine with over a thousand officers and ratings on board and I must admit to slight intimidation by the sheer size of it as the silhouette stood out against the morning sky. Everything was different. I was now alone: this was a real ship and the future was unknown; I had trained as a Radar Plotter but never been inside an Aircraft Carrier; even the smell of Portsmouth Dockyard was so different from the rolling hills of West Wales. The new day really was dawning.

I mounted the gangway and reported to the Duty Petty Officer at the top, from where I was directed to the Regulating Office. This was the place where new arrivals started their 'joining routine' and this was the first challenge – find the Regulating Office.

My first day was spent in trying to find the place where I would live (and sleep)– the mess deck; the place where I would use my specialist knowledge – the operations room; the place where I would work when not on duty in front of a radar set – the quarterdeck; the place where I would eat – the dining area and the place where I was expected to be during Action Stations – the Radar Room. There was a lot to learn and many different people to meet or 'report to' as part of a 'joining routine'. Once completed, I hoped that I would be able to retain all that information. One of the advantages of joining a ship that has been in commission for a while is that everybody else had been there for several months, knew the routine, and were generally eager to help out any new arrivals. Everybody seemed to remember what it was like when they joined there first ship and were very friendly.

H.M.S.Bulwark with Seahawks on deck

I soon found my 'mess' – it was Number 15, halfway along the ship on the starboard side and four decks down. It was a small mess, no bigger than 20' long and 8' wide but fifteen of us had to sleep there in a three-tier arrangement of bunk beds. We were an eclectic bunch covering the whole range of social strata – I was the youngest, and the oldest was a knarled old seaman of 35! Leading Seaman, (Soapy) Watson was in charge of the mess and he ruled it with an iron fist. And thank God he did, for anyone weaker than Soapy would have had a very difficult time and anarchy would have reigned. His opposite number was Leading Seaman Jimmy James - also a 'three-badged' Leading Seaman. (Three badges meant that he had done over twelve years of 'man's service' (over 18) and was at least 30 years old. Jimmy was short, bald, kind, had a great sense of humour and with his wife, ran a dancing school in Portsmouth.

Bulwark sailed within a week of my arrival, and we were on our way to Rotterdam. This was my first experience of a 'foreign visit' and I still remember the excitement I felt when 'going ashore'. My first job was to find a shop to buy a present for my mum. I settled on an Edam cheese, looking lovely with its Red Wax coating. When I got home, I sadly had to apologise to Mum for my failure to deliver her present. I had experienced a period of immense hunger, so I had eaten it! She was quite understanding. Our next 'foreign visit' was to Belfast. We all went ashore to the Saturday dance at the local 'Palais' or whatever its' name was. A group of us had great fun for many of the girls worked in the local Shirt factory, so it was a bit of a competition to see who could dance with someone from each department – sleeves, collars, buttons, ironing/pressing, backs or fronts. I seem to remember that Dance Hall was in a suburb called 'Hollywood'! Our Rugby team had a good outing in Belfast too, and we won the match and got presented with an engraved medal, which, miraculously, I still have.

We returned to Portsmouth for Christmas leave and as soon as the New Year arrived, we were off again, but this time to warmer climes.

Once out of the Channel and Western approaches, we headed in a South Westerly direction. We were off to the West Indies and our first port of call was Trinidad. Leaving Portsmouth covered in snow soon became a distant memory as we bathed in tropical seas beneath swaying palms. Our first port of call was Port-of-Spain, Trinidad where we anchored in the harbour with the local church clearly visible on the nearby hill. My duties when in harbour were principally involved in being crew for the liberty boat. As we were anchored off, whenever anyone wanted to go ashore, they had to use one of the several boats that the ship carried for such eventualities. I enjoyed that job very much, especially as our first trip was usually for fresh provisions at 5.30 in the morning when the harbour was quiet and beautiful against the rising sun and our pinnace had to provide the shuttle service for all the people going ashore. It was my first 'real job' and although the hours were long it was an amazing experience.

When in Grenada, our next stop, volunteers were invited to join the crew of a whaler (just like I'd sailed at Shotley) which a Leading seaman wanted to sail up the Grenadines. I put my name down and was told I could go. Brilliant! We would leave the ship in Granada and sail up as far as Bequia where HMS Bulwark would meet up with us a week later. That was a fantastic trip. We sailed by day and camped on a different beach every evening. Many of the small islands were deserted (not now – they now have much concrete, many hotels and many tourists) and on the ones that were inhabited we always had a very friendly welcome.

On several occasions, when I tried to find the post office or shop which sold stamps for my collection, I was frequently asked 'What's it like back home, or How's the Queen?'. The locals seemed to think that 'The Queen' mixed with everybody – a bit like Island life.

Whalers Crew – me on the left

Sailing between the Islands was idyllic, and it was on this trip that I first encountered flying fish. I never discovered why they do it, but they skim along the surface of the water, from wave to wave and as the whaler doesn't stick out of the water very much, they often miscalculated and finished up inside the boat.

We sailed north to Bequia, Island hopping on the way and staying overnight on most beautiful and often deserted tropical beaches. When the islands were inhabited, the people were wonderfully friendly, but all too soon Bulwark appeared over the horizon, and it was time to be back on board.

Jamaica and Bermuda were next in line for our company, and we had a wonderful time in both places. I met my first 'girlfriend' in Jamaica.

Bulwark was too big to go alongside the harbour in Kingston, so we had to anchor off the town which meant that a shuttle service was provided to take sailors ashore and bring them back and to carry provisions and, once again, as Boats Crew, this was my job.

Vivienne was working in Victoria Market, where we disembarked our passengers, and whilst waiting to fill up for the return journey I used to go to her market stall and chat with her. When off duty I went to see her, and she took me home to meet her parents who were very friendly and hospitable. They cooked a typical meal of fish and ackee rice and they made my stay in Jamaica one of great happiness and one that I will never forget.

I was very sad to leave Jamaica as our visit there was over all too quickly and we then headed north to Halifax, Nova Scotia where it was many degrees lower than sunny Jamaica, in fact it was several degrees below freezing – normal weather for this part of Canada in February.

The First Lieutenant wanted the ship to be smart when we arrived, so we stopped well out of sight of the harbour entrance in order that we could paint that side of the ship that would be seen by the public when we moored in Halifax. Because of the height of the ship's side, wire nets had to be rigged to stop people falling in the water, and rigging the nets was not hazard free. But it had to be done. And as a member of 'the Bosun's Party', that was my job. The net was secured on the flight deck and then thrown over the side. Bosun's party then had to climb down and, in a similar manner to the swing under the apple tree in the garden, get the nets swinging backwards and forwards until as they got close to the ship's side, we could hold on to one of the projecting 'eyes' into which we could attach a rope to hold the net close to the side of the ship.

Before the side can be painted, all the salt that had accumulated since the last time the ship was painted, has to be removed before fresh paint can be applied. This is normally done by a sailor, with a bucket of warm fresh water and a cloth. With one arm holding on to the net and the bucket, the free hand washes the salt off the ship's side. During the time that we were doing this, it was snowing, and the ambient temperature was so low that the water which we used to wash the salt off, quickly froze as it met with the steel hull on the ship. There was no way that the salt could be removed by this simple method and all that we were achieving was the addition of a layer of ice on top of the salt. But the ship had to look nice and to this end, paint was then applied by roller and paint brush on top of the thin layer of ice and once the nets were hauled back aboard, we slowly crept into our berth, presenting to the assembled reception committee of the Mayor and Local Dignitaries, a freshly painted ship and gleaming ship that was a credit to the Royal Navy.

The visit was a huge success. There were hundreds and hundreds of families queuing up to take the sailors to their homes and give them some hospitality. Many of those who had not intended going ashore because of the cold, were actually ordered to change into their best uniforms and go and grab a family.

I met some wonderful people with whom I kept in touch for many years. Ten years after that visit, that family came over to England and I caught up with them in their home in Surrey.

As soon as we sailed from Halifax, we met some awful Atlantic weather. It was quite amusing for those of us who had endured that cold and miserable activity of washing the side and applying the paint, to watch great sheets of grey paint float past as the waves removed it from the side of the ship.

It is not the policy of the Navy to allow members of the ship's company too much free time. We had to be kept busy and once we had cleared the Canadian coast we prepared for the activity.

As we crossed the Atlantic heading for Gibraltar, we joined in a NATO Exercise with our Canadian friends, American cousins and the rest of the Home Fleet. Our aircraft flew many sorties both day and night and our helicopters were continuously operating as anti-submarine patrols. The radar room was manned continuously as was the operations room, which meant that we had to work a 'two watch system'. A 'two watch system' meant that you did four hours on watch, and four hours off. That wouldn't be too bad to keep up, but during the day, when you were 'off watch' you still had to do the other jobs that were your responsibility.

At the end of a ten-day exercise, you're pretty tired. Four hours on, followed by four hours off is not much fun after the novelty has worn off and after a week of this routine one becomes a bit of a zombie, because during the four hours 'on', you are sitting in front of a radar screen for the whole period without a break. It's all done differently now, thank goodness.

We lost several aircraft during that exercise – mostly Venoms (single seat night fighters). One was lost as it ditched from the catapult, and two others collided at nighttime. Although we searched for many hours for survivors, we found none. We were all very glad to get to Gibraltar and have a rest.

Bulwark had to go into dry dock in Gibraltar, for maintenance below the waterline which meant that toilets and bathrooms had to be provided ashore.

The toilet block was a strange building, consisting of about 20 cubicles, side by side, constructed over a fast-flowing stream of water that provided the flushing arrangements. The water passing beneath each seat was more than a trickle – it flowed quite quickly, and the volume was more than adequate.

Each morning – often after a hard night ashore in the 'Trocadera' or similar Flamenco themed bar, all the sailors had to 'fall in' in a regimented fashion on the quay side before being allocated jobs for the day. Once this was over, and when the order 'fall out' was given, everyone was expected to disperse to whichever part of the ship they worked and start their tasks.

Instead of everyone going off to work, there would be a mass movement of bodies towards the toilet block and for the next 30 minutes or so all cubicles were fully occupied and functioning.

One morning a particularly nasty member of the ships company (or might even have been a Spaniard (or Gibraltarian) with a grudge against the British) decided to have a bit of fun.

Occupying the first cubicle at the head of the 'stream', he crumbled up a newspaper, lit it, put it in the stream, let it go then vacated the cubicle. Once on its journey, the lighted paper passed through each cubicle in turn, and at some speed.

Fortunately, the speed with which the flames passed under the bare bums prevented damage of too serious a nature, but there were not many in the cubicles that morning who didn't have cause to be very annoyed at the prankster who, by this time his victims were in a condition to look for him, had disappeared without trace.

From Gibraltar we went through the Mediterranean to Malta, through the Suez Canal and then to Aden.

I was glad to see Malta, where Mum and Dad had met and the passage through the Suez Canal was a most interesting time.

Aden is an unattractive place at the best of times – its only saving grace is that it was a duty-free port so many luxury goods such as cameras and watches, could be purchased much cheaper than in the UK. It is essentially a bunkering port where ships stop to pick up fuel. The water supply was dreadful and the only way to disguise the taste was to lace it with lemon powder.

Whilst we were in Aden, my brother Leonard was doing his National Service in the Veterinary Corps and had been tasked to go to British Somalia (as it was then) to collect a load of donkeys and deliver them to the Sultan of Muscat as a present from the British people!

Whilst we were in Aden Leonard came aboard the Bulwark and we enjoyed a trip ashore together and then we met up again at our next port of call, Muscat. Leonard had delivered his donkeys and was waiting to go home, and we were anchored off the port, so he was able to come aboard again. That was a huge bonus, seeing my brother in such a remote and inhospitable part of the world.

Onward to Ceylon – Sri Lanka – where we anchored off Trincomalee. Whilst there, Captain Gick decided that he wanted to try and break a few records with his new boat. It was a 27' sailing dinghy with a huge area of sail and theoretically possible, when on 'the plane' to be fast enough to enable a water skier to get up on his skis behind the boat. The boat had been designed by Uffa Fox, the foremost boat designer in the country and who was a friend of the Duke of Edinburgh, for whom a similar boat had been built. As I was a frequent sailor during off duty times, my Divisional Officer nominated me to go with the Captain and it was a great experience, especially as Captain Gick's theory was proved correct. One of the officers was able to get up on his skis behind the boat but only for a few minutes. Had the wind been stronger, the record would have been in trouble!

Whilst in the Indian Ocean two ships collided – one a large tanker and the other a passenger boat carrying pilgrims from Mecca. The tanker was disabled, and we had to take her in tow until a tug could come out and take over. I was told to join the 'Bosun's Party' which was a team of four sailors who looked after all the wire ropes on board and did all the splicing. The Leading Seaman in charge didn't believe in doing any of the work himself if there was someone else available to do it. I was by then an 'Able Seaman' so it soon became apparent that I was in for a lot of work.

But I didn't mind.

I knew how to splice a wire rope in a number of different ways, but because of lack of practice I was quite slow. Leading Seaman

Whyman saw to it that by the end of the week I was able to perfectly splice a thimble into a wire rope within five minutes and I was really very proud of that skill that I had acquired in HMS Bulwark.

Years later, at the surgery in Meadowside, Eye, a contractor had parted a wire rope which needed splicing. When he returned to work the next morning, he could not believe that, not only had his wire been repaired, but it had been done by the Dentist!

After Sri Lanka we went to Singapore, The Philippines and Hong Kong.

I managed to get a seat in a Venom for the Fly Past of Manila and the experience of going off the deck of an aircraft carrier via the catapult, and then returning courtesy of the arrester wires, was a great thrill, which reinforced my ambition to be a Naval pilot.

Hong Kong Harbour

Hong Kong is famous for being a duty-free port where all RN ships call so that their ship's companies can buy their presents to take home (rabbits as they are called).

I was no different. I bought some beautiful silk brocade for my Mum as she was a skilled dressmaker, and I also bought a superb tea service which I thought that she would like. The shop specialised in packaging too and agreed to pack up my precious tea service ready for the homeward journey. This box was then taken aboard the ship and stowed away until we got back to Portsmouth.

Back home in Eye, I proudly presented this box to my Mum and when she opened it, I realised that I had been duped. The lovely tea service that I had carefully selected and paid for in Hong Kong, wasn't there. In its place was a box full of broken crockery!

On the way home, we were diverted to the Red Sea and the Gulf of Akabar to show a bit of military strength in the area, and then we sailed for Mombasa.

A few of us had asked for permission to take our annual leave in East Africa and one of the group, a National Serviceman whose dad was an official at the Bank of England, had a friend who was an officer in the Kenya Police, based in Moshi, in the foothills of Kilimanjaro.

Our request for leave was approved and we decided to have a go and climb Mt Kilimanjaro. With rucksacks packed with tents and spare clothes and naval boots on our feet, we headed for the local bus station to catch the next bus to Moshi. That journey was an unforgettable experience.

The other passengers consisted of travellers from the rural areas who had been to the city to buy goats, chickens and other interesting creatures, as well as provisions and utensils, which they were then taking back to their villages and homesteads. The bus was full to the roof and beyond, with colourful tribesmen and women in their native clothing and body decorations, together with a whole menagerie of assorted animals. At one point along the dusty road the bus stopped as a local baboon hunt was taking place, and we couldn't get past until the baboons had gone into the bush with the hunters behind them.

We eventually got to Moshi and were met by a Constable of the Kenya Police who took us to the place where we would make our base camp before setting out to climb the mountain.

Nowadays, large parties go up Kilimanjaro, in well organised groups arranged by Travel Companies with guides and porters in attendance. We did have a guide of course, provided by the Kenya Police but we certainly had to carry all our own gear.

The long march from the dusty plains through the tropical rain forest into the high-altitude scrub became more difficult as we gained altitude. Our final camp, before setting off for the summit at 2 in the morning, was at around 18,000 feet and from then on, each step took enormous effort.

At the summit – me with the ice ace.

We got to the summit before the sun rose and to have the experience of seeing the sun rise over the extinct volcano that was once active in Kilimanjaro, was unforgettable.

There was no snow and ice on the summit (it seemed that the snow was blown off the top) and I now regret not going down into the ice filled crater before descending.

Coming down the mountain was thrilling. Extensive scree slopes could be utilised for rapid descent and once one had got the hang of it, one could descend in a few minutes what it had taken a couple of days to climb. It was similar to skiing but without skis or snow.

Our final camp was within the grounds of the Police Headquarters where a barbeque had been laid out for us. Stuffing ourselves with local game cooked over an open fire was a great treat after four days of Naval Survival Rations and I still remember the smell of the meat cooking over the barbeque on the plains beneath Mount Kilimanjaro.

We were taken on a mini-Safari in the Police Land-rovers before returning to Mombasa on the local bus. It had been an unforgettable experience made more so because we had very little in the way of 'organised' or 'official' support, and we relied on the local buses for transport. That certainly was the best way to do it.

The South African leg of our ' World Cruise' had to cancelled for political reasons, so we came back through the Suez Canal and the Mediterranean, calling at Famagusta (Cyprus) where we were offered the opportunity for some R&R (Rest and Recreation).

I took up the offer and went with Ivor, a friend from Ganges days who had retrained as an electrician. We had a few days on the beach before heading off to Gibraltar again (for a final 'Rabbit Run' – a chance to buy last minute presents) and then home to Portsmouth.

My Mum came down to Portsmouth to see Bulwark enter Harbour and when I took her to my mess deck to show her where I had spent the last 18 months, I think she was a little taken aback! It would have been nice if my father had also come to meet the ship but sadly, he didn't consider it important.

I wasn't too unhappy about leaving the Bulwark. The mess was very cramped; the other occupants were a mixed lot - some of whom were verging on the criminal class.

My next move was to HMS Dryad where I was to go on another course to train as a Radar Operator 2nd Class and after that a course to become a Leading Seaman, all in preparation for the next big move to Scotland and H.M.S. Temeraire where, if selected, I would commence training to become a Sub Lieutenant. My Divisional Officer had blocked my request to apply for a Short Service Commission to train as a Naval Pilot, but had put, in its place, a system whereby I could go to Dartmouth as an Upper Yardman, if I passed all the exams.

Getting promoted to a Leading Seaman RP2 was the first step on that path.

6
H.M.S. DRYAD and H.M.S VICTORY
(Able Seaman to Leading Seaman)

I was glad to leave Bulwark.

My Divisional Officer had blocked my attempt to apply for a Short Service Commission in the Fleet Air-Arm, so it looked as though I would have to try and succeed as an Upper Yardman, get to Dartmouth and, once promoted, try and get on to a flying course and train as a Pilot.

The first step in this direction was a course at HMS Dryad in Portsmouth to become an RP2 – a Radar Plotter Second Class – one up from where I was, and after that, a course to become a Leading Seaman, all in preparation for the next big move to Scotland and H.M.S.Temeraire- but only if I was selected and to make it to Temeraire, But first, I had to pass the infamous Admiralty Interview Board (AIB)

H.M.S. Dryad was a very unusual place. It had been a stately home with extensive gardens and an estate which had been taken over during the war and from here that the planning of many of the great military campaigns was organised. It had been Eisenhour's Command and Control Centre, so it had lots of history. Post war it was turned into a Radar training base.

Perched up on the top of Portsdown Hill it commanded a magnificent view of the coast and the English Channel. As soon as a new group of trainees arrived and placed their kit in the mess, they had to be allocated a 'part of ship' job which would be carried out when not undergoing their training in the classroom, and which contributed to the overall running of the establishment.

I arrived at Dryad with about 30 others and when the Petty officer was allocating jobs, he asked us all if anyone had any experience with horses.

Thinking that this offer might have some potential I raised a hand – after all I had ridden Albert, the lovely old cob owned by Uncle Sydney all those years ago in Cornwall. I was the only one.

'Fine' he said 'You report to the stables'.

Every four days, (we worked a four-watch system) when the members of my mess were weeding; cleaning up; painting; or doing any one of the many mundane jobs that were on offer, my duty involved saddling the horse and riding him for about an hour, just to give him exercise and because this was considered a very special responsibility, I was given the coveted 'Blue Card'. This meant that whenever there were any unpleasant tasks to be done by the duty watch, I could say that I had a Blue Card and had to attend to the horses.

It just so happened that 'The Chair Makers Arms' a delightful country pub was well within the exercise range of me and the horse, at least when I was on duty. We enjoyed a quick trot to the pub once I'd saddled him up and given him a brush and the locals soon got used to seeing him tied up outside whilst I went in and ordered a pint for me and a bucket of water for the horse. The horse soon became a local celebrity.

When guard duty came around (again on a four -night cycle and everybody had to contribute,) we had to get dressed in boots, gaiters, webbing belt and a tin hat and carry a truncheon – very much like Private Pike in Dad's Army. We had to sleep in the 'Guard House' when not on patrol and we had to take it in turns to patrol the perimeter in pairs throughout the night and record, in the ships log, any unusual happenings. In the summer months this was indeed a most enjoyable experience – at least it was for me who loved being in the countryside. The Estate on which Dryad had been built was extensive and walking the perimeter was no great hardship, through fields, woods and open country.

There was pig farm too, and when a sow was about to have piglets, we had to be particularly vigilant and record the exact time the piglets arrived. As we didn't have direct access to the Pigs House (which was locked) the only way we could get an update on the delivery was by crawling up a tunnel from the yard into the sty. As you can imagine, a very pregnant sow is hugely territorial and very protective of her babies and on one occasion I had to make an emergency exit from the tunnel as the angry sow raised her huge body and turned to confront the intruder.

I was almost eighteen when I started in Dryad, so had a provisional driving licence which enabled me to drive a motorbike or a three-wheeled vehicle. The Dryad Car Park was full of cars of all shapes and sizes. Usually, the Navy in their considerate and compassionate manner, gave us all of two weeks' notice of being required to join a ship in Singapore, Cape town or any other part of the world– and often it was less than that. This lack of notice meant that some unsuspecting car owners had little or no time to dispose of or sell their vehicles. And those that did, frequently had to accept very low offers.

My first car was a Morgan three-wheeler, bought for £17 from a chap who had to go off to Cape Town in a hurry and it was a lovely little machine and got me around very nicely .I was allowed to drive this on a provisional licence because it didn't have reverse gear .This was at a time when I had no idea of what the name Morgan meant and neither did I fully appreciate how the value of this little car, would escalate over the years. I still don't remember what happened to it when I left HMS Dryad – maybe it's still in the car park. I had my moneys- worth out of it so maybe I just gave it away.

I often think of how times have changed since that course.

One of the subjects that I had to learn during my course was the correct switching procedure to bring the Early Warning Radar from its 'Off position' to be fully operational. Bearing in mind, all the electronic equipment associated with this machine filled a 10' by 10' room and if incorrectly sequenced, fuses would be blown, and the system made unserviceable. The entire procedure was designed so that the central technical bit to the Radar - the Thyrotron Valve was warmed up and brought into service in the intended way and at the correct time. The correct procedure had to be followed, and this took some time to learn.

Thirty years later, I had a radar system in my boat which, although not as powerful as the Early Warning Radar that I learned to operate at HMS Dryad, but non-the-less a very sophisticated piece of electronic gear as it linked the radar to the chart, and this could be switched on by the flick of a switch!

After the RP2 course I was sent to HMS Victory – Portsmouth Barracks- for a Leading Seaman's course.

It was unusual for someone so young to be on the course, (I was 18 at the time) but this was only because of the Upper Yardman Scheme, and I became the youngest Leading Seaman in the Royal Navy.

Once I had qualified as a Leading Seaman the next hurdle was the Admiralty Interview Board to select suitable candidates for the Upper Yardman Course which, if successfully completed would lead to promotion to Sub Lieutenant and a career as an Officer.

If my memory serves me correctly there were about a dozen of us at the preliminary course in Portsmouth and they were from all branches of the Royal Navy. Once again, I was the youngest in the class. The course culminated in the AIB and the twelve or so who managed to pass were soon on their way to HMS Temeraire in South Queensferry, on the banks of the River Forth and to ensure that I was elevated to the correct status for the course, I was promoted to Leading Seaman.

I travelled up to Scotland with Gareth Jones whose dad was an MP. Gareth was an Electrical Mechanic who had been to a posh Private School, and he was the proud owner of an MG Sports car. The journey to Scotland was great fun.

Essentially a 'knife and fork' course, the main purpose of Temeraire was to knock the many rough edges off us simple sailors and turn us (hopefully) into Officers.

By any standards, a considerable challenge, and involved much study and examinations.

7
LEADING SEAMAN to SUB LIEUTENANT

My life came to a crossroads when I was a Leading Seaman, aged 20, stationed in Scotland at H.M.S. Temeraire. There is no doubt in my mind that the path that my life was ultimately to take was determined by a gale in the Bristol Channel. Had it not been for that very rough night when HMS Chaplet went to the aid of a vessel in distress, I could well have spent my life in Cornwall and in farming.

H.M.S. Temeraire was a very select Naval Establishment set in the very rural and tranquil acres in the shadow of the Forth Bridge at South Queensferry. The residents were young men from the lower deck who, having passed through the many and varied selection processes that the powers that be had perversely devised, were now on the final bit of the training programme that was aimed at converting them from rough sailors to cultivated members of the officer class. I was the youngest of four sailors on the course and the only one who had joined the Navy at 15.

The other three were adult entrants and who had had other jobs before arriving at this place. Rodney had been an officer in the Merchant Navy; Peter had been in the sixth form at a Secondary Modern near Plymouth; Colin had enjoyed a varied career already - as a trainee Naval Pilot; as crew on a boat that sailed to the West Indies and finally as a miner in the Uranium mines in Canada.

The other 15 students had come from the Artificer route – a better educated lot than us sailors and to illustrate it they wore a much smarter uniform with shirt, jacket, tie and peaked cap.

We were supervised by a small number of hand-picked staff, whose job it was to mould us, very quickly, into Naval Officers and allow a seamless transition from the lower deck to the wardroom. In some cases, this presented a considerable challenge. Not only did we have to improve our standard of education (school classes every day), but we were also expected to play our part on the sports field too.

Me, Colin, Peter and Rodney.
(I came across this picture at a recent reunion, celebrating 60 years since this photo was taken. It illustrates the bond that existed between us then and is just as strong now.)

As one time there were no more than 20 of on the course, so if we had a rugby and hockey fixture, with the help of the staff we could field both teams. Meals were formal affairs – mess dress every evening, with drinks in the anteroom before going into the wardroom for dinner with the staff and probably the captain too, so by the end of the course the staff knew each one of us quite well.

With the Highlands on our doorstep the temptation to go into the hills every weekend was strong and most of us took every opportunity to get away. Weekends were spent in the Highlands whenever possible, not just for the love of camping and the great outdoors, but it was an acceptable way to escape Divisions and Church so as often as I could, I would head north with a rucksack and a tent and tackle a Scottish Mountain.

Bruno, John and I in the Highlands

Had 'Bagging Munros' been popular at that time, I would have been a serious contender as I loved nothing better than being up there in that beautiful part of Scotland and I climbed Ben Lomond, Ben MacDuhie, Schiehallion, Ben Nevis and several other Munroes. I would love to have bagged a few more had I been aware of this challenge.

The photograph shows most of the students turning up for Rugby Team duty!

At the end of our academic course, which was at roughly 'A 'level standard, we had our final examination. Once they were over, but before the results were published, we were sent to training ships for a bit of sea time. This practical experience (our first as an embryo officer) was a valuable indicator as to how successful the course had been. At the end of that 'sea time' whilst the results were collated, reports were prepared for our graduation. Although our uniforms were consistent with the rank that we occupied before being elevated to HMS Temeraire (I was a Leading Seaman so wore the traditional 'Square Rig) but the white patches on our shoulders indicated to everyone else that we were 'Upper Yardmen' and were training to become 'Officers'. If all went well for us, and we completed the training, we would soon be donning the uniform of a Sub Lieutenant. The give-away white patches on our shoulder frequently resulted in hostility of varying degrees from some members of the ship's company who were suspicious of anyone who aspired to 'be an officer'.

When the exam was over, I was sent as a Leading Seaman with Upper Yardman white flashes, to HMS Chaplet for three weeks sea time.

Chaplet was a 'CH' class destroyer which had seen service on the Atlantic Convoys during the war and was currently employed in the Western Approaches.

During the three weeks sea time, we were attached to each department in turn so that once back in Temeraire we could write up a 'Sea Journal' with not only a record of all that we experienced during that trip but a detailed account of how each department functioned, how it was staffed and how the equipment was operated. It was a formidable task and one that took many hours of burning midnight oil to complete.

One night, on duty in the Bristol Channel, a severe gale came in from the west. Just after midnight, a 'Mayday' distress call was received from a yacht off the North Devon coast and off we went to its aid. Someone on the yacht had been injured in the wild weather and was in need of a doctor.

Our sea boat was a 27' whaler – propelled by oars and steered by the coxswain and which had to be lowered from its davits into the sea by the 'duty watch on deck'. I was included in this team.

The First Lieutenant, an experienced Lieutenant Commander was in charge of the operation but after many attempts was having difficulty in getting the whaler away from the ship's side. In order to get the sea-boat away and over to the sinking yacht, HMS Chaplet was stationery in the water and at the mercy of the wind. The wind and waves had turned the ship beam-on to the sea and the uncontrolled rolling and pitching were forcing the whaler back on to the ships side with potentially very dangerous consequences. His orders were not having the desired effect, and I could see that unless something was done, and done pretty soon, we would have another emergency.

I asked the First Lieutenant if I could take over, for I knew how to sort this out.

Hugely surprisingly, he said 'yes' so I took charge and, under my direction, using ropes to aid them, I had the sea boat away on its journey to the stricken yacht in no time.

The Sea Journal.

When the emergency had been dealt with and the sea boat returned to its secure position on deck, HMS Chaplet proceeded to the Irish Sea and I returned to my cabin. It was only then that I began to realise how impertinent I had been in suggesting to the First Lieutenant that I could deal with that situation better than he. I was only a Leading Seaman, and he was a Lieutenant Commander. I was under training, and he was the 'second-in-command' of a Naval Warship. But what I didn't know was that this action, by me, on this stormy night in the Bristol Channel would determine my future career in the Royal Navy. I went to bed and gave it no more thought.

When this period of sea time came to an end, I went back to Temeraire, and the next big task was to write up the 'Sea Journal' and once that had been completed the results of the exams had been posted.

I had failed.

I was the only one not to have made the grade.

Closer inspection of the individual results showed that I had passed every subject except one. Naval History.

I was not surprised.

Some people have a flair for languages; some for science; others have a complete block when it comes to mathematics. My weakest point was history. I've never passed a history exam; I have no interest in history, I cannot remember dates and (unfortunately) I find the subject, deadly. I knew that if I had to re-sit the exam, I would achieve a similar result.

The procedure for those who fail a final exam in Temeraire involved going before yet another interview board, consisting of a selection of the local high-ranking officers – usually Captains and above who collectively decide the fate of the person summoned to appear before them. This fate usually had only one direction. OUT

The rules of the game stipulated that if any Upper Yardman failed to complete the course (for whatever reason) they were immediately discharged from the service and returned to 'Civvy Street'. It was unknown for anyone to fail the finals and continue with the course or even to return to the lower deck.

I was aware of this, and I must admit to not being too unhappy about the possibility of leaving the Navy and joining my brother Leonard in farming. I had warned Leonard of the situation and had also told him that the probable outcome would be a discharge from the Navy. I was prepared for the outcome, and I was happy to 'leave it in the lap of the Gods'.

And so, my time came – the solitary failure from the Temeraire course appearing in front of a collection of senior officers assembled for the purpose of deciding his future in a posh office in Rosyth Dockyard.

I was accompanied to Rosyth by the First Lieutenant of HMS Temeraire who had to report to the Board of my behaviour and how I had conducted myself throughout my time under officer training. My fate looks sealed until he read out a report from Commander Groom, a highly decorated Destroyer Captain who had been in Command of HMS Chaplet during my sea training.

I was unaware of this report and thought that the decision was a foregone conclusion, so I was quite surprised then the President of the Interview Board called me back in to announce my fate.

'Upper Yardman Barter' he began, in a slow, ponderous tone ' You have not passed your final academic exam and under normal circumstance you would now be discharged from the Royal Navy.

However, in view of Commander Groom's report from your sea training in HMS Chaplet, we have decided to waive the results of your examination, and you will proceed to Britannia Royal Naval College forthwith'.

Apparently, Commander Groom had been impressed with my handling of the sea boat during that gale in the Bristol Channel and had written

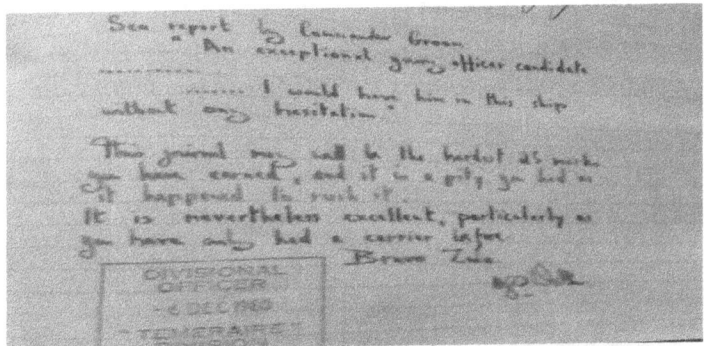

'An exceptional young Officer candidate. I would have him in my ship without a moment's hesitation'.

High praise from such an experienced officer which resulted in me going to Dartmouth with the rest of them. Three months later I was promoted Sub Lieutenant – the youngest ever to have been promoted from the lower deck (I was 20 years old) and the first one for 20 years to have come to Dartmouth from HMS Ganges at Shotley. And it was all due to luck – luck that I had been on that ship at that time and luck that the First Lieutenant had sufficient confidence in me to allow me to take this action.

I often think of 'what might have been' (as I'm sure that everyone does) and I am in no doubt that had it not been for that night in the Bristol Channel and the subsequent good report that was passed to the Review Board, I would have failed to make the grade and discharged from the Royal Navy (as no officer candidate who failed the course was allowed back into service on the lower deck). Maybe I would now be writing the musings of a retired farmer!

When we' passed out' -Graduated from- Dartmouth we were awarded a promotion grant of £120 to cover the cost of buying a Uniform, Greatcoat and Ceremonial Sword. As I already had my father's sword and his uniform which I had altered to fit me, I was able to use that grant for other things.

We had just bought the farm, and it needed stocking, so the Admiralty Promotion Grant went to buy a Pedigree Friesian Cow and a Landrace Cross Large White Pig who within three months would produce a litter of thirteen piglets! Leonard and I did a huge amount of work renovating the farm. We acquired some moulds that enabled us to make our own 4" concrete blocks from which we built pigs houses and other outbuildings and very soon the farm was a functioning unit with pedigree Frisian Cows, several pigs and some chickens. It was a great pity that the dice fell in favour of the RN!

Tregolls Farm (naval uniform with hat!)

Before we could accurately call ourselves 'Sub-Lieutenants' we had to complete three months at the Royal Naval College at Greenwich, after which we did the standard 'Subs Courses' when we visited all the establishments which were home to the several specialisations that we could opt for or not.

Peter, Colin, Rodney and I graduated from Britannia Royal Naval College, Dartmouth as Sub Lieutenants on 1st January 1961 and the next stage in our progression to fully qualified Officers in the Royal Navy, was a three month 'cultural course' at Greenwich. Having meals in the Painted Hall and with everything that London has to offer on the doorstep, and with the freedom to enjoy it, was a huge change from the strict discipline that we had experienced up until now. Of course, we had classes to attend and homework to complete, but the lecturers were civilians and the routine more like a university. Naval History was high on the agenda, and so was History of Art and we also spent many hours on the roof tops of the college, learning how to use a sextant and take sun and star sights. When we had passed though these famous portals not only had we had a better idea of advanced navigation but also had a good working knowledge of the London Art Galleries, Theatreland and Soho!

At the end of the working day, Colin and Rodney went home to their wives, as they lived locally, whilst Peter and I explored the West End and took in many visits to the theatre, art galleries and other places of interest. One of which was 'The Coach and Horse' in Greenwich Market.

This pub was unusual in that it had a licence to open at 5am – to serve the workers in Greenwich Market. Peter and I became friendly with the Landlord who encouraged us to work behind the bar. Having completed a speedy apprenticeship we frequently ran the pub so that the landlord and his wife could have an evening off.

I celebrated my 21st birthday whilst at Greenwich and to start the day, Peter and I went to the 'Coach and Horses' for a couple of pints before returning for breakfast in the 'Painted Hall'. Later that day, Colin came in to play me at squash. Because it was my 21st birthday, I had hoped that he would let me win. He didn't.

I often wonder what the true purpose of the Greenwich Course was, and I have yet to come up with a very convincing answer. Maybe it was to round off our 'education' with a bit of culture and combine it with a bit of 'Astro Navigation'. Or maybe it was simply to allow us to adjust to the new position in life within the Royal Navy that we now found ourselves in. Whatever the justification, our time in Greenwich was memorable and very enjoyable.

This three-month passed very quickly and we were soon off to other destinations as part of the 'Sub Lieutenant's Courses'. We visited various Naval Establishments which were home to the individual specialisations that were open to us, and to others as well. HMS Vernon the home of Sonar; HMS Dryad the home of Navigation; HMS Excellent the home of Naval Gunnery and RNAS Culdrose, the home of Naval Aviation all hosted us for two to three weeks at a time and when all these had been completed, we were given a week's leave before being sent off to our first ship. Peter, Colin and I all went off to Stanstead where we boarded a plane for Singapore to join the 6th Minesweeper Squadron, whilst Rodney went to Malta.

We were now fully-fledged Sub Lieutenants.

8
HMS Houghton, Woodbridge Haven, and Exmouth

I arrived in Houghton in Singapore in time to join the captain, Commander Gus Halliday and the rest of the officers for breakfast in the very small wardroom that was to be my home for the next 18 months.

I was taking over from Sub Lieutenant Brian Adams who would leave later that day for a flying course in England, so we quickly went through my duties, met the other officers and the crew and off he went. As far as I could determine, my duties included looking after the Ship's Office, all the correspondence, pay, confidential books, and money changing when we went to other countries. I was also the Divisional Officer for most of the crew. I would be the Education Officer if anybody wanted educating; I would be Sports Officer and responsible for arranging sports fixtures whenever necessary and last but not least, I was film officer and had to go to the Fleet Film Library in Singapore to select suitable films for the entertainment of the ship's company. The expression 'Dog's Body' came to mind, but I dare not articulate it!

It seemed that I would be kept busy and that is how it turned out, especially when Gus Halliday was relieved by Commander William Staveley.

Commander Staveley was the youngest Commander in the Navy who, at the age of 31 was promoted at the earliest possible opportunity. And it soon became apparent why this was so.

He was very fond of writing reports, especially after minesweeping exercises which involved the use or evaluation of equipment. Frequently this information was considered sensitive enough to be 'Classified' which meant that the report could only be typed by me and not by Writer Michael LeStrange who normally worked as my assistant and occupied the only chair in the office.

We had no computers, laptops, tablets or printers. Each letter was typed on a skin which could then be placed in a duplicating machine and copies could be run off by turning the drum by hand. A spelling mistake involving a single letter could easily be corrected with correcting fluid but any mistakes involving more than a few letters usually meant starting again and, on several occasions, as I typed well into the night to get a report out the following morning, as I approached the final paragraph I discovered that I had omitted a sentence, or word and that I'd have to start again.

HMS Woodbridge Haven was our support ship – the 'mother ship' to the 104th Minesweeping Squadron and generally speaking their officers covered our needs and dealt with much of the administration, especially involving pay and stores.

An official visit had been planned to Manila in the Philippines and unfortunately this coincided with Woodbridge Haven going into dry dock for routine maintenance. This meant that HMS Houghton as Senior Ship (with Commander Staveley on board) had to take over the responsibility of some of these services, especially pay and the cash account. As I was responsible for this in our ship, (the senior ship) when we went to Manila, I had to cover this duty for all the ships in that visit. And during that visit there was a pay day, so I had to carry enough money to cover this and more.

As we left Singapore, we had more than £5,000 in Malayan Dollars in the safe, together with the same amount in Philippine Pesos which I had drawn from the Bank at an exchange rate of 10.47 Pesos to the Pound Sterling. The currency of the account for which I was responsible was Malayan Dollars, which then had to be converted to Sterling at the end of the visit as this was the main currency of the account. Introducing the Philippine Peso just added another complication which I could deal with. Unfortunately, during the visit, we ran out of money (the sailors were spending far more than we had anticipated) and I had to go to the local bank in Manila and get another 50,000 Pesos. The exchange rate was now 10.72 to the Pound Sterling.

At the end of our visit, as we headed back to Singapore. I had to change back any unused pesos to Malayan Dollars and once in Singapore I had to reconcile the account and return any remaining money to the Supply Officer in Woodbridge Haven. And this took many hours of midnight oil!

I was secretly very pleased with myself as much as relieved when, a day or so later I was informed by the accounting team in Woodbridge Haven, who had been through the account, that the books balanced, and the account was correct.

On a visit to Saigon, as Sports Officer, I organised a Rugby match against a local French team. This was at a time when Vietnam was still under French control, shortly before they left, and the Americans came. The Viet Cong were a problem but not near enough to Saigon to trouble the city. We could hear the crack of gun fire, but it was considered too far away to be of any importance and the game of rugby went ahead.

Normally, at half time, especially in that heat, you get a glass of squash, or water, or an orange to suck. Not in French Saigon.

It appeared that the local tradition was to give the opposition a glass or two of Ouzo to quench their thirst, which, as we quickly discovered, was a very clever and enjoyable way of overcoming any superiority that the visiting team may have demonstrated before the interval. We lost the match but had a happy time!

Commander Staveley celebrated his birthday on the evening before we left Hong Kong to return to Singapore. He preferred to dine on board as it was less expensive than taking his fellow officers ashore and instructed our Chinese Steward to go ashore and collect the ingredients which the chef would then turn into a Birthday Dinner. We sailed early the next morning and as we settled into our watchkeeping roster the symptoms started to appear.

It was a most awful passage south to Singapore. Not only was the weather bad and our little minesweeper rolled about drunkenly but all the watchkeeping Officers were stricken by severe diarrhoea and vomiting. Coke Cola was the only thing that I could keep down long enough to cope with a four-hour trick on the bridge and the others were no better off. We eventually arrived in Singapore when three of us were admitted to hospital at the Naval Base. Commander Staveley and Jim Weatherall, the Navigator both had

Hepatitis B (severe jaundice) and I had contracted Dengue fever which is quite a serious illness. It later transpired that the Steward had bought the Oysters for Commander Staveley's Birthday Dinner from the local market. Further investigation suggested that the oysters had been harvested from the area adjacent to the sewerage outfall!

Whilst we were in hospital Communists from Indonesia invaded Sarawak and Brunei and HM Ships Houghton and Maryton were dispatched to Brunei.

I joined them two weeks later when I had been discharged from Hospital and when Commander Staveley arrived a few days later he took command and directed operations. We had no maps of the area other than aerial photos taken by the RAF.

There were no roads through the jungles of Borneo as the rivers were the conduits along which boats (mostly primitive canoes) carried people and goods. The first task, in Bill Staveley's mind, was to patrol the rivers and search for obvious areas where insurgents were accessing the rivers from their training ground (if these existed at all).

John Hickman, a fellow officer in Houghton and I, were given this task. Our duties involved taking a local dug-out canoe with a large outboard on the back and, together with a local policeman who would act as interpreter and a sailor armed with a lee Enfield .303 rifle as crew, we would each take one of the major rivers each and go as far as we could, investigating any suspicious landing area or pathway which might give access to a possible training area. Once we had covered the length of the river we would then report back to the Gurkha Commander, especially if we discovered anything unusual.

One would have thought that, in the absence of jungle greens, or camouflage, it would have been desirable to for us to wear something unobtrusive.

Not a bit of it. Bill Staveley thought that as we were representing Her Britannic Majesty, we should wear white uniform! It's a wonder he didn't insist on us wearing swords as well. So off we went, offering ourselves as easy targets, in white uniform against the green/brown of the jungle and the river! Fortunately, there was no sign of any insurgents as we landed at every riverside clearing to investigate possible access. On return, having covered all of the navigable part of the river, I had to report to the Gurkha Commander to be debriefed. Whilst I was talking to him, my sailor, Mechanical Engineer Gargett, was being given hospitality by the Gurkhas in the shape of a tot or two of rum (presumably the one that he had missed whilst out in the canoe with me).

Back on board, I reported to Commander Staveley, had something to eat then, as it had been a long tiring day, went to bed and I was soon asleep.

About an hour or so later I was awoken by the First Lieutenant (the Officer on duty) who informed me that Marine Engineer (Stoker!) Gargett had acquired a knife and was threatening to kill the Duty Petty Officer and that, since he had been with me all day, he was my responsibility. I should go and sort him out. I was furious. I was furious on a number of counts.

Firstly, I was furious that the First Lieutenant had awakened me. He was Officer of the Day and as such, he was solely responsible for what happened to the ship or its crew. Any problems he should deal with them.

Secondly, I was annoyed that the duty Petty Officer wasn't dealing appropriately with a Junior Rating as he should, and thirdly, I was annoyed that ME Gargett, who had behaved very well all day, was now involved in a fracas with the Duty P.O.

Clad only in a sarong, I stormed into the galley, where Gargett, evidently under the influence of alcohol, had indeed got the Duty PO pinned against the bulkhead with a knife at his throat. My annoyance and anger drove me straight to Gargett where I took the knife off him, gave him a clip around the ear and a verbal dressing down then repeated it for the Duty PO before returning to my cabin and bed, but not before handing the situation to the incompetent and ineffectual First Lieutenant. The incident had to be logged and went through the usual disciplinary channels, and I was involved in the trial. ME Gargett didn't have much of a defence and was sentenced to fourteen days in the glasshouse.

During this emergency we (the British Forces) had the power to requisition (i.e. take over) any useful piece of kit that we needed to help fight the insurgents.

When John Hickman and I were on Patrol we came across the car used by the leader of the Partai Ryatt – the Communist mob, so we requisitioned it! It was a Karmann Ghia (V.W. Sports car) which suited us well. We would chuck the sten guns in the back and head off to the beach!

In the meantime, the fight against the insurgents was hotting up. I was sent to join 42 Royal Marine Commando as their Boat Officer. They had a camp high in the jungle from where all patrols and surveillance was mounted. I had four Sailors in my group and together we had to provide all water borne transport for the operations conducted by the Royal Marines, one of whom, Paddy Ashdown of the Liberal Democrats was a young Captain. I went on several patrols with them and became part of the operational unit of 42 Commando.

It was the rainy season for most of the time that I was with 42 Commando in the jungle, and after a particularly wet period, a flood alert was received, and it appeared that many of the indigenous Dayak people (who lived in long houses and whose ancestors had been head hunting cannibals) were in danger of being swept away by the rising water levels.

The war stopped as we turned to help them. Unfortunately, the only boats that we had at our disposal were the canoes that we had requisitioned from the local fishermen and a redundant barge that was moored on our jetty. What it had been previously used for I have no idea but the mechanical Engineer in our small party went below, worked out how to start the beast, fired the engine up and off we went up the river to assist in any way we could. As the only Naval Officer, I was in charge of the barge, and it was a new experience for me. Progress was painfully slow – we could, at best make 6 knots mostly against a current of 5 knots. But we eventually made it up the river, rescued some Dayaks whose 'long houses' had become submerged in the rising flood, and brought them back to relative safety of the 42 Commando base.

When the time came for me to finish my posting with 42 Commando, and return to my ship two months later, I was presented with a Royal Marine Green Beret and Badge and made an Honorary member of 42 Commando. I still treasure that badge.

A Visit to a Dyak 'Long House' *The 'barge' used for the rescue.*

When the time was up for return to the UK (and a place on a Flying Course, I hoped) I was told that HMS Woodbridge Haven had to go back to the UK and be scrapped. Her navigating officer, Lt Cmdr. Gordon Marshall from Eye, Suffolk would be remaining in Singapore to join the ship that would replace the Woodbridge Haven, so I was directed to navigate the Woodbridge Haven home to the UK.

Woodbridge Haven must have been one of the oldest ships in service in The Royal Navy and was one of the last ships in the Navy to have had reciprocating engines. Her plates were getting dangerously thin and, to cap it all she had no modern navigational equipment on board. We had charts of course but nothing other than a compass, a depth sounder, a sextant and a stopwatch.

I had learned Astronomical Navigation from the rooftops of Greenwich, practising the art of sun sights over the rooftops of the Royal College, but I hadn't had much practical experience, so this was a fantastic opportunity and one which I relished. Taking morning and evening stars, plus a sun sight or two during the day gave me the opportunity to use 'astro nav' in a serious environment. Since then, I have been asked on a couple pf occasions 'what action are you most proud of?' and I frequently think that is was bringing this old ship home to England from Singapore, with the minimum of navigational aids, that I especially proud of.

We refuelled in Ghan, a small island at the southerly tip of the Maldives with a maximum height above sea level of only two metres. An RAF staging base had been established there during the Second World War and we knew that we were not going to get a 'run ashore' during our visit as this was just a refuelling stop. When Captain Townley asked me, as we approached the island, 'What time should we sight Ghan, Peter?' Ghan is just a clump of palms and an airstrip and if the visibility is below par, it would be easy to miss her and sail right past. However I was confident of my sights and calculations.

'At 3.10 this afternoon, Gan will appear 15 degrees on the starboard bow, sir' I replied. The horizon was empty, we had been out of sight of land for several days, so the other officers took my statement with a pinch of salt.

As the time approached a crowd gathered on the bridge expecting to enjoy my humiliation when there was no sign of anything other than the odd seabird, and a cloud. Many binoculars appeared as the Officers congregated on the bridge. They even ran a sweepstake hoping that my calculations would be hopelessly out.

It was with immense arrogant self-satisfaction that I was able to report at 3.10 that a palm tree was visible, (with the aid of binoculars), on the starboard bow!

We refuelled, transited the Red Sea and then the Suez Canal and refuelled again in Gibraltar.

We anchored off Portsmouth to await entry to our final berth. We knew that many relatives were waiting to greet the ships company, and they were ferried out to the ship from the Dockyard. I was not expecting anyone to come and meet me, so when my Mum appeared amongst the passengers coming on board, I was very pleased, and she was pleased to see me. It was disappointing that I had volunteered to be duty officer for that night so couldn't go ashore with her. When the time came for me to go on leave, I was still waiting for an appointment to a Flying Course as I had been promised. Instead I received notification that I was to join HMS Exmouth in Helensborough where I would be 'Additional for Seaman Duties' or words to that effect which really meant that I was to be a general dog's body.

Exmouth was a target- ship employed in the training of submarine crews, particularly Submarine captains so we were destined to spend a lot of time at sea and it was a sad reminder of the past for

The Admiralty planners are all heart. When we needed a break from the relentlessly monotonous task of being a target for submariners to fire torpedoes at, The Admiralty sent us for a bit of Rest and Recreation as Fishery Protection off Iceland where the Icelandic Gunboats were still flexing their muscles whenever a British Registered Fishing vessel strayed into their territorial waters. There were some benefits to this job. A run ashore in Reykjavik was great fun as the sun was still visible at Midnight and the locals, after spending half the year in darkness, knew a thing or two about partying in the summer. The midges were a huge nuisance.

At sea we were there to assist the British Trawlers if the Icelandic Gunboats (Thor, in particular, whose captain was trigger happy) got aggressive. When the British Trawlers radar broke down or they had any other problems we would send an engineer over and he would return with baskets full of Halibut as payment for his services. I've never eaten so much beautiful fish since.

When we got back to Rosyth, I had developed Mumps so had to be transferred to an isolation hospital in the Vale of Leven. When able to, I returned to my ship and on the way back I was sent for by the Base Surgeon Captain who ushered me into his office and with an over melancholy expression said that he had some very bad news for me.

'I'm very sorry to tell you, Lieutenant Barter, that because of your recent illness, you are now sterile and will never have children'.

Just goes to show that even Surgeon Captains talk rubbish at times!

9.
A Lifelong Partnership

In July 1964, H.M.S. Exmouth was moored near to the Forth bridge, waiting for a berth the next day in Rosyth Dockyard. David Codd, the Navigating Officer, suggested that he and I go ashore that evening to meet up with a couple of girls who he knew and who were completing their midwifery training at a Hospital in Ayrshire.

It sounded like a great idea, despite Ayrshire being on the other side of Scotland.

We took the boat ashore, hired a car and set off for Irving.

Pat and Rosemary had completed their SRN training at Hammersmith Hospital and were in the middle of getting their Midwifery qualification. David had known them from London through a mutual friend and thought it would be a good idea if I would pair up with Rosemary for an evening out. David's girlfriend Clare, (who he eventually married) was working in America and giving him a bit of a run-around so he was pleased to have an evening out with an old friend. We had a lovely evening and at the end of it, we returned to Rosyth.

On the way back, we were talking about the enjoyable evening that we'd just had, and I realised that David had a fondness for Pat, and in view of the currently strained relationship between him and Clare, I gave him a bit of advice.

As we were approaching that age when one starts thinking of settling down, I said 'David, old fruit, I suggest you forget about Clare and marry Pat.

Then I added 'If you don't, then I will'.

Pat and Rosemary returned to London having completed their training and HMS Exmouth continued on to Iceland and the Cod war. I left the ship in September and went off to complete the Aircrew Survival Course in the New Forest and after that a NATO Tactical Course at the Royal Naval College Greenwich. My next appointment was to be the basic Flying Course at Linton on Ouse, Yorkshire.

As soon as I had left Exmouth, I contacted Pat and went to see her at her flat in Earls Court which she shared with Rosemary and another colleague, Jane.

On every occasion that I was free, I went to Earls Court to see Pat, and the fact that I was at Greenwich made life easy in that respect. I bought a car – not a very sensible one I admit but it was a car none the less. It was a 1937 Austin Ruby – Registration ANO 101 and I was soon to appreciate the impracticality of this machine.

On the day that I was to take Pat out in my new car I didn't make our date on time. It broke down soon after leaving Greenwich and I had to resort to the Tube and taxis. I lost all confidence in the beast and Pat and I never had an outing in it.

At the end of the course at Greenwich, I had to make my way to Linton on Ouse and I decided to go by car. The problem that I'd had with the engine had been fixed, so I set off from Greenwich in pouring rain at 9 o'clock on a Saturday evening. I decided to travel overnight to avoid the traffic, but I hadn't accounted for the weather. As I headed north out of London the windscreen wipers decided to have a rest. With the rain lashing down and the headlights of a 1937 vehicle at peak performance, keeping on the right side of the road was a challenge.

But providence was looking kindly upon me.

In the gloom I caught sight of a hitch hiker, thumbing a lift on the A1. I stopped, and he very gratefully accepted the offer of a lift to York, his destination.

Then I told him the bad news. With no windscreen wipers, if I gave him a towel to stem the flow of water through the open window, would he keep the windscreen clear?

'Of course,' he replied cheerfully and that's exactly what he did. With his left arm out of the window he worked the wipers all night until we got to York where, having dropped my passenger off, I went to RAF Linton-on-Ouse and parked the car. As I reversed into an empty space, there was an expensive sounding bang which turned out to be the fracturing of the 'half shafts' – the rear axle. Fortunately, I had arrived at my destination otherwise it would have been a very expensive exercise.

Pat and I decided that we didn't want to be apart and although Naval Officers were not officially allowed to either get married before the age of 25 without special permission, nor live ashore, we rented a flat in the Clifton area of York and Pat came to join me and she took up a post at York Maternity Hospital. My appearing in her life upset her plans somewhat. Before we met, she had intended going with 'Save the Children' to Shimla, in the foothills of the Himalayas, to use her qualifications for the benefit of those in that part of the world. Sadly, they were deprived of her enormous skills and expertise and the Barter family were the beneficiaries.

We decided to get married and would have preferred a quiet ceremony in a Registry Office but in deference to the wishes of our families we agreed to get married in Wales. After the Christmas holiday Pat went home to arrange the wedding and settle the argument between her stepfather and two uncles as to who should give her away.

During the week before the wedding I was night flying, so I was tired before I set out for Wales on the Friday evening.

The wedding day dawned white in Wales. Heavy snow had fallen over much of Wales and the West of England, and it soon became clear that my family would not make it. Only Ivor and Gwen got through and arrived just in time for Ivor to fill in as Best Man.

The following day we set off for York where I had another week of night flying to look forward to. During our time in York, Pat worked as a Staff Midwife in the Maternity Hospital which helped considerably with our finances.

I passed the flying course and when that was done, we decamped to Cornwall, to join RNAS Culdrose for the helicopter conversion course and a summary of our life in Cornwall is written elsewhere. Basically I was grounded medically on the same day that Sarah arrived and that meant that we had to move to Belfast where I was appointed as Flight Deck Officer to HMS Fearless which was being built by Harland and Wolf.

Sarah was born prematurely at the end of July and very soon we were off to Belfast. Then another quick move to Dorset as the Admiralty thoughtlessly sent me to cover for a sick Navigating Officer. We lived in a mobile home in Portland for my last eighteen months in the Navy and that was where Nick was born. Much of that time I was at sea, on Exercise in the Atlantic or training the fleet in Portland, but I spent a lot of time away and Pat had two young children to bring up on her own. Without my presence, it was a hard and lonely life, but we had a wonderful neighbour – 'Bligh' who loved Pat and the children and was very much like a surrogate 'Mum' in my absence. When I was at home, and had to leave early in the morning, there would be a knock on the caravan window and when I opened it, Bligh would pass me a cup of tea, to get me going!

When Nick was six months old, I was released from the Navy, and we moved to Exeter.

I was a student at St Luke's college during the day and in the evenings, when I was at home to look after the children, Pat worked in the A & E Department of the Exeter Royal Infirmary. This was a very busy hospital, especially during the holiday season when accidents on the new Exeter by-pass were all too frequent.

And that set the pattern for the next fifty years. Pat and I have shared the responsibilities of family life as much as possible. She has been the mainstay of the family, adapting quickly to any change in environment and always contributing hugely when necessary.

This meant that whenever a new surgery was started, Pat would recruit and train the staff and fill in as necessary until they were all 'bedded in'. She would always be the first to be called when staff were sick and it is difficult to imagine how I would have coped with the many and various situations that I have been in, without the constant help and steadfast support of Pat. Unfortunately because we moved frequently and with the responsibilities of a family, Pat's ambitions were never realised. She had wanted to work with deprived families in Shimla and had signed on with Save the Children, but I came along and all that was changed.

A family group just before I left The Navy

And Pat and the children with dear old 'Bligh' who was such a friend in Portland.

Pat was devastated by the loss of her brother Graham who died on a squash court at the age of 50. He was super fit and after his Rugby career, which included caps for Wales and the British and Irish Lions, he coached a club near Liverpool.

Pat was very ill during the latter part of our time at Meadowside but when we moved to Tattingstone she had improved sufficiently to take up a part time job as Deputy Matron at a Residential Home in Needham Market and she remained in that post until we moved to Cornwall. In her free time, she became a Samaritan and took her turn on the roster for Ipswich. This training with the Samaritans was of immense value for Pat as when we had settled in Cornwall, she enrolled in a Course to become a Counsellor, run by the University of Plymouth. We had a lovely house in PenPol, overlooking Restronguet Creek and it was a new beginning for Pat and two years later she graduated. She enjoyed it immensely and felt very fulfilled when she had completed it. Unfortunately, the move back to Norfolk made it more difficult for her to find a satisfactory position, especially as she willingly gave her time to help in the new practice in Diss. Now that we have retired, Pat's time is totally taken up with giving love and attention to the grandchildren. Sarah has found it very difficult bringing up her four children without the help of a husband -in fact he is more of a hindrance than anything as he still exerts, or tries to exert, his compulsive controlling influence on her and the children. The children, fortunately, are now seeing through their father and are beginning to resist his demands that they spend more time with him.

Emily is the only one who looks forward to spending time with her father. Lorca and Lucia are both very excited about going to Spain with him for a holiday as they have their own friends there and want to see them and catch up. But I feel it won't be long before they won't want to go (except for Emily who will always want to be with daddy for a holiday – not, I think because he does anything exciting with her, for the others say that Emily is not allowed out and spends all day on her iPad – which Emily enjoys!

We have now been married for almost 53 years (although we have yet to celebrate the Golden!) and the amazing thing is that we still talk to one another; we still enjoy each other's company; we are great friends, and we are still tolerant of the others' bad habits!

When we sit and cogitate and reminisce, we come to the conclusion that our marriage has been successful largely due to the fact that each has allowed the other to pursue an independent path with the freedom to travel along that path unhindered. We are two individuals who have lived as such, but each supporting the other at all times, with love and understanding. It is of great sadness that neither of our children have found such happiness in their partners.

We have had to adjust, quite dramatically, our standard of living since the disastrous effect of the credit crunch and the failure of the business, but despite that we are very fortunate in having a nice house to live in where we can offer love and support to our family and our grandchildren who spend a lot of time under this roof. I hope that we are able to continue to do so for many years to come as our children and grandchildren are such a huge, huge source of joy to us both. But one thing that has been so important to me over the course of the last fiftynine years, is the constant and unfailing love and support that Pat has given to me and which has enabled me to live this rather 'Random Life'.

10
On Flying

The seeds were sown in Cornwall where, at the age of 12, I had a holiday job. This often involved working on the farm that had been created as part of the land occupied by RNAS Culdrose and for which, my dad was, amongst other duties, the 'farm manager'.

Leonard and I picked potatoes, helped with the pigs or any other tasks that needed doing. At other times, we worked for a flower grower whose acres of anemones on the Lizard peninsular needed hand weeding.

This didn't just involve weeding a patch of flowers in the back garden – but weeding on an industrial scale.

I remember being shown a field of about 3 acres or more and the rows and rows of emerging shoots, all of which had to be hand weeded with the aid of a small hoe. These shoots were emerging anemones, a cut flower very popular for growers who supplied the London Markets with early Cornish flowers.

We started at the top of the field and worked our way down, coping with two or three rows at a time. We always worked backwards – so that our feet did not tread the soil that we had just hoed. At the end of the day we had hardly made any impression on the field but at the end of a week we were working more efficiently and covering the ground. Anyway, the farmer was pleased with our efforts.

This was, as you might imagine, a boring, monotonous and soul-destroying job. But we did earn some pocket money – ten shillings (now 50p) a day and that was the reason why we were there. But for me, the bonus was that this particular field lay under the flight path for RNAS Culdrose, and I had a bird's eye view as the latest naval fighter jets came into land.

Culdrose was a very busy airfield for we had at that time (1950) a very impressive Royal Navy including several Aircraft carriers.

Sea Venoms, Sky raiders, Hawker Hunters, Seahawks and various other fixed wing aircraft together with a whole range of helicopters were frequently in the airspace over the Lizard Peninsular and I was hooked.

My first flight was in a Venom whilst at HMS Harrier, and further flights from RNAS Brawdy really got me hooked on a career as a Naval Pilot. As an Able Seaman in HMS Bulwark I had persuaded one of the Venom pilots (who had known my dad from Culdrose,) to allow me to have a flight in the left-hand seat of his aircraft when the opportunity arose. We visited Manila in the Philippines and as part of the arrival celebrations, HMS Bulwark's aircraft were to do a fly-past over the city. And I could go along as a passenger!

I collected my flying overalls and headgear and after a quick briefing was strapped into the cockpit of the Venom. The excitement got worse as the engine was fired up and we taxied to the launch position on the catapult. One end of a wire strop was attached to the aircraft and the other end fitted over the 'dolly' of the catapult. When the pilot had indicated that his engine was a full revs, the controller would drop his flag. The 'dolly', with the underside of the aircraft attached, was then fired along the track towards the bow. Three seconds later, when the 'dolly' had reached the end of the track, and the aircraft was at 'flying speed' the wire strop dropped away, and we were airborne. It felt as if we had been 'squirted' into the air – which, in fact, just as it was.

This alone was a fantastic experience and being part of the flypast was very thrilling. The 45-minute sortie was rounded off when we returned to the flight deck and caught the arrester wire and taxied to our parking slot.

The Admiralty were advertising for trainee short service, aircrew, and I immediately volunteered. I was the right age; I had the necessary qualifications and, I was already in the RN. I was tremendously excited.

All requests like this had to passed through the Divisional Officer who, if he supported it or agreed with it, then passed it up the chain to the Commander then the Captain. If all agreed, the path was clear for me to apply.

My request got no further than my Divisional Officer.

His argument was that I had so much potential for a long-term career as an officer it would not be in my interest to apply for a short service commission as a Pilot. He thought that I should go through the system as an Upper Yardman, go to Dartmouth and once through that I could then train as a Pilot and have a long career and possibly reach fairly high rank. A short service career would end after five years and then I would be looking for another job. That arrangement suited me as five years of flying would be amazing .My views were not taken into account, so my application was rejected.

I have never forgiven him.

Once I had been through Dartmouth, at every conceivable opportunity I reminded my senior officers that I wanted to fly. I was sent to Singapore in a minesweeper and when the time was fast approaching for me to return to the UK I applied again for the flying course only to be told that as an Upper Yardman with my history, I had far too much experience as a Seaman officer to be allowed to fly, and I should set my sights on a career in Navigation or Gunnery.

I was furious and very frustrated.

It seemed as though everyone was against me. My flight home was cancelled, and I was sent for by the Senior Officer who said 'Barter, the Navigating Officer of HMS Woodbridge Haven (who lived opposite me in Eye) could not be spared to go home with Woodbridge Haven which has to go back to England. You will join her tomorrow and be the Navigating Officer for her passage to the UK. Peter Ford was also in that 'steaming crew' to bring the old lady back to the UK for scrapping.

Woodbridge Haven was on old ship and destined for the scrap yard. Her hull was paper thin in places as a result of decades of corrosion. She had no navigational aids other than charts, a sextant and a chronometer. Her reciprocating engines were nothing short of museum pieces and she had a top speed of ten knots. When asked to push a bit harder the vibration of her old engines created more leaks in the hull. But we got home safely. I frequently think of the old 'Woodbridge Haven' and my time in her as Navigating Officer. If anybody asked me what was my proudest moment, I often replied that it was that I had Navigated an old ship from

Singapore with only the most primitive of navigational aids. On the way across the Pacific Ocean, we had to call in at Ghan to refuel. Ghan was a redundant airstrip used as a staging and refuelling base for the RAF and the Royal Navy. I suspect it was only a few metres above sea level so from a navigational point of view, it could easily be missed especially if the visibility wasn't too special. The risk of actually missing it was quite high – high enough for the rest of the officers to take bets on whether my navigational skills were going to come up with the goods and we would actually berth on a jetty in Ghan. I was on the bridge with binoculars and the remainder of the Officers crowded round the captain's chair waiting to see Ghan or not, depending upon my latest sun-sight.

The captain asked the important question 'Peter, when will we arrive in Ghan?'

I went to the chart. Then fiddled about with the parallel ruler.

'At 3.15 this afternoon, Ghan will appear at 20 degrees on the starboard bow, sir' I replied. About ten pairs of binoculars suddenly appeared and were distributed amongst the spectators as they also kept an eye on their watches.

With the tension mounting, although I was quite confident in my calculation, the sweat began to appear on my brow and my palms. With a minute to go, one of the spectators let out a cheer for at 20 degrees on the starboard bow, just above the horizon, were the fronds of a palm tree. It was Ghan!

We took Woodbridge Haven into Portsmouth Harbour when a lot of families came aboard to celebrate our return. I wasn't expecting anyone so when my Mum appeared on the upper deck, I was more than a little surprised. After a few days leave we all set to and decommissioned the old ship and then waited for our next posting. When mine came through, I couldn't have been more disappointed. I was to go to HMS Exmouth which was based in the Clyde at Helensborough as we were the target ship for Nuclear Submarine Practice for the new captains. It was called 'The Perisher Course' and by all accounts it wasn't much fun.

I still wanted to fly but it looked as though this would never happen. I was 25 – the top end for flying training and I had been told to join HMS Exmouth. There was no mention of a flying course and I was very frustrated.

When I got back to London I went up to the Admiralty and demanded to see the Second Sea Lord.

Admiral LeFanu had been my Captain at HMS Ganges and had taken a great interest in my career. I knew that if anyone could help, it was him.

The staff surrounding an Admiral, especially in such a rarefied atmosphere as the Admiralty tend to protect their boss like Rottweilers, and I was told by any number of Commanders that no, I could not see Admiral LeFanu without an appointment and because I hadn't got an appointment it looked as though I would never penetrate this defensive wall. Eventually I persuaded one of them to get a message to the Admiral that I was here to see him. A few minutes later the Second Sea Lord came bounding down the stairs and as soon as he saw me, he shouted 'Peter, how good to see you, do come up'. There were several scowling Commanders on the stairs as the Admiral escorted me up to his office!

I explained the situation and said that despite my constant requests to be allowed to fly I had been refused on a number of grounds without even the luxury of the flying aptitude test which was mandatory for all aircrew. I was now to go to HMS Exmouth at Faslane, near Helensborough and by the time I had finished that job I would be too old to fly.

He was most sympathetic and told me that he would do what he could. Sure enough, true to his word, the Admiral had fixed it. Later that week I received notice that I was to join the flying course at the end of the year.

At the start of the flying course I had to undergo survival training where we spent seven days in the New Forest with no food, whilst travelling between designated map reference points and avoiding 'capture'. We had a parachute from which we could make a shelter in order to simulate a crash landing in inhospitable terrain. I lost a stone and a half in that time but felt a lot better for it! This survival training took place in the New Forest but before I started it, HMS Exmouth was tasked to go to Rosyth (the other side of Scotland where there were dockyard and repair facilities, but not much in the way of entertainment, especially as we, HMS Exmouth, were anchored in the middle of the River Forth.

David Codd, the navigator had a girlfriend but she was in New York. I was unattached and free as a bird, so David suggested that as there wasn't much going on in Rosyth, ought we to go and take a couple of 'birds' out for dinner whom he knew because they were nurses on a course in Ayrshire. They were based in London, in Hammersmith Hospital but had gone North to Ayrshire General to get their midwifery qualification. Of course I agreed, so we rented a car from a firm in Rosyth, had a shower and went ashore. Even in those days, it was a crazy idea to cross Scotland just to take a couple of girls out to dinner, especially when I hadn't even met them. Anyway, I was paired with Rosemary and David with Pat. We had a great evening and, on the way home to the ship, in the early hours of the next morning I said to David 'David, as Claire is in New York and has been buggering you about for the last six months, I suggest you ditch her and marry Pat. And furthermore, if you don't want to do that, I shall marry Pat.' And that is exactly what I did.

The following week I went on the Survival Training course and as soon as that was over, I went to see Pat in London as she had returned from her course in Scotland. As soon as I had returned from the survival course, I said my farewells to those in HMS Exmouth and joined the RAF for basic flying training.

Initial Flying Training was carried out at RAF Linton on Ouse, on the outskirts of York and the course started in November, not the most ideal time to start this sort of thing. When civilian pilots do the Private Pilot's Licence course, they opt to go to sunny climes where the good weather makes a heck of a difference when learning to fly. The Navy, however, didn't consider this important so off we went in November.

The aircraft of choice was the Chipmunk on which thousands of pilots have trained and it's a lovely little aircraft to learn on. I went solo in 10 hours which is normal for most students after which it was just a case of doing the work in ground school, completing the required navigational tasks in the air and then the final handling checks and exam. We practiced simple aerobatics – the loop, barrel rolls and other basic manoeuvres which helped in making the course very exciting – which it was. It was all that I had hoped it would be and more!

All of this was weather dependant, and it was wintertime.

Chipmunk Trainer

One day I took off solo for an extended navigational exercise and I headed north for the first reference point. I was airborne for 45 minutes and when I returned to Linton I had a bit of a shock. In my absence, there had been a significant snowstorm, and the complete airfield was under a few inches of snow. I could only guess where the runway was as it hadn't yet been cleared. My first attempt to land did not go well, so I opened up the throttle and went around again. The second time I came down on the grass at the side of the concrete which gave me much better control of the brakes and after a couple of spins I stopped outside the crew room where the window was full of the anxious faces of students and instructors all of whom were waiting for the last man home. I was quite pleased that I hadn't disgraced myself.

At this stage, Pat and I thought it would be a good idea if she moved from London to be with me in York . We shared a flat and Pat started work at York Maternity Hospital. We thought that as we were together, we might as well get married and planned to do just that. We foolishly arranged our wedding to be in January and in Wales. Pat had chosen a lovely old church up a mountain in Glamorgan and all the arrangements were made although the difficult bit was getting the various factions of her family to agree to doing certain things on the big day. Both her uncle, and her Stepfather wanted to give her away so one of them had to be disappointed.

I was night flying the week before the wedding but just managed to get there in the early hours of the appointed day. I stayed overnight with an aunt, and when I woke up, everywhere was white with snow. All of South Wales and the West country had been hit by a severe snowstorm, and as the morning wore on, messages came through that my dad had turned back, so had my brother and his wife; my mother couldn't make it and the only member of my family to actually get there was Ivor, my best man! It was all a bit of a shambles really, but the nuptials were duly carried out and we set ff back to York. That journey wasn't without incident for we were stopped by a Police car for driving too slowly! I was night flying again in the week after the wedding but we soon settled down to married life in York although there was a minor problem that I hadn't bargained for. According to Navy Rules, Officers under the age of 25 have to get their Commanding Officer's permission to get married and Officers under 25 were not allowed to sleep ashore! Somehow, we overcame these difficulties and at the end of March, I completed my 'fixed wing' training and then went off to Cornwall for the 'Rotary' part of the course.

The journey South was pure delight, and it was wonderful to be arriving in the relative warmth of Cornwall with the roadside banks covered in spring flowers.

We had been allocated a married quarter in Helston (next door to where my parents had lived) and we soon got to know our neighbours. We were especially friendly with John and Mary who we had first met at Linton. John was an ex-Merchant Navy Officer and Mary was a midwife and, surprisingly also, was pregnant. John was younger than me so didn't qualify for a married quarter, so they elected to rent a property in Stithians where my brother had his farm.

John and Mary were ready to enjoy everything that life in Cornwall had to offer and their rented cottage had an empty pig sty in the garden. After a glass or two of wine one evening John and I thought it would be a great idea to have a couple of pigs in the sty. We could let them have a litter of piglets, sell them off and make a few pounds.

And so we did. Sophie and Phaedra arrived and soon settled in to life in Stithians. We were assured that they were pregnant, so we just had to wait until the piglets arrived.

There were twelve students on this conversion course – converting from fixed-wing flying to the helicopter. We learnt on the Hiller 12E, a lovely little machine with a glass bubble front and skids underneath and as summer approached it was sheer heaven to be flying these attractive little machines around the countryside of Cornwall, and sometimes further afield.

The Hiller 12E

Culdrose has a 'satellite' airfield a few miles south towards The Lizard, called Predannick. This was a deserted airfield, used solely for training purposes and we frequently took off from Culdrose and flew south to Predannick where we would spend a couple of hours on flying practice - especially learning to hover. Hovering, to the uninitiated, would appear to be a very simple task but in fact until one had mastered it, it was quite a challenge. Like many things in life once it had been learned it then became second nature.

When returning from Predannick to Culdrose it was great fun to fly along the main road at eye level height only to lift up before getting too close to the lorries!

We trained in navigation, instrument flying, night flying and emergency landing, but it was whilst night flying that my flying career ended. And it was the week before I was due to graduate. I was on good form. I'd had good marks in all my assessments and life was good. I had yet to learn that it was not to last.

Night flying in July was always enjoyable, principally because even at 11 pm it wasn't very dark. I'd been on a Night navigation exercise, and I came in to refuel. Once that had been completed, I was told to take off again. For some reason, I didn't hear the instruction from the tower. And I didn't hear the second instruction either. The first that I knew about it was when an aircraft handler appeared with illuminated battens and instructed me to shut the engine down. I was sent home whilst the aircraft radio was given a thorough check.

The next morning, as there appeared to be no fault in the aircraft communication system, I was told that my hearing would have to be checked and for this I had to report to the Air Medical School at Seafield Park, in Hampshire and from there I was told that I could not fly again.

The perforations to my eardrum that I had experienced all those years ago, had left scarring which, over time were hardening with the subsequent loss of elasticity to the tympanic membrane in the ear. My hearing was now below the level required for flying and my flying career was over.

It was a devastating time and one which took many years to come to terms with, and to get over. I was heartbroken.

But I didn't have time to brood. As soon as we got back home from the Air Medical Board, Pat went into Penzance Hospital and Sarah was born the day after I was grounded.

But in true Naval fashion, within a week I was told to pack my bags and go to Northern Ireland to stand by HMS Fearless which was being built by Harland and Wolf. And that's just what we did.

11
The Transition – from Flying, through Teaching to Dentistry

The news that accompanied my visit to the Centre for Aviation Medicine was devastating.

I was to be permanently grounded from flying.

I couldn't think of doing anything else, nor did I want to. I had fought so long and hard to get on to the flying course and just as I was completing it, I was to be stopped flying.

But Pat was heavily pregnant, and we needed to get home to Cornwall. We jumped into our mini-van and headed west from Hampshire.

It was a long drive, and we got home absolutely exhausted. The suspension of the van was not at its best when we set out from Hampshire, and it certainly was a lot worse some 400 miles later as pulled up outside our married quarters in Helston. In the back of the van there were six small Suffolk oak trees in large terracotta pots that had been grown from acorns from the Oak Tree at Meadowside and were destined to spend the rest of their lives in Cornwall. These had definitely contributed to the deterioration of the suspension and the closer we got to home, the rougher the ride became.

Ordinarily this would have been not worth mentioning, but from Pat's perspective it was the most significant part of the journey.

She had just got to bed, exhausted, when her waters broke so we had to get back into the van and head off to Penzance hospital. It was a forty-five-minute journey but seemed so much longer, but when we did arrive, the staff were kind and caring and as they were probably aware their patient was herself a midwife, so they gave her special treatment.

Sarah was born the following day, so I didn't have much time to sit and feel sorry for myself, especially as a letter arrived the next morning informing me that in two weeks' time I was to join HMS Fearless in Belfast. Fearless was being built by Harland and Wolf and was soon be taken over by the Royal Navy.

I was to be part of the crew who accepted her from the builders, carry out sea trials and get her ready to be a fully trained up fighting unit, at which point she would be taken over from Harland and Wolf and enter service in the Royal Navy and take her place as the very first Amphibious Warfare Ship. I just had time to hand in my resignation before we packed up and left for Belfast. I didn't want to do anything other than continue to fly but as this was to be denied to me, I had no alternative but to resign.

The Royal Navy, in their usual caring and compassionate way, had not factored in that I had a wife and baby daughter when they sent me off to Belfast and when we arrived no accommodation was available for us. We had to find our own which was not easy. I have a suspicion that because I had resigned my commission they felt that they could treat me as though I didn't matter to them.

We settled for a largish caravan on a site in Donagadhee which was a short drive from Harland and Wolf's yard. We soon settled in and Sarah and Pat quickly became friends with the residents of Groomsport, the small town adjacent to the caravan site.

Two weeks after our arrival in Belfast, and just as we were settling in to a basic routine, I was told that I had to return to England for a Flight Deck Officers Course as I was to be responsible for this side of the operation of Fearless. So off I went.

The following night, whilst I was away in England, a severe storm was forecast for Northern Ireland and the friends that Pat had made in Groomsport advised that the caravan site was no place for a young mum and new baby. They insisted that she stay with them during my absence, and they took it in turns to give her accommodation whilst I was away.

That night, during the severe storm that had been forecast, the caravan next to the one that Pat and Sarah should have been in, was blown over the cliff on to the beach. Had Pat and Sarah stayed in their caravan, heaven knows what might have happened, but for sure, they would have had a terrifyingly dreadful night. We shall always be grateful to the kind people from Groomsport for their generous hospitality whilst I was away.

I got back at the weekend and settled down to my new job and I enjoyed meeting the Naval Architects who had designed the ship and the engineers who were constructing her. But it wasn't to last. It began to appear that the administrators in the Admiralty were determined to make life as difficult as possible for Lieutenant Barter.

Two weeks later, on the Tuesday, I was sent for by the Captain of Fearless who casually informed me that the Navigating Officer of HMS Pellew, based in Portland, had gone sick. As I was a qualified Navigating Officer, I was to replace him.

The ship was an operational one, engaged in the training of submarine crews in the Western Approaches so it was vital that she was kept operational and at sea. It just so happened that the chap I had to replace was my old friend Rodney Cave, who had been an Upper Yardman at Temeraire at the same time.

The captain then told me that I had to catch the ferry in two days' time. Once again, there was no mention of accommodation, so we relied on friends to put us up at places where the journey to Portland took us, and when we arrived we still had the problem of accommodation to sort out. As we had been quite comfortable in a caravan in Belfast we opted for the same in Portland. We soon found a van for sale on a nice quiet and convenient site on the Isle of Portland not far from the Harbour. Within a week of leaving Belfast, we had settled down to a new life in Dorset.

When the Admiralty had accepted my resignation, the terms of it were that I had to serve a further two years before my discharge, so I started thinking about the future. Pat was pregnant and that Christmas, Nicholas arrived and was born in the caravan.

With two young children, the responsibilities and economic need for future employment increased. I couldn't imagine there being much demand for an ex navigating Officer or a grounded helicopter pilot. I thought that I'd be cautious and opted to take advantage of the newly announced Government scheme. To attract more ex-servicemen into the Teaching Profession a course was designed in which one could get a Certificate in Education in two years.

I'd had some experience in teaching, as one of my duties in HMS Houghton in Singapore was as Education Officer which involved helping ratings achieve better level of education for promotion and I quite enjoyed that.

I applied for and was awarded a place at St. Luke's College, Exeter to study Physics for secondary school and the Primary course. I asked for this combination so that I would be well placed for any opportunity that arose, be it in Primary School or Secondary and, as the Middle School was very popular in Suffolk, I thought that my choice of study would be good for that too.

My teaching practice was at a village Primary School in Tedburn St Mary, on the Cornwall side of Exeter. The head teacher was fantastic and gave me full rein right from the first day and he also said that he expected me to teach the children how to play the recorder.

'But I don't play the recorder, sir' I replied.

'That's not a problem' he said. 'Take a school recorder home; buy the book and keep one step ahead'.

That was very sound advice.

I did what he said, and in the evenings, I would sit Sarah and Nick on the table in our modest kitchen in Exeter and play to them, starting on page one and gradually working through the book. By the time I completed that first teaching practice, my class could play a recognisable tune on the recorder, and so could I.

I thought that I would do a bit of pottery with them too – I hadn't done any of that either, so we would all learn together.

The headmaster's philosophy helped again, and I bought the book. The school didn't have a kiln to fire the precious items that the children had made, so, with the help of a friend from St Lukes, I made one.

It consisted of a dustbin inside an oil drum. The dustbin had shelves on which the precious items rested, and this was then stood on bar across the oil drum about 9" from the base. A fire could then be made in the oil drum, around the dustbin and hopefully the contents could be cooked not unlike the firing of a pukka kiln. The children were very excited by this project. They helped with every little bit and after much experiment and fun various items were created, then dried, before packing them carefully in the newly constructed, but totally untested, kiln.

It was a carefully planned operation with everyone providing an opinion on the best way to proceed.

The fire was eventually lit, and it burned with great gusto. We couldn't measure the temperature, but it was soon glowing like a workman's brazier and at the end of the school day the children went home buzzing with excitement and anticipation for the next morning. If it needed high temperature to fire the priceless earthenware pieces placed inside by their artistic creators, the kiln was doing the job!

We were all at the school gates early the next morning, well before the official starting bell.

Every child was there, well before the school opened. Even the ones who were not in my class or involved with the project could not stay away from witnessing this milestone in the creativity of the school. It was a small school so they all knew what the top class were doing, so everyone turned up to see the opening of the dustbin!

Nobody could say I hadn't warned them!

They knew, as much as their youthful enthusiasm would permit, that real potters have a proper kiln and pottery has to be fired at a certain temperature to achieve the best results. And to achieve even better results they understood the need to control the timing of those temperatures. They also understood that our 'rough and ready' firing chamber had none of the refinements of even the most primitive of kilns and that we really had very little control of any part of our firing process.

Despite the psychological preparation for total failure, the excitement was loud and unrestrained. The oil drum was cold, so the lid came off. The cinders of the once roaring fire were cold too, and much reduced in size. The dustbin with its precious contents was carefully lifted out of the oil drum and placed on the grass. It was a tense moment and suddenly everyone was very quiet. Breaths were held as the lid of the 'dustbin firing chamber' was lifted and the internal 'oven' was carefully removed by the two 'class leaders'.

It wasn't as bad as I had feared. Most of the pieces had some part that was recognisable although very few were totally intact. Piece by piece they were rescued from the rubble -like heap within the oven and each piece passed along the line until its creator claimed it.

It was a dirty and dusty business so at Morning Assembly many of the children wore distinctive dirt and dust inspired facial paint as testament to the activities earlier in the playground.

The opening of the 'Kiln'

Most of the children had something to show for their efforts. Admittedly what they took home was not especially inspiring neither from an artistic point of view nor an educational one, but we all had had enormous fun in the process and if they are anything like me, then they still remember it and talk about it!

My course at St Luke's finished and I was soon on my way to a new job. The Times Educational Supplement is where all teaching post are advertised, and I was quite excited to read of a vacancy in my old school.

RHS were advertising for a Physics teacher, so I applied and was invited for interview.

Three of us turned up for interview and because I was an 'Old Boy' I'm sure this helped me into the job. Another of the interviewees that day was for the Head of the Physics Department- effectively my new boss. Alex Marshall who got the job, and I, became firm friends. He was a very gifted teacher; highly amusing, original, and inspiring, who ran the department very efficiently and very professionally whilst at the same time being very kind, considerate, and supportive. As a very green teacher, I relied upon him enormously since the teacher training course that I had just completed did not, in my opinion, equip me for facing a class of teenagers. Having said that, I've always asked the question 'Can you really teach anyone to teach?'

I believe that success as a teacher is more to do with personality than specifics learnt in college. Anyway, Alex was always encouraging and supportive and he became a great friend, adviser and mentor. A deep friendship also developed between Alex and his wife Christine and Pat and I during those two years at The Royal Hospital School and that friendship has lasted almost 50 years.

RHS is a comprehensive school, not just in name but as they should be and were designed to be.

Each school year was divided into five or six academic levels and catered for this range of ability. If a child started off in year one at the bottom of the pack in 1D but achieved good results at the end of the year, he would be elevated to form 2C. If he did well in that year, he would go up to 3B at the end of that academic year and so on.

My teaching career started with a bang.

My first class was 6D/E. These boys were the true products of the comprehensive system in that they had come up from the lower streams and had taken an extra year to attain 'O' level standard. They were sixth formers doing 'O' levels. Many were 17 and some were a year older, so they had muscles to flex. And there's no better place to flex these muscles than on a new teacher, especially an 'old boy' and one who had been in the RN. They couldn't have asked for a better target at the beginning of a new term!

The classroom was an old- fashioned lecture theatre. My desk was at the front and the pupils sat in tiered seats rising to the back after about ten rows, all accessed from the side.

I was, not unnaturally, a bit nervous. This was my first real class; this was a REAL teaching situation, and I was expected to start with a meaningful part of the 'O 'level Physics syllabus.

I sensed potential difficulties. There was a certain 'atmosphere' to the room.

It wasn't long before a tall boy with sandy hair and stubble on his chin made some disparaging remark which suggested that he and I weren't going to get on. It caused some merriment amongst his peers, and I realised quite quickly that action had to be taken otherwise I was going to lose control, and lose it quite quickly.

Maybe I was psychologically and sub-consciously prepared for this. I don't really know.

Maybe my reaction was instinctive, I don't know that either. Maybe previous situations that I had been in had given me the experience, confidence and ability to deal with this little incident so early in my career. After all, it was my first day!

Whatever it was, I calmly and slowly walked up the steps at the side of the seated class until I was alongside the offending pupil. Fortunately (for me especially) he was seated at the end of the row which made my task so much easier.

With both hands, (and without a word said), and to his startled surprise, (as well as the astonishment of the rest of the class) I grasped his uniform on both shoulders, lifted him out of the seat, and dragged him down the steps to the entrance to the classroom. With one hand still on his shoulder I opened the door then helped him into the corridor outside.

In a quiet and controlled voice, but not quiet enough for the rest of the class not to hear, I advised him that my duty was to teach him some physics and that is what I intended to do. If he didn't want that to happen then every lesson that he was in my class, and scheduled for a session of Physics, he would spend it outside the door in the corridor. And that is where I left him whilst I returned inside to the classroom.

I closed the door and picked up the lesson where I had left off. Out in the corridor he would soon be ridiculed by other pupils as they walked past and hopefully, would have to explain himself if the Head came along. The Head was not a sympathetic man and would most likely have punished the boy further.

It had the desired effect. From then on, he was as quiet as a lamb and I had no more trouble with him, nor with anyone else for that matter, and the nickname that was circulated for the new Physics master was 'Bovver Barter'.

The first year for a new teacher is always 'on probation'.

During his or her first year the Head Teacher has to sit in on the Probationer's lesson and if satisfied with the newly qualified's performance, he or she can endorse the certificate, and the new teacher can then be deemed to be 'fully certified'.

The lesson that the head sits in on is chosen at random and with no warning, but I knew that this was going to take place sometime during that first year.

The headmaster was a large, intimidating individual, (to the staff as well as the boys) and he could be a bit of a bully. He was a Cambridge Blue for Rugby and used his six-foot three frame to his advantage.

I explained to all my classes my status as a probationer and explained about the Head coming in to assess me and they were very quickly on my side. We rehearsed the situation where, if he came through the door unannounced, we would all know why he was in the classroom. They all understood that he would not be there to pick up a few intellectual gems from me, but to observe not only my ability as a teacher but to see how the class reacted to my deliberations.

All my classes understood the situation and were soon on my side. We rehearsed the routine a number of times so that, should he appear unannounced, I would immediately switch from whatever topic we were working on to that of 'The Moving Coil Galvanometer'. This was in the 'O' level syllabus, and we had already covered it, so we all knew it backwards and I really liked teaching it.

As planned, one morning when I was teaching in the same lecture theatre that I had been in when I had been christened 'Bovver', the door was opened without the usual 'knock' and in walked the Head.

He strode slowly up the steps to the side and took his place at the back of the class. As he mounted the steps, with his back to me, I indicated to the class that their moment had come and got their immediate understanding.

With a clean blackboard and an attentive Headmaster, we were soon discussing the scientific principles involved in the Moving Coil Galvanometer.

At the end of the lesson, the pupils departed, several winking at me as they left, and the Head slowly moved his bulk down the stairs to confront me as I was packing up to go.

'Well Barter' he started, looking menacingly over the rims of his 'half- moon' spectacles

'Not how I would have taught it, but you did a very good job. Well done'.

I was flabbergasted and when I next taught Upper 5, they all wanted to know what he said, so they were thrilled when I told them that, thanks to them, I was soon to be a 'Certified Teacher'.

David Dixon was my equivalent in the Chemistry Department and at times, we shared the top floor of the teaching block when we were scheduled for adjacent laboratories. The Physics lab was next to the Chemistry lab with a connecting door and whenever he had an exciting experiment going on, David would tell me, and I'd take my class in to witness it.

When we had something that might be of interest in the Physics lab, David would bring his class in to join in. He was a bit of a pyromaniac and enjoyed explosive experiments – whilst I enjoyed electrical experiments especially the effects of static electricity. and so did the children, so together we made science interesting and entertaining for them. His nickname was similar to mine – so the science teachers were often linked together - Bovver Barter and Aggro Dixon!

I enjoyed teaching immensely and had come to RHS in the belief that I could really make a difference. I hadn't been too happy there as a boy, so I thought, mistakenly as it happened, that I would be able to change all that.

I quickly realised that the system was greater than the individual and that I ought to think about improving my qualification to get a better job. Candidates for a Head of a Science Department would need, as a minimum, a BSc, and for that I ought to either go to university or take an external degree. I applied for a BSc at the University of East Anglia as they were pioneering the modular degree. To study meteorology, oceanography and geology as part the BSc syllabus was a very attractive idea and one that would have suited me admirably, so I applied.

But they told me I was too old! I was all of 27!

This made me consider alternatives.

Life was slipping me by!

12
From Teaching to Bristol

Sarah and Nick, both at Holbrook Primary School were going, with their friends, to the Dentist for the first time. They were all quite apprehensive and I couldn't understand why. I had never been afraid of dental treatment, and I couldn't understand why my children should think this way and it troubled me somewhat. It then occurred to me that if I were thinking of going to university (to improve my chances of a better job) then perhaps dentistry might be a good idea. If I became a dentist, my aim would be to make it so that people generally, (my patients) and children in particular, were not afraid of visiting a dental surgery.

A great friend of mine, who had been on a flying course with me, was a Doctor in the Royal Navy so I telephoned him and asked, 'If you wanted to be a dentist, where would you go?'

'Bristol', he replied, 'That's the best Dental School'

'How do I do that?' I asked

'Write to them' he replied.

I did just that.

I was called for an interview and at the end of an hour's chat, they announced that they would give me a place starting in the following September, if I could get two passes at 'A' level (in Biology and Chemistry) before then.

'Thank you' I said as I left. 'I'll see you in September'.

I caught the train back to Ipswich and before I drove home, I went along to the Civic College and enrolled as a student at the evening class for 'A' level Chemistry and then I put my name down for the exam at the end of November, just six weeks' away.

I took some comfort in the fact that I had got an 'O' level in that subject some thirteen years before.

I bought the last ten years of past papers, grouped the questions and, assuming that the person who wrote the questions was a fallible human being and had a liking for some parts of the syllabus over the others, started on the process of 'spotting' the questions. I also assumed that the same person who was setting the questions over the last ten years, still occupied that position and would be involved in the paper that I would be sitting in a few weeks' time.

And so, after six weeks of early morning swatting; late night swatting and the weekly classes in Ipswich, I sat the exam.

Of course, I had revised the written part but not the practical – principally because I had overlooked it.

On the day of the practical, I was confronted by a rack of test tubes, some unknown chemicals, a Bunsen burner and a paper with some questions on it, some of which asked the identity of the chemicals.

Thirteen years ago, I had been involved in Chemistry Practicals, but in those days the test tubes were about six inches long and they took a minute or two to get warmed up. The ones on display on this very special occasion were very small and required a different and more precise technique for their use. I have a feeling it was called 'microanalysis'.

And I was unfamiliar with this.

I put the appropriate powders in the tube, added a bit of water, held it in a pair of forceps and showed it to the Bunsen flame. The lab was in silence other than the noise of a dozen other Bunsen flames, carefully heating little test tubes.

The silence was abruptly shattered by the sound of glass on glass.

Not gentle or deliberate glass on glass, but high velocity glass on glass.

Everyone looked up. The adjudicator walked slowly over to me as I looked at my forceps. The test tube that I had been heating had vanished.

Evidently, I had applied too much heat and far too quickly, and the little glass tube went off like a rocket and exploded on contact with the double-glazed window of the lab.

Despite this little mishap, I managed to scrape a pass and then, after a few days to get used to the idea that I had passed 'A' level Chemistry, set about learning a bit of Biology.

In theory, I had the luxury of more time for Biology.

The exam was in four and a half months' time, as opposed to six weeks, but I had more to learn.

I hadn't even got an 'O' level as I had never studied the subject.

As before, I bought the last ten years of papers, I studied them and made a plan.

I needed to know one subject inside out; I needed to do quite well with two further questions and then to be able to know a few essential facts on another two.

However, it wasn't as simple or as easy as that. During the spring term the second-year pupils were taken on an educational cruise and staff had to take it in turns to supervise them. This term was my turn.

In addition to that, the rules were that during the absence of that teacher, his classes would be supervised by another member of staff, but the class teacher was to prepare sufficient lessons to cover his absence, and, on his return, he was to mark the work and include those marks in the pupils' end of term assessment.

This meant that, in reality, I was so busy during that spring term that I could do very little preparation for my forthcoming exam, and I had to work so much harder when we got back and throughout the Easter holiday.

Under the terms of my contract, I had to give three months' notice of leaving so my letter had to be in before the start of the summer term. I was soon the object of ridicule throughout the staff room.

'What an idiot' they would say ' to give up such a good position when he hasn't a hope of getting the 'A' levels in such a short time. I had kept secret that I already had passed one.

The headmaster visited Pat at home on several occasions when I wasn't there and tried to get her to make me see sense.

Part of my responsibilities at RHS was to take the GCSE boys away from the school whilst the GCE examinations were taking place. The rationale for this was to remove the so-called 'rowdy element' whilst the more academic pupils were doing exams. We camped in Thetford Forest and when I had got them settled down in their tents, I brought out the book and other paraphernalia that I'd brought along and learnt how to dissect a rat; a dogfish and a cockroach. This was all done with the light of a 'Tilley' lamp; in a tent in Thetford Forest; and after all the children in my care had gone to sleep!

I took the exam in Ipswich and at the end of term, packed up everything and departed for Bristol.

Rumour also circulated that I was leaving because I was a rubbish teacher but right up to the final days, the headmaster kept trying to persuade me to stay. I had made up my mind to go to Bristol and study Dentistry and nothing would have made me deviate from that decision. I later learned that the headmaster was leaving RHS and, horror of horrors, his replacement was to be Norman Worswick – the Housemaster who I didn't get on with and was instrumental in my leaving the first time!

I had persuaded the local Building Society to allow me a mortgage, so I bought a small bungalow in Ashton Vale, and it was here that we sat and waited for the results to come through and as we did so, I mentally assessed our situation.

I had given up a perfectly good job, and one which I really enjoyed, in a lovely part of the country, and moved to Bristol to a house that we couldn't afford, and at that particular moment I had no job, no income and our future was totally dependent upon the results of an 'A' Level examination that I had taken a month or so previously.

When that brown envelope fell on to the mat on that morning of 15th August, 1971, it was hugely gratifying to see that I had indeed, satisfied the University entrance requirements and the next stage of our lives could begin. All was well with the world.

It was just as satisfying to hear that every one of my 'O' level pupils, including those from 6D/E had passed Physics at 'O' Level. I hoped that those who had said I was leaving because I was a rubbish teacher saw those results. But I doubt that they did.

The next thing to think about was a job. I went to the labour Exchange to 'sign on' and whilst waiting in the queue got chatting to the regulars. On hearing that I was new to all of this they gave me advice about what to say and assured me that there was no need to worry, I wouldn't get a job, and I would soon be going home with my dole money.

At the window, the young lady looked at the form that I had just completed and said ' Good news, a job has just come up at a bakery in Bishopston. You start this evening'

The night shift at a bakery wasn't the most appealing of jobs but the wages were better than the dole money, so I started that evening.

I returned to the labour Exchange every holiday from then on. And every time it was the same. The old lags who were regulars seemed never to be offered work, so that they could continue collecting the dole money and go back to plucking turkeys or working on building sites.

Every time I appeared at the window the cheery voice would say 'Oh, good news,……..' and I would be sent off to deliver ice cream for Walls, or work in a Dolls Hospital or do whatever job was top of the pile that day. But it didn't matter. At the beginning of the Michaelmas term, I started life as a student at Bristol University.

Once we had got over the shock of me actually getting into Bristol we settled down to a five-year spell. The children started in a lovely little Primary School at the end of the Road in Ashton Vale; Pat got a position as the District Nurse at a very busy Practice in Bedminster, and I began my course as a student at Bristol University.

Mature students were quite uncommon in those days – hence the UEA in Norwich telling me that at 29 I was 'too old'. I was the oldest on my course by several years and it initially felt very strange sitting in a lecture theatre amongst all these very young but clever young men and women. I was paired up with Tim Hayward – son of the Pickles Empire – who just happened to be the youngest on the course but a very bright lad and the difference between us became apparent on the first day.

He was a straight 'A' at 'A' levels and covered all the syllabus, but my studies had concentrated at only a fraction of the whole. Tim knew what the lecturer was talking about and I didn't. I had to take copious notes which I then researched at home before writing them up again. On Fridays – the day for experiments in Biochemistry or Physiology, I would ask the lab technicians if they would leave one set of gear out so that I could go back to the lab on the Saturday morning and run the experiment a second time.

Tim would spend the weekend on hedonistic pleasure and often call in on a Sunday evening to borrow my notes so that he could write up the last experiment for the following day.

The first year passed very quickly. I had to burn the midnight oil to keep up with the academic side and I also took an evening job, two evenings a week, repairing Antique Dolls at the local 'Dolls Hospital'. The owner had two young children and a very boisterous Spaniel and had no control over any of them. My life at the Dolls Hospital was made more difficult because between the three of the – the dog and the kids, it was a challenge to safeguard the completed work. Frequently I had to carry out additional repairs that had been inflicted whilst the doll was a 'patient'.

At the beginning of the first holiday I went to the 'Labour Exchange' (Job Centre) to sign on. It was crowded with old lags who I chatted to whilst in the queue. When I got to the next available 'window' I was quite confident that I would be treated no differently from my new acquaintances.

'Nah, you won't get a job mate, just sign on, collect your cash and then go out and earn a bit of Christmas money'. And that is what I expected to do.

The young lady on the other side thought differently.

'Ah' she said, looking up from her desk' You are the lucky one. We've just got a vacancy at a bakery in Bishopsworth. Start tonight. Sign here'.

And that's what I did. I worked nights in a bakery for the Christmas holiday.

My job was to take hot loaves off a trolley and place them in a slicer. One loaf every 5 seconds. I stood one side of the machine, and a younger man of Pakistani origin stood the other. Nothing very taxing until you've been at it for eight hours.

The first couple of hours there was a novelty to it but then monotony set in. The noise was such that making conversation was such a huge effort that after a short while we both realised that this was not going to happen. So we worked with only our thoughts for company. The first night I went through all the poetry I could remember; the second night much the same; the third night I remembered a teacher once saying, 'when you are waiting for a bus, try to differentiate Sine x in your head'. That wasn't a huge success and after a while, my mind went blank as I just watched the clock until break time.

I'm glad I worked in the bakery. From then on, I never begrudged the relatively high wages that factory workers get. They sell their soul to monotonous repetition and consequently sacrifice much of what is good about working in the company of and for the benefit of, fellow human beings.

The Bristol years were enjoyable. Keeping University hours fitted in very well to family life. If Pat was unable to collect the children from school, then I could, and vice versa. If Pat hadn't finished her very busy patient list, she would go back to finish off when I came home. Our neighbours were lovely and very helpful too.

Stan and Shirley had three children and Sally Anne went to the same school as Sarah and Nick. Stan was a postman, a very happy and jovial man who would do anything for anyone whilst Shirley, much the same in personality, worked in the Office at the Post Office Headquarters. Stan's Mum – Nanny Piper – would come and baby sit if either of the children were ill and couldn't go to school. We were very fortunate with our immediate neighbours too. George and Elsie Plaice were retired. Elsie was a Bristolian and George was from Gateshead. He had been involved in shipbuilding all his life and had come back to Bristol to work on the restoration of the SS Great Britain, now in dry dock in the city centre. George was a riveter and plater, and his skills were vital in bringing the Great Britain back to life. I admired George's weekend routine. Every Saturday without fail, just before mid-day, he would dress up in his best suit and go to the 'Hen and Chicken' for several pints of beer. I suspect that he had lunch there too, but always returned home between 2 and 2.30 when he would undress, get into his pyjamas and go to bed.

At the University, we had the benefit of a visiting Professor from the United States. I think that he irritated a number of the academic staff during his tenure, but he dictated how our course was to be run. His philosophy was simple. A dentist is part of the medical team. He should not treat a patient's head and neck in isolation from the rest of the body. Dentists should be trained like doctors and treat the whole person. The mouth is but the window of the body, so he thought that we ought to know what we were dealing with.

We spent a lot of time with the medics at the Bristol Royal Infirmary, including ward rounds, tutorials and a spell on call in Accident and Emergency. We also dissected the whole body – a part of my course I really disliked.

Every Thursday afternoon anatomy was on the timetable when we had to attend the dissecting room where a cadaver (or parts thereof) would be on the bench and we would be expected, under the direction of an Anatomy Tutor, to dissect part of it.

All the bodies were stored in Formalin, the smell of which was so strong that it lasted for days. Until the effects of the formalin wore off every stimulation of the olfactory nerve was received in the brain as 'Formalin'. It wasn't until the Sunday evening that the sense of smell returned to normal.

The other issue was the origin of the bodies. I did some investigation for my own peace of mind and was in some small way put at ease when I discovered that the previous occupants had bequeathed their bodies to medical research – and for which they had received a fee. Tim knew that I disliked anatomy and made a special effort to always get to the dissecting rooms before I arrived after lunch on Thursday. Often, as I entered the swing doors of the lab, I would hear Tim shout 'Pete' and a human body part would be thrown, rather like a cricket ball, for me to catch.

With the academic year behind us, the pre-clinical year involved the practical side of fillings, making dentures and porcelain work either in the technical laboratory or on the 'phantom head'. Once we had passed this hurdle we were let loose on our first patients.

Treatment was provided free to all patients and no expense was spared when deciding what would be best for them. There were about 300 students on the clinical side of the course at any one time but because the Bristol Dental Hospital was in the City Centre, there was no shortage of patients.

Because of my situation (with two young children) I was under a certain amount of pressure. Firstly, I couldn't afford to fail any of my exams and, what is more, when I had completed my training, I wanted to be experienced enough to have my own surgery, and this was my motivation.

I chatted up the lady who was responsible for the allocation of patients to the students so that anyone who required complex treatment was put on my list and I was hungry for cases which involved laboratory work. I was also friendly with many of the technicians who allowed me into the lab so that I could make the porcelain crowns and bridges as well as do all the technical stuff in denture construction. In my final year I had made over 200 porcelain crowns and 35 dentures, so I was very confident that if required, I could do the laboratory work for much of what might be required in General Practice.

At home, during the weekends and evenings, if not out with the children exploring the countryside around us, or what the city had to offer, I did a bit of building at home. I added two bedrooms and a sunroom to the bungalow and built a new porch over the front door. I was fortunate in that the double garage at the end of the garden had an inspection pit, so I was able to do all the repairs on our ageing car and even changed an engine. Of course, at that time cars were pretty simple machines, especially the Morris Minor and the Austin A35 and I could quite easily do an engine change on either of those. Motoring is now quite different, and I wouldn't have a clue where to start on our car now if it broke down, and in any case when you open the bonnet there's no room to work!

It was a wonderful period in my life. Although it was hard – I worked hard at university and held down a couple of jobs to bring in a bit of extra cash, whilst Pat worked for that busy Medical Practice and worked long hours at her job and in the home. Despite all of that we still had time for the children and every weekend we did something as a family. Our great luxury was a coloured Television – but with a slot machine. It required 50p pieces to keep the picture alive and on many occasions, we missed the last few minutes of a play or a show because we didn't have a 50pence piece to feed it!

During my final year I started thinking about the future. One of my tutors was a Surgeon Rear Admiral and an Honorary Dentist to Her Majesty the Queen. He tried desperately hard to persuade me to go back into the Royal Navy as a Dental Surgeon with the rank of Surgeon Lieutenant Commander. After the way in which they had treated me during the final two years of my service I was not very keen. I knew that despite what was on offer, and despite all the assurances to the contrary, I would be posted to a large ship, probably a County Class cruiser where, because I had a Bridge watchkeeping certificate and I had completed the Destroyers Navigating Course, much of my non-surgery time would be spent on the bridge. I was also aware that lots of sea-time beckoned and I wasn't too keen on that.

With the children fast approaching secondary school age, I wanted to be at home for them and Pat. We are all wise with hindsight and now, looking back I often wonder how our lives might have turned out had I taken the Navy route. I would probably have retired as a Surgeon Commander or Captain, on a full pension at the age of 50. I had lost all my pension rights when I had resigned my commission, so this may have been a very crafty way of getting my pension back.

Rightly or wrongly I decided to go into General Practice, so I was delighted when the results of the final were published. All my hard work had paid off. I had been awarded an Honours Degree (only three in our year) and I had won the gold medal as the best student. I had also collected every prize on offer! Orthodontic prize, Children's dentistry prize; BDA medal; Claudius Ash Prize and other minor awards. Quite a haul for an old chap like me!

I had arranged to join the dentist in Eye, and during my last year in Bristol, whenever I could I visited Eye and spent some time with him. Our plan was that I should join him in Eye, and together we would open a branch Practice in Framlingham which he would run until he finally retired.

Sadly, he died a couple of months before I had finished in Bristol and his wife wouldn't wait for me and sold it to someone else.

But our family plan still held, and we moved to Suffolk, and I started work for the new owner of the Practice, in January, 1976.

13
On Dental Practice

Before I qualified, I had decided to move to Eye where the Dentist was soon to retire. He had a busy practice and welcomed the idea of me joining him and was quite fired up by the thought that together we would expand into Framlingham where there wasn't a dentist. He would run the new practice there and I would take over in Eye.

With this in mind, every opportunity that I had in my final year to come up to Eye and visit him, I took, and he was always pleased to see me.

One Friday during one of my visits, we were enjoying a Gin and Tonic (large) when the phone rang. It was someone who needed emergency treatment. Although he had consumed several large glasses of General Gordon's Cough Medicine, he advised the patient to come over and he would do the necessary.

I was about to take my leave as he enjoined 'Hang around and I'll show you how it's REALLY done!' I declined his offer and went to my mum's house. I never really found out how that particular session went as he died the following week.

Although we had had this arrangement about me taking over his practice, his widow wouldn't wait for me and sold the practice.

I kept to my plans to move to Eye, but instead of joining the Practice as a partner, I was going to be working as an associate.

The New Year dawned, and I began work with a full book of appointments. For any new graduate, their first practice is a huge learning curve. Providing Dental Treatment in a Hospital environment is quite different from General Practice where the equipment, materials and methods are at the whim of the Practice owner, and every surgery is different.

I still had a lot to learn and because of this I was not as quick at delivering the treatment as the boss. This meant that I was earning less money – certainly much less than he was expecting of me. My contract stated that he took 50% of my earnings and he was expecting a whole lot more than I was delivering.

There was also another problem. I was born in Eye; I had been to school in Eye; I knew many of my patients. And they all wanted to chat.

Going to the dentist isn't something that many people enjoy – in fact most people, whether they admit it or not, do have some degree of fear or apprehension. Talking, relieves much of this and it's a good thing to have a rapport with one's patients.

But the boss didn't agree.

At the end of the first week he took me into the staff room and told me that he wasn't too happy. He wasn't happy that I was earning less than my nurse and that I would have to speed up if I wanted to stay with him.

The next week, despite my best efforts, he still wasn't happy. He began to put the pressure on me. Whenever I took time to chat to my patients about Dental Hygiene and ways of preventing the need for dental treatment, I used floss, tape and interdens and other materials to reinforce the message.

From the end of the second week, he said he would not provide those materials, as I wasn't earning enough to cover them, so I would have to buy them myself.

This was obviously meant to not only reduce the overhead but to discourage me from giving this advice to my patients because there was no money in it!

So life was not easy.

I was being asked to work in a way that was totally alien to me and in a way that I did not agree with. My ambition had always been to make my patients less apprehensive than they had been about visiting a Dentist, but the way that I was being obliged to work did nothing to assist me in goal.

A friend had told me of a redundant surgery in Harleston some 12 miles away, so I considered starting my own surgery here. When a new dentist joins a practice, he/she signs a contract which has a 'binding out clause' which restricts that new dentist from setting up a surgery within a given distance. My binding out clause was for 10 miles from Eye, so Harleston, at 12 miles, was OK.

Although the boss didn't like it much.

The surgery had last been used by an ex-Army Dentist whose equipment and methods could only be described as primitive. He didn't have a great reputation either.

The building had been unoccupied for a number of years and was desperate for a makeover.

The boss had complained that I hadn't earned much in the practice in Eye and he was right. There wasn't too much in my bank account either. I had no alternative - I had to do much of the decorating and refurbishment myself.

In the evenings and at weekend, I donned my overalls and with rollers and brushes, applied paint to every surface until it began to look like a surgery. I handed in my notice and put a big sign on the building in Harleston saying that this was soon to open as an NHS Dental Practice and that if anyone wanted to become a patient, they could leave their name and address inside. Many people did so, by putting a card through the letter box but many spoke to me whilst I was doing the painting and cleaning, so I stopped what I was doing and took down their details.

I bought good, second-hand equipment, installed it, recruited my staff and, as I finished in Eye, began the next phase of my life as a Principal of a Dental Practice.

I was inundated with patients, - many of them had last seen me in overalls with a paint brush in my hand and were somewhat startled to see me now in surgery attire and standing beside the chair. For some I had to do some smooth talking to convince them that I had appropriate qualifications and to prevent them getting out of the chair!

I was soon seeing 30 to 40 people a day and it was hard going. The first winter was hard with lots of snow and ice. One morning I was heading across the Waveney at Scole when I hit a patch of black ice and lost control of the car completely. My car slid across the road into the path of a lorry heading south. I thought that my time had come.

For no apparent reason the car veered back to my side of the road and the lorry sped past as my car hit the curb. I had escaped death by pure chance.

My blood pressure was sky high and as soon as I got to the surgery,

I phoned the Suffolk Highways Department and gave them both barrels of my tension and frustration as this incident had been caused because Suffolk Highways had not salted their side of the Waveney, whilst Norfolk had salted up to the bridge.

In those days we all had to provide our own emergency cover, and this aspect of life was very demanding. As patient numbers grew quickly to over 5,000, the phone was rarely quiet when the surgery was closed especially at a weekend.

On Saturday morning the first call would come early and often I would go out to Harleston, treat a patient and return home, only for it to ring again and I'd have a quick coffee before setting off again. Frequently Sundays would be the same, especially as patient numbers grew.

I used to open on Boxing Day to cover the emergencies that arose as a result of the excesses of the festive season. One Boxing morning as I approached the surgery, I could see several people waiting outside for me to open up, and my heart sank.

However, at the end of the session when I was closing the surgery to go home and reflecting on the morning's activity, I came to the conclusion that every one of the patients could have waited until after the holiday and the surgery was open again.

They had attended because they were lonely and needed something to do!

For many people, especially those living alone, the Christmas period can be a very lonely and miserable time, and it seems odd that some people would come to the surgery to relieve their loneliness.

After about 18 months, the landlord decided to sell the property and as I didn't want to pay the amount that he was asking, he put the rent up. This made me think that perhaps it would be better if I owned the building that I worked in. A small, terraced house, just up the road from my surgery, came up for sale, so I made an offer, applied for planning consent and decided to buy it. Unfortunately,

Barclays were not very sympathetic. They wouldn't give me a mortgage as I wasn't earning enough – so much for the 'Rich Dentist' myth. The only way that I could raise the money to buy this house and turn it into a surgery was to take out a second mortgage on our house in Eye.

Citibank Trust were willing to lend me the money and I bought the house and set about the conversion to a surgery, and we soon moved in.

 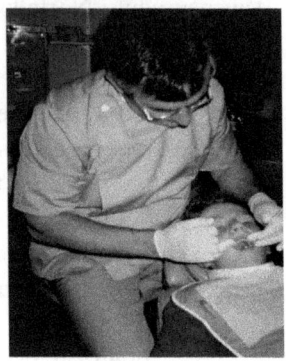

The 'Credit Card Surgery'   *and me working in it.*

I was very happy. I now owned my own practice and the building it was in (with the help of Financial Institutions!) Now that I was established, there was one thing that I needed to do.

In Dentistry, there are two recognisable graduate qualifications – the BDS (Bachelor of Dental Surgery) and the LDSRCS(Eng) - (Licentiate in Dental Surgery at The Royal College of Surgeons in England).

At the end of our course in Bristol, most of my classmates, me included, applied to take the LDS exam which was held in London. The exam date was a week after our results had been announced and the night before we were due to travel to London, the Clinical Dean was wishing us all well and said to me 'Peter, as our best student we are expecting a good showing at the Exam from you'. That remark made me lose all confidence and I didn't travel to London the next day for fear of letting everyone down.

But that is something that I always regretted so once I'd settled into my surgery, I applied to sit the Exam in London at the next available date. The exam was due to start at 10.30 so if I caught the 8.15 train, I would be fine. At 7 .30, just as I was about to leave to catch the train, I received a call from a patient (all calls were diverted to my home) who needed urgent treatment which I could not ignore. So off I went to Harleston, treated the patient then caught the next available train to London. By the time I got to Lincolns Inn Fields, the venue for the exam, the candidates had been working at their papers for 40 minutes. It took a bit of persuasion to get them to allow me access to the exam room, but I eventually convinced them and was allowed to start, although no extra time was allowed. After lunch we had to treat a patient and then be examined by Professorial Staff in a viva voce. I came home truly concerned as to whether I had passed.

But when the results were published, all was well, and I had been awarded a LDSRCS(ENG). I had a new plate made and proudly hung it outside my new surgery.

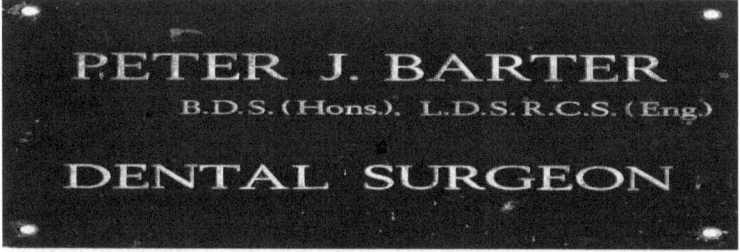

My euphoria and self-satisfaction at having my own surgery didn't last long. Interest rates started rising and in no time at all, Citibank Trust had put up their rates to 24.8%.

In today's terms, it was like buying a house with a Credit Card! I had to pedal very hard just to keep the mortgage payments up.

Patient numbers rose to 10,000 and I was in desperate need of help. I was working a ten-hour day, and I felt that I couldn't keep going like this.

I recruited two dentists to help me out. One was straight from university and the other was an experienced practitioner who had moved up from Essex to enjoy the good life of Norfolk.

I was, at the time, spending half a day a week at Wayland Hospital doing a session of Oral Surgery which I enjoyed immensely. I assisted the Oral Surgery Consultant from the Norfolk & Norwich Hospital, and we dealt with surgery referrals from a wide area, and it took me out of the surgery and back into a hospital environment which I enjoyed. Because of the demands of the surgery it often meant that after a session at the Hospital doing Oral Surgery, I had to return to my practice and deal with the emergencies. With a patient list of the size that I had, there was always someone with pain, or a broken tooth, or broken denture and the recruitment of two associates would help the practice to flourish whilst I was at The Wayland.

That was the plan!

Some plans just don't work out.

Despite having all this help, things got no better. I was working harder than ever and when either of the dentists called in sick, it was me who had to sort out the mess, especially as many of our patients travelled a long way by bus to visit the surgery.

Friday sickies seemed to be a common occurrence and when a patient reported seeing the 'sick' dentist at the market with his pigs for sale, I realised that I was being taken for a ride. He was more interested in developing his pig breeding business than attending to his patients.

The other dentist, straight from university, was the son of a Bank Manager in Mid Wales. Although he had passed his University Finals his enthusiasm for Dentistry was not as strong as what his fathers had been. His work was appalling, and I often had to re-do the work that he had done on his patients (and at no cost to them, of course).

Many years later, when he had a Practice of his own and was employing an associate, we met at a Dental Seminar. During a break in a lecture that we were both attending, he came over and shook my hand and thanked me for being so patient with him. He confessed that at that time he had no interest in continuing in the profession and it was not until he married and had a family that his enthusiasm for work improved. He admitted that had he been in my shoes, he would have given himself the sack!

The high interest rates coupled with the increasing workload meant that my life was completely taken over by work. My two associates were of little help – in fact they made things worse, and I began to have health problems. I really couldn't see a way out of it. Patient numbers were increasing daily. If I sacked the two associates, looking after all those patients single handed would be a huge challenge so I concluded that the only solution was to sell the practice.

I had been friendly with the boss of the Community Service

and when he heard that my practice was up for sale, he contacted me to offer me a post in the Community Service. Although quite different now, at that time the Community Service inspected all school children in the county, in their schools and offered treatment at Community Clinics. This appealed to me, so I accepted the post, and I was due to take over from a Dentist who had recently undergone heart surgery and was soon to retire.

I was happy to take on his workload and spent some time in preparation for this. My Practice was sold, and the new owners (Simon and Judith Sykes) moved up from London and started work in Harleston.

I was due to start my job in the community the following week when I had a call from the Boss.

'Sorry', he said, 'but the Community Position is no longer available'.

That was a bit of a blow. I was now 'out of work!

It appears that the chap who had had the heart surgery had come to the conclusion that being at home with his wife was more stressful than being at work, so he decided against early retirement and returned to his position.

I had to act quickly so I put in a Planning Application to convert my garage to a surgery so that I could work from home. The surgery was designed to be deliberately small so the problem I had with thousands of patients would not arise. How I thought that the physical size of the building would limit the number of patients, I don't know!

When I left my boss, he quickly recruited a replacement associate and when I bumped into him shortly after I'd opened up in Harleston, he took great pleasure in telling me that he had found 'the perfect associate' and that together they were opening up surgeries in Framlingham and Debenham.

Sadly, this honeymoon period was soon over. One of his nurses came to me and asked for a job and when she started work told us how difficult it was now that her old boss had fallen out with his new associate. When the new chap placed an order for materials to the suppliers, He would get on the phone and cancel the order!

The associate left to take over the Framlingham Practice and the Debenham Surgery was allowed to decline and was then put up for sale.

The Planning Application was running for my surgery at home, but these things take time, so I thought that the Debenham Surgery would give me something to do whilst my garage was being converted.

So I bought it, and as he handed me the keys he said sneeringly 'You are welcome to it. I've never been able to get it to work, and neither will you!

I recruited two local girls, Alison and Dawn and once again I found myself painting and decorating and installing new equipment. Within two weeks of opening we had an appointment book full for the next three weeks and we had to open on Saturdays to keep pace with the demand.

Debenham was a great place to work. Not only was it a lovely village but the people were very friendly and supportive, and we made many friends from the village. It was a very busy practice which I had not anticipated. The Planning Permission had been approved so we started on the conversion of the garage and when that was ready, I had two very busy practices to run.

Many patients from Harleston had heard that I had opened up in Eye so happily made the journey to my new surgery. Debenham had to go.

I took on an associate to run Debenham 'with a view to buying it after 3 months'. That was an acceptable way of doing things in Dentistry and when he started, he had a very full book of patients, and it was his intention to buy the busy surgery. At the end of the three-month period he had run the place down to almost nothing, so I had to get rid of him and go back and build it up again. Never again would I recruit someone 'with a view to buying'.

With the associate gone, I got the surgery back to profitability and then sold it to a chap from Southampton who had spent much of his working life in The Congo! He didn't do very well in Debenham!

Dentistry is a very funny business, and success depends largely on the personality of the dentist and the staff. I've always been very lucky with my staff and all my surgeries have been great places to work with lots of fun and lots of laughter. The girls have remained loyal, and several have worked for me for many years.

Our surgeries were happy places, and the waiting rooms would be full of laughter, and maybe that is why we were always so busy. Sadly that industrious activity wasn't translated into money and that is why I failed my children who always wanted their father to be a 'rich dentist'.

The equipment that I had installed in Eye was straight from the Dental Exhibition and I think I was one of the first dentists in the country to have Fibre Optics on the handpieces. These are like little headlights on the drill, so you can see what you are doing. Working in the back of the mouth, in a dark, wet environment is much less of a strain when everything is lit up!

Despite my impractical ideas on how to keep the patient numbers down, I soon needed help.

Bernard arrived straight from university, and I became a Registered Vocational Trainer. Bernard didn't contribute much to the practice, but I hadn't expected him to. He was here to learn, and I was in a teaching role – unlike mine with my boss! But I enjoyed having Bernard in the next surgery for he brought a new dimension to Dental Practice. He really ought to have been an actor because his interests lay in theatrical activity, be it singing or dancing or straight performing. But he was a good dentist and kind and sympathetic too and I felt that my patients would be well looked after if Bernard ever wanted to take them over.

Sarah and Nick were both attending Thomas Mills Grammar School in Framlingham which had a very active exchange programme with a school in France. Both had exchange students come and stay at ours and they in return went over to Modane. Nick fell in love with Skiing -Modane is in the Alps so that wasn't surprising. He wanted to go skiing at every opportunity but disappointingly for him, who had spent much time and energy looking forward to the time when 'Dad was a rich Dentist', I didn't have sufficient spare cash to fund his skiing exploits. But we did have some land. Meadowside stood in an acre of meadow so I persuaded Nick that if I provided the tubers, he could grow Dahlias and sell them at the gate. We ploughed the meadow, planted the tubers then when they were in flower, Nick picked and bunched them and sold them at the gate for 10p per bunch. That first year he sold enough flowers to fund a ski trip during the

Christmas holiday; at half term and again at Easter.

On Saturday mornings, if I didn't have a surgery, I would work in the Dahlia field with Nick and one morning, dressed in overalls, I was hoeing between the rows of flowers.

A man came over and asked if he could have £5 worth of flowers, but of the colours of his choosing. Always happy to oblige, I suggested he walk with me and tell me what colours he would like.

As we walked around picking the flowers of his choice, I asked him where he lived and how long he had lived here. It transpired that he was an 'incomer' from Essex and really loved this area.

'What especially do you like about living here? I asked.

He thought about that for a moment, then said 'Well, I love the fact there's no class distinction here'.

'Gosh, that's interesting' I replied 'Tell me how it affects you'

'Well', he said, 'Where I've just come from, a man like me would never be spending time with a gardener like you'.

I said that I was very pleased to hear that and gave him his flowers and carried on hoeing!

Unbeknown to me life was soon to become a challenge.

Pat and I went to Scotland for a wedding and whilst staying in a Hotel near Loch Lomond, Pat became very ill.

We came home, and Pat's condition got worse. I had to call the local GP out at night for fear that Pat was having a heart attack, but they were not very supportive. This was hugely disappointing as she had been their Practice Nurse and Midwife for several years and one could have expected better support from them.

She was totally exhausted, devoid of strength and energy and at times was unable to lift a cup of tea. She was seen by several consultants, but nobody could give a diagnosis. We had an appointment at the Masonic Hospital in London and had to go in a wheelchair and on the train. The consultant said that she had a heart condition that he could hear without a stethoscope and wanted to take her to theatre and operate. Pat refused to go because he failed to convince her that he knew what he was going to operate on and why!

It transpired that she had a severe bout of ME and for this there was no recognised treatment, so Pat decided to self-medicate and by using homoeopathy and with the help of a few friends, gradually over the next couple of years, got her health back.

My mum had a stroke and came to live with us until she was well enough to return home. She then had a second stroke whilst in a nursing home and died as a result of that episode.

Bernard married his nurse, Teresa, and they expressed a wish to take over the surgery, so we sold Meadowside, sold the surgery to Bernard and Teresa, and we headed off to Tattingstone and another direction!

14
Dentistry for Dogs!

During the course of her treatment at the Debenham surgery, a patient mentioned that she was the owner of an Irish Wolfhound and that the poor dog had toothache. Furthermore, she didn't know what she could do about it. On questioning, it seemed to me that the poor old dog had broken a canine tooth which in turn had become infected and really needed to be treated.

In a moment of weakness, I offered my services.

A friend of mine had become the preferred dentist for the Bristol Zoo and finished up treating a number of animals who had dental problems, and I thought that this might be an interesting area to get involved in and Banham Zoo wasn't all that far away!

But where do you start?

This might be just the opportunity!

I suggested to the lady that she bring her beloved pet into the waiting room one evening after work. I thought that her presence during a normal working day might have an adverse effect upon the other patients, so it was best done when the surgery was empty.

At the agreed time, the patient arrived with its owner, and I was very pleased to see that I would be dealing with an unusually placid and friendly animal, although I was not quite as well prepared for its size. It was a very large dog and although I was a little apprehensive about getting so close to such a large animal, I really needn't have worried.

Lowella allowed me to inspect her teeth as though she knew what she was here for and that she'd had done it before. She opened her mouth, and I poked about until I had satisfied myself that she did have a dental problem and that I was able to fix it.

Not Lowella, but one of a similar breed, size and colour!

Lowella had broken an upper left canine tooth – so aptly named – and it looked as though there was a chronic infection in the gum at the top of the tooth. Obviously, treatment was necessary, and fairly soon too, and the procedure would be similar to what I would be expected to do on the human equivalent.

Lowella's owner asked about my fees.

It was sensible of her to enquire before she was faced with a huge bill, and she expressed great surprise when I gave her my answer. Animal dentistry would be an interesting side-line and one which interested me, and I considered that if we could generate some publicity from the experience that we were about to become involved in, there might be other dog owners whose pets had similar problems, and they might come to me for a solution. I had visions of becoming a 'Dog dentist!' as a lucrative side-line! I proposed that all fees would be waived in return for Lowella's owner writing an article in the local papers (East Anglian Daily Times and The Eastern Daily Press) about a Dentist in Debenham treating an Irish Wolf Hound who had a dental abscess!

She hastily agreed – possibly in case I changed my mind, so I contacted my Vet friend and booked a surgery and a general anaesthetic.

I gave my friend details of the patient and the owner, and he immediately said 'Hey, wait a minute, I'm not booking surgery time until the fee is paid up front. I've had dealings with this lady in the past and I need to have the money in my hand.'

That ought to have flagged up something in my brain, but alas it didn't.

We agreed to delay booking the surgery at his practice until Lowella's owner had paid the Vet.

That having been done, we booked the surgery, organised the support staff and equipment and duly turned up at the appointed time.

Lowella was anaesthetised.

Irish Wolfhounds are very large animals, but the strength of their skeleton is, apparently, less than what might be expected for an animal of that size. Once they have been put to sleep, it is inadvisable to turn them over for fear of breaking one or more bones in the process. Unfortunately, as Lowella was losing consciousness she chose to lay down on her left side on the operating table and because of her long neck, her head was a long way down. As the tooth that I wanted to work on was on that side, it meant that I had to spend the next hour on my knees to gain access to the tooth which was now a few inches from the floor.

Alison my nurse, was an invaluable member of our team. She was a local Suffolk girl and was totally unflappable.

Allison could deal with anything. The fact that we could hardly see the tooth that we were supposed to be operating on and in any case, it was upside down, didn't present a problem. At least not to Alison. What is more she made it perfectly clear that if I couldn't sort it, she could. There was no place for my moaning about how difficult this was going to be.

With the clock ticking – the vet wanted Lowella out of the anaesthetic as quickly as possible – we set about the treatment. The tooth had to opened, the infection drained, the nerve canal cleaned thoroughly and then washed out before sealing a filling at the tip of the root and then rebuilding the tooth. At the end of about 40 minutes – somewhat shorter than I would have allowed had the patient been human and not upside down- I placed a white filling to rebuild the crown of the tooth.

We cleared our equipment out of the way as Lowella regained consciousness and was taken home by her owner.

The following morning, I telephoned the dog's owner and enquired as to how the patient was after a long session under the anaesthetic.

'Just a moment, I'll go and look' was the reply. A few minutes later a breathless owner reported

'All appears to be well, Lowella is at the bottom of the garden, chewing a large bone'. Job Done.

Two weeks later I thought it was about time that the article regarding this treatment appeared in the local papers, or at least a draft ready for my approval, so I duly phoned Lowella's owner to see how it was coming along.

'I've been giving it a lot of thought' she said.

'Unfortunately, I am unable to write that article because as Lowella is a Show Dog, any treatment that she has had might compromise her standing in any competition.'

I never got a fee – and, more importantly, it was another career that failed to take off.

As my wise old Granny used to say, 'Experience is dearly bought'.

15
The Harley Street Experience

One of my patients in Debenham was the wife of the local GP. Her Dad was a dentist, and he was about to retire and was looking for someone to take over his Harley Street Practice.

His daughter approached me one day and asked if I could call her father in London, and when I did, he invited me to come and have a look at his surgery. He explained that he wanted to retire in the next year or so and thought that I might be just the chap to take over from him.

I thanked him for the vote of confidence and for the offer but declined, by saying that I was an NHS dentist through and through and did not intend to venture into the Private sector.

He phoned me several times and asked me to reconsider. When he realised, he wasn't getting very far he then sent an invitation to lunch at the Royal Society of Medicine where he had proposed me for membership.

When the time came, I trotted off to the RSM and met him for lunch in the hallowed halls, and after a most enjoyable lunch, went to his practice in Harley Street. He accused me of being narrow minded in not wanting to expand my horizons into areas that Harley Street could offer.

And so gradually, he wore me down and I reluctantly agreed to give it a try. And I was now a member of the Royal Society of Medicine!

I would be his associate for three months on the usual 50% contract and I would undertake all the necessary surgical and endodontic treatment on his patients. He currently referred these patients out to a specialist, but this was well within my experience so to be able to carry out these procedures 'in house' was very good for his practice.

These patients would be referred to me from him, and from a couple of his friends along the street, who also needed help in this area of General Practice.

The equipment at his practice left a lot to be desired as it was so old and the materials that he wanted me to use were not what I had been trained with nor used in my practice, nor, if I'm honest, wanted to use on my patients.

His nurse wasn't really up to speed either, so Alison agreed to come down to London with me on my days at his surgery, and we took with us a hamper of sterilised equipment and sufficient materials to cope with the treatments for that day. Of course, I had to pay Alison's expenses – he didn't make allowances for those!

In order to make a 9 am appointment, we had to catch the 6 o'clock train from Ipswich. And at the end of the day we usually arrived back in Ipswich at 6pm.

The Harley Street address was sub divided into a number of consulting rooms and surgeries, and out of hours was overseen by a resident 'receptionist' who acted for all the surgeries.

One afternoon our receptionist telephoned me to say that a patient from Reading had phoned and was in pain and as the boss wasn't working that day, could she put the patient in to me in two weeks' time.

'No', I said' 'I'll see her tomorrow'

'Oh no, sir, we don't work that way in Harley Street'

'I don't care how you do it in Harley Street' I replied. 'If she's a patient of this practice and in pain, then I will see her tomorrow'.

I saw the poor lady the next day. She was not a 'regular attender, as such, but came along when she had saved enough money for the anticipated fee.

Her mouth was in a dreadful state and that was due entirely to the fact that her treatment had been dictated, not by her clinical needs but by the fees that could be charged for patching her up. She believed that because she had elected to go to 'Harley Street', she would receive, and was getting, the best treatment possible!

Unfortunately, this was not an isolated case, and I saw several patients whose treatments had been driven by cash as opposed to necessity. It really was an 'eye-opener' and I soon began to notice the pattern of how treatment was proscribed.

The fees dictated the treatment.

One afternoon I had a patient booked in for a root filling on a molar tooth. The Boss had told the patient it would cost him £350, and he was prepared for this amount. I examined him thoroughly, took some X-rays and in the absence of any pain, symptoms, or clinical indication for such treatment, advised the patient that this treatment was unnecessary, and that he could go.

The patient was very cross.

'I am a High Court Judge, and I have taken time out to come here for treatment and you tell me that it is not necessary! I am going on holiday tomorrow to a remote Greek Island, and you may have messed up my holiday by not doing the treatment that was proposed'.

I carefully explained that there was no justification for doing the proposed treatment – he was not in pain; there was no swelling, or any other pathological signs associated with that tooth and there was nothing on the X-ray to indicate the need for treatment. And, I added, 'If I open the tooth needlessly and it becomes infected, your holiday will be ruined because on a remote Greek Island it is unlikely that you will be able to access dental treatment'.

He was not a happy bunny when he left the surgery, despite not having to cough up £350!

The long train journey home gave me ample opportunity to reflect upon the situation and I finished my three months and called it a day.

Patients were coming to Harley Street believing that they were getting the best dental treatment that money could buy. In reality, they were paying over the odds for treatment delivered using old equipment and inferior materials. The charge for a Root filling at this prestigious address was £350. My patients in Eye were being treated in a 'state of the art' surgery, with the most modern of Dental Equipment, with the best materials. The fee for that same treatment, under the NHS was £12!

The Harley Street experience was just that – an experience, and I was glad to return to my humble NHS surgery where, for all its faults, the NHS system is patient driven and the patient's needs determine the treatment provided. Long may it continue.

(When I first wrote this, I had no idea that within ten years, NHS

Dentistry would have reached a low point where it is no longer driven by patient needs, but 'box ticking bureaucracy'.)

16
The Move to Tattingstone

As a child, I spent many hours with my grandparents, and I was often required to help them in their garden. Grandad grew bedding plants for his own use and for sale, and he had many regular customers, so I was quite used to the ways of growing seedlings in greenhouses and planting out flowers in the garden. In fact, I would have been quite happy to have had this as a career, but life has a funny way of unfolding.

My surgery in Eye, despite having been specifically designed to be small and manageable, soon got very busy.

I'd had some experience of 'too many patients' in Harleston and I was determined to avoid a repeat of that. My practice at home was to be small and manageable and furthermore, I wanted to keep it that way.

Sadly, this was not to be.

But it was entirely my fault. I seemed quite incapable of saying 'no' to anyone who wanted treatment. I didn't do this consciously, it just happened, and in no time at all I had more patients than I could cope with. The situation began to affect my health – especially my mental health. I still remember one Saturday lunchtime, after a morning's surgery, going down to the town in Eye for something from the shops. When I returned, there was a lady sitting on the bench outside the surgery with a blanket over her head. She was not a patient of mine but had turned up in the hope that I would see her, which of course I did.

I soon refused to leave the house in case I was needed at the surgery and my life was on a downhill spiral. When the surgery was closed, patients would come around to the back door and plead their case. On Christmas Day, a patient called to see if I would help them out.

Having a practice adjacent to the house had its advantages, but there were many disadvantages.

My mother had had a stroke, from which she recovered by sheer determination and during her recovery period she lived with us at Meadowside.

Pat had been very ill and for a time she could not even raise a cup to her mouth as she was so weak. The local GPs were called out but didn't appear greatly interested and a trip to London to the Royal Masonic Hospital was arranged. I took Pat down by train, in a wheelchair as she couldn't walk and after a short inpatient stay, the surgeon decided that he would operate but when questioned, was far from specific as to what he intended to do. It was obvious that he didn't know!

So we returned home, with Pat determined to be the architect of her own recovery and with the help of homeopathy remedies, determination and help from our friends, especially Gisela, she made a slow recovery. Mum had to go into a Residential Care Home in Yaxley as there was no way that Pat could look after her, and whilst there she had another stroke from which she died three weeks later.

One lunch time, when I had finished a hard session in the surgery, I went up to see Pat who was still in bed.

She had been reading the East Anglian Daily Times and a Thursday is when there is a Properties Supplement.

Amongst the many houses for sale was an established cut flower nursery in Tattingstone. This immediately grabbed our attention. Tattingstone was near to Holbrook where we had lived before; The Shotley Peninsular was the best part of Suffolk or so we thought; a nursery was a most attractive possibility as a substitute for dentistry.

We had to go and see it.

We went that evening and immediately fell in love with it. The following day I made them an offer which was accepted. And over the next few weeks we made several visits to the nursery, especially at weekend when I learned the ropes for growing these special flowers and worked in all aspects of the flower production at the nursery so that when we took it over, I would know everything about growing Alstromeria.

The photos above show (to the right) the nursery from the air and to the left the artic conditions during our second year.

Bernie Mayston, who had been working for me as an associate for about two years, agreed to buy the practice and we put the house on the market.

Mum had died in the October, and we sold Meadowside and moved to Tattingstone during the following February. This was the time at which the flowers were growing so I had a couple of months to get used to everything before marketing began. We had a list of regular customers who had their favourite colours. Being florists, they were very particular about the quality of the flowers that I delivered to them and ensuring that every stem, every flower was top quality was an important part of our work. The florists, especially the largest one in Ipswich took great delight in thoroughly examining each bloom of every delivery in the hope that some fault would be found to justify them paying less than the agreed price.

The nursery was a great joy. I put up several polytunnels and doubled the area under glass or polythene. I opened up+ much of the grassland and increased the number of varieties of flowers that we could offer but despite this, one thing did not change. That was the turnover of the nursery.

Closer investigation of the accounts showed that the previous owner, who had retired from a local chemical company, included his pension as part of the income from the sale of flowers and then took it out again as wages! Sadly, the accounts were not a true reflection of the financial state of the nursery, and I had been sold a pup.

Never mind, it was a most enjoyable pup and after several years we took the income up to ten thousand pounds per year. This was partly due to an increase in varieties that we grew for the cut flower market and the increase in area of Alstromeria. Inside the main glass house one of the varieties that we grew was called Golden Glory.

These were the tallest of the Alstros, and often got to a height of six to seven feet, and the stems were the thickness of a thumb. Arriving in the greenhouse to pick for the days deliveries as the sun was rising, and seeing the sun's rays shining through these magnificent flowers was one of the great delights of the job.

I got planning consent for a temporary building and continued to grow the nursery both in terms of plant varieties and growing houses.

Sods law applies to flowers as it does to every other aspect of life. Whenever there was a Bank Holiday and thus no deliveries on the Monday morning, the weekend would be hot and sunny, and the flowers would be unstoppable. If I picked them on Saturday I had nowhere cool to store them, so I installed an old butcher's storeroom so that the thousands of flowers that had to be picked over the weekend, could be stored and saved for delivery on the Tuesday.

I was interested in the science of micropropagation and went on a couple of courses to learn how to do it properly.

This was an area where laboratory science meets the gardening world, and I found it fascinating, and I built a micropropagation unit of my own. Although I used the technique for Alstromeria I also experimented with Orchids and sweet peas.

One of my patients at the Practice in Debenham was a world authority on miniature geranium. When fully grown, some examples were only two inches high. He achieved this by getting the seeds irradiated by a high dose of radiation. I thought that

I would take it further and, being a member of one of the few professions who can legally own an X-ray machine, decided to make use of this. But I thought that instead of a high dose of radiation to a dormant seed, (which is what my friend did with geraniums) I would get the seeds, (sweet peas in my case) to germinate (when cell division is at its highest rate) then zap them whilst the cells are at their most active.

Unfortunately, I was unable to reach a conclusion with this experiment as we moved to Cornwall in the following year, but the result of this first trial were quite encouraging. Seeds at the point of germination were irradiated with increasing levels of X-rays from the machine in the surgery. When left to grow they exhibited different growth rates depending on the time in the beam. Disappointingly, however, was the fact that by the time they had flowered, all growth differences had disappeared and there was no evidence of any change in them at all. In the following year, I would have doubled the amount of exposure but that was not to be. I had established that irradiation did cause growth retardation, but the plant had the ability to overcome those initial problems and return to full health by the time the flowers appeared.

The Alstromeria were tender flowers and had to be kept frost free during the winter. In our second year we had twelve degrees of frost, and it was a struggle to keep the plants alive. During that winter we spent over three thousand pounds on heating oil alone, just to prevent frost damage to the plants. One third of the profits of the year just to keep the flowers alive!

Alstromeria were a derivative of the Peruvian lily and been produced as a result of genetic engineering in Dutch laboratories. They could only be grown under licence and when my predecessor set up the nursery, he signed an agreement with the Dutch Growers that they would plant them 5 to a square meter; they would grow them on without subdividing them for a period of no more than five years and then, at the end of that period, they would be replaced from the same suppliers.

Fortunately, this agreement was not between me and the suppliers so what I did was no concern of theirs, unless of course I needed to get in touch with them for more plants.

Leonard took a liking to these flowers as well, and on his farm in

Stithians, grew some Alstros which he sold at the gate. He became hooked on them too and erected several large polytunnels just to grow alstromeria.

One year he and I decided to take a day trip over to Amsterdam to have a look at the exhibitors at the big Annual Flower Exhibition at Aalsmeer. That was a most enjoyable trip. We flew from Ipswich Airport's grass strip and had a good look around the horticultural suppliers in Holland and came back with lots of ideas.

At times, when he had too many Alstros to get rid of in Cornwall, he used to box them up and send up to me by TNT, the carrier, and I would then sell them locally. This was quite useful as he grew some varieties that I didn't.

I often considered that life in Tattingstone could not be better.

The Nursery was running efficiently; I loved growing many varieties of flowers and bedding plants; I was enjoying the Dental job at RHS and the Sailing School was doing well. I wasn't aware of the effect that a holiday, later that year in Cornwall, was going to have, and what a terrible mistake I was about to make.

17
On Sailing

I first learnt to sail at the age of 12.

RHS had their own Shipwright who had built a couple of 14' flat bottomed sailing dinghies which were perfect for pottering about in Holbrook creek. I don't remember much in the way of formal instruction, but I do remember taking the boat out and working out how to make it move through the water.

One of the staff members was the proud owner of a motorboat, which had a wheelhouse, cabin and saloon and he was always on the lookout for a crew. And I was always keen to fulfil that role as I really enjoyed being on the water.

HMS Ganges gave me the chance to sail more often (it was compulsory anyway) and I was soon able to sail, with ease, 27' whalers and 32' cutters as well as the ubiquitous R.N. 14 ' Sailing Dinghy. This old workhorse was heavy, clinker-built wooden dinghy which was in use at all Naval Establishments and often carried on ships for recreational purposes.

I was soon heading up the Ganges sailing team which, unfortunately, wasn't as prestigious as it sounds. We only had one fixture and that was always against HMS St. Vincent, the Boys Training Establishment in Portsmouth. But it was great to be involved in this competition as it meant a trip away from Ganges and a bit of fun.

During the summer holidays in Cornwall, when free from holiday jobs, a friend of my father used to take me on the summer regatta circuit as an available crew, so I crewed in a number of different boats in several different regattas, depending which helmsman was short of a crew.

The captain of HMS Bulwark, Captain Percy Gick, was a keen sailor and in addition to the RNSA dinghy we kept aboard, he had his own boat. This was a highly experimental boat, built by Uffa Fox, the greatest boat designer of the time and when we got to Ceylon (Sri Lanka) Percy Gick sent for me to ask if I would crew for him as he wanted to take his boat out in Trincomalee Harbour. Two officers also came with us and in perfect weather the boat was soon planing along at maybe 15 knots. After a couple of trial runs, Percy got out his water skis and was soon skiing behind the boat – a feat that, to my knowledge, had never been tried before.

In Aden, my friend and I took out the ships RNSA dinghy for an afternoon sail. As we bowled along in a freshening breeze, the sky darkened and in no time, we were in a sandstorm, blowing in from the neighbouring desert of Yemen.

We took the sails down, covered our faces and waited for it to blow through before we could return to the ship.

The ship left Aden the following morning and passed through the area where Don and I had been sailing. From the flight deck, I looked down into the water where we had sat out the sandstorm the previous day. Beneath the blue grey of the water surface, a large shadow appeared, and my heart began to race when I realised that I was looking down on a huge hammer-head shark which was lurking in the very spot where we had been the day before.

As an Upper Yardman, I sailed a lot in the Firth of Forth and crewed on boats on long passages whenever I could, but it was not until I had started work as a Dentist that I was able to do some serious sailing.

My first real boat was a 32' Nantucket Clipper, a beautifully designed ketch rigged yacht with a long keel which I bought from the Captain of Dartmouth and sailed her home to Woolverstone. She was a life saver. I had a very busy practice which I largely worked single-handed. To be able to lock the surgery door, get into the car and within an hour be out in the river Orwell on my own was magical.

In those days there was no such thing as a mobile phone so once I was away from the jetty, nobody could get to me. It was heaven.

Just before we moved to Tattingstone, a friend of mine asked if I would like to help him bring his boat back from America. It took me about 30 seconds to consider this before giving him the answer. Yes, I would.

I flew out to Boston where, at the Airport, I had my suitcase cut open by undesirables looking for expensive items. Travelling from Boston to Rhode Island to pick up the boat was a bit of a challenge as the contents of my case didn't want to remain under the temporary repair of the top. I was glad to find the boat and get settled in before setting off for Bermuda.

Whilst in Bermuda it was so uncomfortable sleeping on board that I decided to go to a B&B for a couple of nights. On the Sunday morning I asked the owner if he could recommend a church where I could attend a Sunday service. 'Why not come to my church?' he asked, so I agreed to join him.

It transpired that he was the Pastor and after the sermon, and from the pulpit, he took a trumpet out of its case and accompanied the choir who sang 'Abide with me'. I have never been moved so much by the rendering of that hymn as I was in that little church in Bermuda.

We continued our journey to the Azores and the weather was very kind – in fact too kind and we spent many days completely becalmed. Dolphins frequently joined us and cavorted around the boat giving us a wonderful display of the skills in the water. I got the impression that they knew exactly what they were doing, and the purpose of the display was to impress us, and it certainly did. When they got bored, they suddenly disappeared – one minute they were there, the next they had gone - and they reappeared just as suddenly the next day.

At night when all was quiet and very dark, a sharp smell of rotting seaweed would suddenly fill the air- very reminiscent of low water in a Cornish creek. As we were a thousand mile from land, that explanation was improbable and I concluded that somewhere ahead of the boat, in the darkness, a whale was venting, and I could smell its bad breath! Although I saw several whales during the day, I never caught sight of one at night. I only had the aroma to indicate that they were there.

Francis Prout, the legendary boat designer and boat builder, lived in Debenham. He was a patient when I started the Practice there and he became a good friend, and soon asked me to help him bring his boat, a catamaran, from Canvey Island to Woolverstone

I fell in love with catamarans. They were roomy, stable and quite fast and it occurred to me that this is just what many people would appreciate if they had not sailed before.

When I had moved to Tattingstone I decided to start up a sailing school.

But this would be different.

Instead of using the monohull to teach people to sail, I wanted to do it with a catamaran. Even large mono-hulls pitch and roll and their movement can be very unsettling for some people and put them off sailing for good, whereas the catamaran didn't roll and pitch and there was usually plenty of room to move around. When inside the hull, there was sufficient headroom to stand comfortably in the galley or at the Navigation table and it was altogether a much more comfortable ride than a monohull.

The housing market was booming; house prices were rising at a phenomenal rate. Boat sales are linked to the housing market simply because when parents die, they often leave their property to their children who usually already own their own home. The younger ones then sell off the one that's been left to them. What do they do with the money? If they already have all they need for a comfortable life, they buy a boat.

If you've had some experience in small boats as a child or young adult, you have some idea of what to expect but most of the elderly punters do not. And they don't like the pitching and rolling of the monohull, and it was on this basis that I decided to teach people to sail in a catamaran.

For the equivalent boat length, catamarans are easy to handle; they have spacious accommodation with plenty of headroom and they don't pitch and roll, so that the gin and tonic stays in the glass. They have a shallow draught so can go where other deeper keeled boats cannot.

We had a berth at the East Anglian Boat Show and after that we had many bookings. We offered own boat tuition, day trips in Chiquita, our Prout 26' catamaran, or week length holidays in which we took the punters across the North Sea into the North Sea Canal and down to Amsterdam where the marina is close to the city centre.

At the East Anglian Boat Show

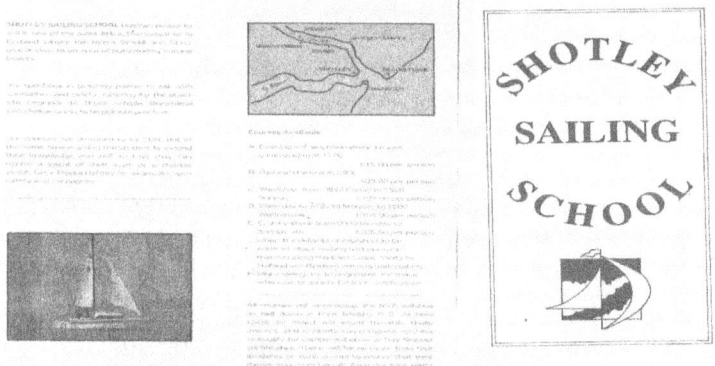

After a bit of Dutch Culture as seen from the centre of Amsterdam, we would head off into the Ijsselmeer which was a perfect spot for teaching sailing. During the day we sailed a lot, then visiting attractive fishing ports like Edam, Monnikerdam and others, in the evening

We also bought a similar boat in Turkey. The idea behind this was that after we had taught our punters to handle a catamaran safely and with confidence, we would give them a discounted rate for hiring our boat in Turkey when we awarded them with certificate.

St. Wardrede was based on the Dalyan river, mid-way between a freshwater lake and the Mediterranean. As the river entered the Mediterranean a sand bar at the entrance made the water very shallow, so it was inaccessible for any boat other than a catamaran, so we were the only boat of any size on the river.

The Turkish government had planned a new motorway from Bodrum to Marmaris and the route would pass over the river above Dalyan. In anticipation of the motorway's arrival, a smart Hotel was built near Dalyan and close to the river, perfectly located for the new motorway slip road that would take the traffic up-stream from Dalyan.

Unfortunately, the motorway project was shelved.

It was cancelled before the bridge was built which meant that this beautiful hotel was completed with no motorway access and no supporting entertainment for the guests. It really was in the middle of nowhere.

The hotel had been taken over by an English Company called 'Turkish Delight' and had been marketed from the standpoint of providing 'total peace and quiet' for the duration of the holiday. This concept was very attractive to many hard-working Brits who wanted a break from the razzmatazz of modern life.

They were fully booked.

However, when most Brits are confronted by peace and quiet, they love the thought of it, but after 24hours they just don't know how to handle it. They need a distraction. They need entertainment. Many of the punters at the hotel were bored witless and this is where we came in. There was no entertainment, no distraction – simply, nothing to do. They couldn't complain because this is just how it was advertised.

Our boat was berthed alongside a jetty at the end of the track, a few minutes' walk from the hotel to the river. We offered day trips; trips up to the freshwater lake where we could overnight whilst visiting the lakeside villages, or week-long trips to visit the fleshpots of Marmaris.

It had huge potential. Nick flew out to run the operation.

The Business Bank Account was in England, and I would get statements fortnightly. For the first month or so, it showed great promise but after that very encouraging start, it began to move in the other direction.

I flew out to see what was going wrong.

Nick was in charge of the operation and when he met me at dawn from Bodrum Airport we went for an early morning sail on Lake Kurgis, and I quickly realised how good a sailor he was.

It only became apparent later that the reason why the bank balance was not heading in the right direction was that he had invited all his friends (and girlfriends too), out for an extended holiday! Many young people enjoyed a boating holiday in Turkey courtesy of Nick Barter's generosity.

Out of the holiday season we offered to deliver yachts for owners or companies, and to tell of all the adventures I had whilst undertaking these deliveries would take too long.

I had agreed to help bring a boat back from Florida but had to pull out of the trip because a couple of weeks before we were due to set off, I was hospitalised with a perforated ulcer.

When the owner got his boat back to the Solent, and I had recovered, he then asked me if I would bring it round to Levington in Suffolk with him.

I agreed to do this but because my surgery appointment book was full the first available time was at the end of October, some three months hence. That was fine by him.

On the Thursday evening, I arrived on the boat in Lymington to find that the weather forecast wasn't too special. Gales were forecast in the channel. A decision had to be made. We either set off and put up with the bad weather or abort the trip and do it another day. The big problem with that was that I would not now be able to do it until the end of December when the weather was probably going to be just as bad.

We decided to go.

We set off and headed into the Channel with reduced sail in the face of strengthening south westerly winds. As we approached Brighton the wind had increased significantly, and we considered pulling into the safety of Brighton Marina to sit it out. That was, until we had seen the waves breaking over the entrance to the harbour. We would never make it past the breakwater.

We had no choice. We had to continue on our journey and hope for the best.

I still have nightmares when I think of the conditions as we went through the Dover Strait. With the wind direction in opposition to the flow of the tide, the surface of the sea was extremely ugly. It was dark with no moon, but just enough residual light to see the weak phosphorescence at the crests of the waves as they broke behind us. From the cockpit looking over the stern, I looked up to see a 30' wall of water towering above me with the white of the breaking surf outlined at the top before it cascaded down the wave front and broke at the stern of the boat. We were 'sailing' under 'bare poles' with no sails set and we were being blown along at about seven knots. It was a horrendous journey and one that remains clearly visible in my thoughts to this day.

I often think that we were lucky to have survived that. We were totally at the mercy of the wind and the sea.

As we passed the Essex coast, we entered a thunder storm and saw lightning hit the water a few hundred meters from the boat. I still have no explanation for why that lightning didn't strike the boat as our mast was the perfect conductor.

Both Guy and I were totally relieved to get in to Levington on the Saturday evening having been in the gale for thirty-six hours.

Guy and I sailed together again when I brought my boat 'Pachinko' from Anglesey to Falmouth. The weather was rough again, but she was a catamaran so less uncomfortable.

A previous owner had been shipwrecked in the Pacific and rescued by a Japanese container ship. During the passage to their next port all he had to do all day was to play a pinball game which had been provided for the crew.

This game in Japanese, is called Pachinko!

When I retired from Dentistry, I decided that I would have more time to sail so, being boatless, I bought a Prout Snowgoose from a couple in Dorset.

He was a retired engineer who had a passion for 'gadgets'. He wouldn't go sailing without his wife.

After one trip across the channel she decided that she didn't want to sail anymore, so they just used the boat as a weekend retreat where she could read and knit whilst he installed the latest bit of boating technical 'must haves'.

They had had 'Renvylle' for sale for a long time when I came along so were happy to take what I thought was a very low price. She had twin diesel engines, a full set of sails, radar with digital charts and every bit of electronic equipment you could possibly think of or want.

And she had been very well looked after. I sailed her home to Shotley Marina and as I sailed her around the East Coast I was planning a serious cruise in the future. She was an ocean-going boat and I had ambitions to do another transatlantic!

Sadly, the final cruise was in the direction of her new owner in Southern Brittany, brought about by the credit crunch and the downturn in the economy which meant that I had to sell her to pay some of the bills. It nearly broke my heart to have to sell that lovely boat which represented, to me, the rewards of a lifetime of hard work. All gone in the blink of an eye. The end of a long association with boats of all sizes.

'Renvylle' was bought by a young French man who wanted it to live aboard as he couldn't afford a house in Southern Brittany where he was a Community Nurse, similar in role to our 'District Nurse', and he visited and treated his patients in their own homes. The boat had to be delivered to Belle Isle from where he would collect it and sail it to its new home.

It was an interesting trip.

Ivor and I set off from Shotley and the weather was not nice. Passing through the Dover Strait we blew out the genoa (the large sail at the front) so had to put in to Portsmouth for a repair. Ivor had to get back home, so once the sail was back on board, I recruited a crew from an agency. All my usual sailing companions were unavailable, so I had no alternative. He was a young man called Mike who hailed from Newcastle and had considerable experience with yachts of all sizes, and I was really thankful that I had him aboard.

We sailed from Portsmouth and the wind dropped, and the sea was like a mill pond. We motored down the channel under a canopy of the Milky Way. Visibility was perfect, and not only could we see the lights of vessels as they came over the horizon, but we could also hear the throb of their engines too, so crossing the busy traffic separation lanes as we headed towards the coast of Brittany wouldn't be a problem.

It was a beautiful night and as we turned to cross the shipping lanes the engine failed.

We were in the middle of the separation lanes with both engines down. I radioed Brixham coastguard who advised us that we were just inside the British sector of the separation zone and if we needed assistance, they would send a lifeboat to bring us back. If however, we drifted over into the French Sector, they would also send a boat out, but we would have to pay. And it wasn't cheap.

Mike and I worked very hard and repaired one engine so that we had enough power to limp into Guernsey where we were able to get both engines working again. It had all been caused by fungal growth in the fuel tanks which we soon sorted out and were on our way again.

As we approached Belle Isle, I called the harbour Control and was advised that there were no berths available alongside the jetty, so I would have to go to a buoy in the harbour.

Pierre, the new owner of the boat was waiting ashore for his navigator who would then come aboard and take the boat to its destination. He couldn't come aboard immediately as he was waiting for Yvonne, his navigator.

When Mike and I heard this, we began to think that the rest of the trip would be rather more enjoyable than it had been up to now as the prospect of a French lady navigator on board for the next ten hours or so would liven things up a bit. Our imaginations went into overdrive, and we drew lots to see who would have the privilege of going ashore in the Dinghy to collect the new owner and his navigator.

After about an hour or so, we were advised by radio that we had to go alongside a moored fishing vessel so that we could embark our passengers.

It then became apparent as to why 'Yvonne' had not required the services of our tender to bring 'her' from the jetty to the boat.

'Yvonne' turned out to be a very geriatric French Fisherman who had spent much of his life in these waters. As we were about to experience tides of up to nine knots at times, it was a prudent move of Pierre to recruit such an experienced sailor to help us through this difficult stretch of water. The severe disappointment that Mike and I felt was due entirely to the fact that we had not appreciated that in French, 'Yvonne' was a man's name. And, to cap it all, Yvonne was so geriatric he was unable to get aboard other than by climbing over the side of a fishing boat.

Back in England I realised that for the first time in thirty years I was boat-less.

And now, who was going to teach my grandchildren to sail?

I couldn't bear it - but money was the problem.

In the local paper I saw an advert for a 'Hurley 20' a well-respected production boat that I had last used in teaching sailing to sailors at HMS Raleigh. It was for sale for £500 so I suggested to Nick that he and I go half- each and we bought it.

And then I had the accident. With all the injuries that I sustained I never thought that I would ever be able to get into a boat again, let alone sail one. I therefore made arrangement for my boat to be taken out of the water and stored in Ipswich until I was well enough to sell her.

Sarah had a friend come over from Spain to stay. She was recovering from a bad accident too and expressed a wish to learn to sail. This gave me the impetus that I needed, and I offered my services. First, we had to paint the boat and get it ready for sea. Initially it was a struggle, but the more I did it, the easier it became and soon I was able to get in and out of the boat without too much difficulty.

Within a month or so, 'Make and Mend' was ready for the water and Christina began her sailing lessons.

She, (Christina)was remarkable. Although she said that she had never sailed before I still don't quite believe it as she made extremely rapid progress, and I could see that she was possibly the Spanish equivalent of Christophe, and I was looking forward to her advancing quickly towards her Yachtmaster Qualification.

It was somewhat disappointing that she decided to return to Madrid for a holiday and she never came back. I believe that her father was very much against her coming over to England so may have pressurised her to stay in Spain.

'Make and Mend' was looking good, so I decided to advertise her and quickly sold her for £800. I then bought a bigger boat for £1,000, painted her up and sold her for £4,000 as I had my eye on a Heavenly Twins catamaran in a yard in Woodbridge. I borrowed £4K and bought her for £8,000. She needed a lot of work doing to her, but I felt that when finished she would enable me to do 'one more serious sail' before I popped the clogs. I really wanted to sail to the West Indies – the Grenadines in particular-

and I thought that this boat would take me there. Doing her up was great distraction from the other less palatable aspects of life which were constantly coming to the surface.

The Dental Company had been hit by the Credit Crunch and changes within the NHS, so effectively we were in serious financial difficulties.

Being on the boat in Woodbridge enabled me to mentally escape the gloom and depression of the financial situation. We had sold almost everything that we had worked for and I just could not see how we could pay the obscene fees that the law firms were adding on to the bill.

When Nick and I sailed 'Sassi' from Woodbridge to Ipswich against the wind and tide, the seven-hour trip was a good illustration as to why I ought to consider giving up the idea of 'one more serious sail' and get rid of this boat.

The effects of age and my accident sadly meant that I just was not agile enough to be safe in a boat on my own.

Although unused to bowing to common sense, I did so this time, and 'Sassi' now has a home off Southend. My sailing days are over.

18
Cornish Rebellion

In July of 1992, Virginia Bottomley, the then Conservative Health Secretary decided that Dentists were being paid too much and announced, (without consultation) that as from the 1st August all Dental salaries were to be reduced by 7%.

Seven per cent may not sound very much but if it's a reduction in pay, it can be very painful. At least that is what the dental profession thought and, not unnaturally, there was a lot of unhappiness, right across the country, about that decision.

The difficulty, however, was what to do about it.

The Cornish dentists didn't appear to have that difficulty. I don't really know what is was about the dentists in Cornwall, but they decided, within a matter of days of the announcement, that they were going to withdraw their services from the NHS and withdraw them completely. And true to their word, from the 1st August, all dental treatment in Cornwall would be provided under Private Contract. To have got their act together so quickly and to have arrived at this decision without dissenters was an admirable achievement and once the news had broken many other areas throughout the UK had their eyes on Cornwall to see how this would be dealt with. Questions were even asked in the Houses of Parliament in case this was followed by a nationwide response and a similar withdrawal of NHS Dental Services across the country.

Pat and I were in Cornwall during the first week in August for our summer holiday, and Cornwall has a very special place in our hearts. We had spent some very happy time there just after we were married whilst I was stationed at RNAS Culdrose and Sarah had been born in Penzance so when the advert appeared in the 'West Briton' whilst we were on holiday, I had some serious thinking to do.

The Cornwall Health Authority were seeking to recruit an experienced Dentist who could help them solve the problem that had suddenly appeared – namely that NHS Dental Treatment was no longer available in Cornwall because all the dentists had withdrawn their services and gone over to the Private Sector. The Health Authority have a Statutory Duty to provide access to Dental Services (like all other services, Medical, Pharmaceutical, Opticians etc) under the NHS and to have all the dentists suddenly withdraw their services was indeed a huge problem, and one which had never been faced before and one they had to solve. And they needed to solve it quickly. The Cornish health Authority had missed the deadline for advertising in the Dental Journal, so they put one in the West Briton and that is where I saw it.

I have always been a passionate supporter of the NHS.

I refused to provide Private Treatment and I turned down the opportunity to have a lucrative career in Harley Street simply because of my belief in the NHS. In my opinion, the action of the dentists in Cornwall was immoral. I know that they were more than a little peeved at Virginia Bottomly's action, but we, as a profession, were very lucky people. We had been trained by the State, at no expense to ourselves; our patients had paid their National Insurance and Taxes and the fees that we received were set by the Government who considered the payment we received for each and every item of treatment, was fair.

I'm aware that many of my colleagues disagreed with this, thinking that we were not paid enough, and by and large, those of the profession who thought that, opted out of the NHS anyway and went 'Private' which they were free to do whenever they felt that such a move was in their best interests.

When this happened, as it did quite often, all the patients of the practice would be advised of the changes that were about to take place and would then have the opportunity to move to another NHS surgery, or stay with that dentist and pay Private Fees. They had a choice.

However, on 1st August 1992 they had no choice.

NHS Dentistry was effectively withdrawn, and everyone had to be Private Patients.

Cornwall at that time, was not an affluent county. This was in the days before the EU grants and handouts, and this action would affect many families who relied upon the Tourist Industry or Agriculture for their wages and very few would be in position to afford Private fees. This action would affect those who could least afford it and I was very upset by the decision of my profession which I considered to be solely motivated by greed.

My mind was made up. I borrowed my niece, Helen's typewriter and tapped out a c.v. which I delivered to the Office of the Health Authority the very next day.

It was not an easy decision to apply for this job as I had a perfect life in Suffolk. I was the dentist to the school, where I had been a pupil and where also, some years later before going on to University to study dentistry, I had taught Physics. We lived in a beautiful bungalow near to the school and I had a five-acre plot on which I grew Alstromerias, and other cut flowers and I also had a facility for indulging my hobby of micro propagation. As if this wasn't enough, there was also the sailing school based in nearby Shotley.

I really had it made. Living in a beautiful part of the world, doing all the things I love doing – life was wonderful.

But despite all of this, I felt enraged that my profession should abandon their patients because they were going to be on a reduced salary.

What about the people who couldn't afford their new fees? Were they consulted? No, they weren't.

From the very moment I saw that advert, I knew how to deal with the problem; I knew how to find a solution and I felt that here was a chance for me to really make a difference.

The Cornish Dentists were wrong, and I was ashamed of my profession for being so avaricious and greedy. I felt sorry for the residents of Cornwall who were being held to ransom. If they cared about their teeth and those of their children, they were being forced into paying two or three times the NHS fees to unscrupulous dentists. Many would not be able to afford it.

I was short listed for the position and then at the second round of interviews I was offered the job.

I started the job on 1st January 1993 and I had a very clear plan. I intended to set up a new dental surgery in each of the major towns in Cornwall. Once they were established with trained staff and patients booked in, I would them sell them at cost to Dentists who would be given incentives to move to Cornwall. The new Practice owner would also be required to provide dental treatment under the NHS for a period of 10 years and would be required to sign a contract to this effect.

Everyone would be a winner. NHS dentistry would be restored in Cornwall; the incoming Dentists would have their own Practice, at a very reduced cost and with a cash incentive to come to Cornwall, and everyone, including the children, the elderly, the unemployed and those receiving benefits, would again be able to access NHS Dental Treatment. Once the surgeries were up and running, the problem would have been solved and solved for another 10 years.

The only people not to benefit by this arrangement were, of course, the dentists who had abandoned their NHS lists and gone Private.

Whilst the planning applications were being considered and the conversion of those properties to new dental surgeries was taking place, I worked out of a mobile unit (an old Schools Dental Service Caravan) and existing Community Dental Surgeries, to give as much emergency cover throughout the county as possible. The Community Services moved the Caravan as required and within a short time we had long lists of patients waiting for treatment in every town.

I convened a meeting with all the Cornish Dentists and the Health Authority to explain what I was doing and to give them an opportunity to change their mind if they wanted to. It was not well received, and I was looked upon as the enemy. I was booed off the stage!

But they were getting worried.

I started in January and shortly after Easter I opened the first new surgery in Callington, on the Devon border. I had planning applications running for many other towns and it was my intention to create new surgeries as quickly as possible. Within a year, (or so I thought), NHS Dental treatment would once again be available throughout Cornwall and would remain like that for at least ten years.

It didn't take the resident dentists too long to realise that this bloke meant business.

He'd only been here for three months and already one surgery was open, and more were in the pipeline. The publicity given to the project by the local media (including the local BBC and ITV networks) was helping our cause enormously. The patients, annoyed at being held to ransom by the 'greedy dentists' were waiting to switch to the new NHS surgeries as soon as they were open. This was hugely troubling to the newly Private Practices. As new surgeries opened, offering the full range of NHS treatment, there would be a massive exodus of patients to the new surgeries. An immediate demise of the surgeries that had abandoned the NHS would occur for they could not expect any patient loyalty, for they hadn't demonstrated any to them!

They, the Cornish Dentists, were very worried. And quite rightly so. Their greed was about to bite them. They called a meeting with the Health Authority where they informed the Chief Executive that unless he stopped this scheme and withdrew me, they would refuse to participate in any clinical activity other than within their surgeries; they would not attend meetings, and they would withdraw all emergency services too.

The Senior Management at the Health Authority were spineless. They appear to have forgotten that they had a Statutory Duty to provide Dental Services for the Population of Cornwall and as the dentists were not prepared to do this, they had no place at the discussion. They had also forgotten that I had been appointed to deal with the problem and that is exactly what I was doing.

My plan was working. New surgeries would come online and once again, the people of Cornwall would have access to NHS Dental Treatment.

Had the Health Authority not been so spineless, they would have stood their ground and continued with the plan that was working well and was on track to solve the problem once and for all. The Department of Health too, was watching to see how things were working out in Cornwall and so too were the MPs in case their constituents were faced with a similar problem.

Regrettably, instead of standing up to the bullying tactics of the Cornish BDA (British Dental Association), they capitulated.

They told me that the rolling out of new surgeries was to cease and to finish with this plan, and to continue to work out of the Community Clinics until the end of my contract.

It was a disaster. The tail wagged the dog and the people of Cornwall suffered. And they are still suffering.

The problem still exists but after they terminated my contract the Health Authority then tried to recruit a team of dentists to work out of the Community Clinics which proved to be another wasted opportunity. The dentists who had left the NHS were a powerful bunch and the influence that they had over the Health Authority was unhealthy. The Health Authority were toothless cowards who refused to stand up to the bullying and failed to consider the interests of the local population.

Cornwall is still a county with a poor record of NHS Dentistry, but it is of some comfort that the surgery that I set up in Callington, all those years ago, is still going strong and is one of the very few NHS Surgeries in Cornwall.

Our house in Cornwall at Penpol

View from the sitting room window.

With my contract terminated we had to decide on the next course of action. We lived in a most beautiful house overlooking the Devoran River at Penpol and the Catamaran was moored at the bottom of the garden. Pat loved it there and had completed a counselling course with the University of Plymouth and had a circle of lovely friends. Sarah had been married in Devoran Parish Church and we had spent a lot of money on an extension to the house as we expected to be there for a long time. It was good to be near my brother and I was hoping that the weekly painting sessions with him would be a fruitful and an enjoyable diversion to dentistry.

I took on an empty surgery in Mullion and got that working four days a week under the NHS, whilst I was waiting for Planning Permission for a new Denture Clinic in Truro. One thing that had come out of the dentist's disputes with the Health Authority was that there were an awful lot of people in Cornwall who had dentures.

A dental practice, specialising solely in the provision of dentures, had, to my knowledge, never been tried before but because of the current situation in Cornwall, it was difficult for a patient to get replacement dentures. I thought that there would be a demand for an NHS Clinic that specialised in dentures, and I opened one in the middle of Truro and employed a full-time dental technician. It was very successful, and we were very busy from day one.

One morning the staff asked if I had seen a programme on Westward TV the previous evening during which a lady being interviewed had complained that she had been to every dentist in the Torquay area, and nobody could provide her with a denture to her satisfaction. I got my receptionist to contact the TV Company and pass our details to the lady in question. She eventually arrived in Truro at my clinic.

Her story was really quite sad. Although she was in her 60s her younger husband had taken an interest in Amateur Dramatics and had joined the local group whereupon he was cast as the male lead against a very glamorous counterpart. My patient, sensing a reduction in the attention that her husband was paying her, felt that she ought to have a new set of teeth which would then result in the return of her husband affections.

She had a number of appointments, and we pulled out all the stops to make her dreams come true. If fact a new denture is a wonderful opportunity to provide the wearer with a 'non-surgical face lift' as a lot can be done to support the sagging facial muscles without picking up a scalpel. I added bits here and there to the trial denture until I felt that we had done everything possible to roll back the years without involving surgery.

The day came to fit the new denture. She was delighted (and so were we) and after a few adjustments to ensure the fit was as close to perfect as possible, we all adjourned to the front steps where we had a series of photos taken with a happy smiling patient surrounded by beaming staff. Our very happy patient then returned to Torquay.

When a new denture has been fitted, as it beds itself in, it frequently causes small areas of soreness which can be quickly remedied in the surgery. I had taken a lot of trouble to ensure that this eventuality was minimised before she left the surgery so that she didn't have to come back from Torquay for an 'ease' of the denture which would take 20 seconds. As she didn't come back during the following week we telephoned her to see if all was well. She was very positive. No soreness, she was delighted with the appearance and overall, very, very happy. We wished her well and got on with life.

Some three months later, we received a small parcel in the post which was a bit of a puzzle. On opening it, out fell a set of teeth. Quickly followed by a letter.

It didn't take long to read.

'You can keep these bloody teeth as they are no use to me. My husband has left me'.

I didn't consider it prudent to continue the correspondence as I felt to do so would have resulted in the blurring and overlapping of the boundaries between dentistry, social work and marriage counselling.

During this period whilst I was running the surgery in Mullion and the clinic in Truro, I had an unexpected visitor. A dentist came to see me who wanted a job. Nothing unusual about that you might think, but there was.

Dentists do go looking for jobs and when you want some help you advertise in the British Dental Journal and normally you can wait for weeks or months before getting a single response. So this really was special. Here we had a dentist, banging on my door and asking for a job. Very unusual.

Not only was that unusual, but also were his qualifications. He was an experienced dental surgeon with a master's degree, so he was top drawer.

His natural home would have been in a hospital environment or teaching at a university, but here he was, asking for a job. At the time I was running both Mullion and Truro, so it would be good if he could look after Mullion for me whilst I concentrated on the Truro Clinic. The problem was that he couldn't drive! So that was the first obstacle. It later transpired that he had lost his licence.

The regulations were changing in the area of Infection Control, and we now were expected to wear latex gloves and one day I noticed he wasn't, so I instructed him to do so. It was only then as he put these on in front of me, that I realised that he was missing two digits on each hand.

To be missing one finger is unfortunate, but to have two absent could be considered a bit of a handicap. But how do you manage with two missing on each hand? There was a story waiting to be told,

One of his hands was short of the thumb and index finger and on the other hand the ring finger and the little neighbour were absent.

Evidently, he'd been able to disguise this when not wearing gloves but now all had been revealed as attention was immediately drawn to the unfilled fingers of both gloves! Despite this apparently enormous handicap it didn't affect his dexterity and he could perform any dental procedure to a high standard.

Pat and I had already decided that we would return to Suffolk where we felt that the provision of Health Services, especially hospital services were better than those in Cornwall. I'd had a bit of heart trouble which meant a couple of trips to Treliske Hospital in Truro. We were not impressed and felt that the best solution would be to go back to Suffolk where we knew the Hospital services to be better. I needed to sell the Truro Clinic. I had given the Mullion Surgery to a colleague who had another practice in Redruth and the Truro Clinic would be taken over by my colleague with damaged hands who had agreed to pay a nominal sum for the surgery and the equipment. Just before we left the house for the final time, the local pharmacist telephoned me on Saturday afternoon. 'Did you know that someone is trying to forge your signature on a prescription'.

Of course, I had no idea, but it later transpired that it was my highly qualified assistant who had taken over my surgery and who was trying to get Class A drugs on a prescription using my signature.

The police were involved, and we eventually learned that this chap, a highly qualified Dental Surgeon, had a bit of a history.

He was a drug addict – well disguised, I'm the first to admit as I had no idea he was a user.

His elderly parents lived close by and it transpired that he was attempting to get drugs on a Prescription with my forged signature. It was his intention to administer these drugs to his parents and upon their death, use his inheritance to buy drugs for his own use. It also transpired that he had lost the digits on his hands in order to fund his drug habit. He had been working in Alaska and, like most dentists insured his hands. When short of cash to pay for his narcotics, he took an axe and removed two fingers from one hand and the insurance company paid up, believing it to have been an 'accident'. Sometime later he repeated the procedure but targeted the thumb and one finger on the other hand. Whether the insurance company paid up a second time I never knew, but I would be surprised if they had been fooled twice.

We later learned that his brother lived in Stithians, and my brother knew him well. They didn't get on, which is perfectly understandable especially as the brother in Stithians phoned the police when he heard that his Dentist brother was driving a car whilst banned.

We moved to Suffolk before the money for the surgery had been transferred. I suppose that I shouldn't have been too surprised when I was later told that he had fled the country and was now working in the Persian Gulf!

He still owes me for the surgery!

19
AUSTRALIA

We were living in Penpol, near Truro and as the Health Authority in Cornwall lost their nerve, my contract was terminated, and we decided to move back to Suffolk. I was in the final stages of disposing of the Practice in Mullion and in Truro. One morning the phone rang.

It was Tim Hayward, who I had been paired with for all our preclinical work at Bristol Dental School. He was now in Sydney, Australia but we had kept in touch since our Bristol days. After a few moments of chat, Tim asked me if we had any plans for Christmas. Why? Because he wanted to take his family on holiday and asked me if I would cover his practice for the holiday period – do a locum in fact.

The idea appealed to me so, without hesitation, I agreed to travel to Australia in December so that I would have time to get to grips with his practice before he took Chrissie and the girls away for a Christmas break.

The first obstacle to overcome was that of a Work permit and Visa. Australia only wanted young people and wanted them to be skilled or experienced in job categories that were acceptable to their government. Dentistry was not – they had enough of their own and in any case, I wasn't a youngster. Tim wrote endless letters but to no avail, they wouldn't grant me a visa. In the end, using a stack of notepaper with his surgery address, I wrote many letters to the Australian Embassy on Tim's behalf until at last they accepted one. I was being invited over to Australia, as a Consultant,'.... to educate and advise my dental colleagues on the latest techniques for the provision of full dentures!' As it so happens, there is a much lower demand for full dentures in Australia than in the UK but those at the Australian Embassy weren't to know that.

In the intervening period, we had sold the house in Cornwall and moved to Diss, into a Victorian Terraced house on Victoria Road. The house required a lot of work to get it into a shape that Pat found acceptable, and right up to the moment we took our cases out to the taxi and closed the door behind us, we had been working to get 'Albion House' as we wanted it.

We felt that we could do with a holiday too.

We broke the journey in Singapore where Ivor (another naval friend from Ganges days) had kindly arranged for us to use a friend's flat during our stopover. Three days of sightseeing in Singapore and we were ready for the next bit of the journey to Sydney. We flew with Singapore Airlines, so the flights were as comfortable and stress free as humanly possible. Singapore Airlines looked after us very well and we arrived in Sydney refreshed and excited.

Tim met us and we were soon in his beautiful house in Roseville Chase on the Northern outskirts of Sydney getting to know Chrissie and their two children, Heather and Lauren. It was late afternoon and when we had been there about an hour, Tim thought that I would like a bit of activity so off we went in his car with a two-seater canoe on the roof rack to the Paramatta river for a bit of sightseeing. I've done a lot of sailing and rowing, but I've never been in a canoe before and to have your first trip in what seemed to be a very unstable and uncomfortable water borne vehicle in what was well known as a breeding ground for sharks, did not fill me with much enthusiasm or confidence especially as I was familiar with Tim's carefree and cavalier take on life.

Anyway, despite everything it was a great trip and a wonderful way to start the Australian visit.

Their house was essentially built on a rock outcrop. The front entrance was off a road that wound its way around this modern estate, but the back of the garden, which included a double garage was on a higher level and fronted the road as it climbed higher into the estate. The garden which lay between the house and the garage had a significant but attractive slope through which ran a stream. Beneath the house a room had been excavated out of the rock and Tim made very good use of this as his wine cellar!

The garage had been converted into a flat of sorts for our visit, and this was to be our accommodation. Unfortunately, it had been designed as a garage and there was no way to disguise that, and during the high summer temperatures it was almost unbearable and even well into the night it wasn't much better. The stream though the garden, whilst having the appearance of a delightful addition to any recreational space, concealed a more sinister use. It was a breeding ground for mosquitoes.

Everyone knows what mozzies are, and of course we all get irritated by them during the English summer. Australian mozzies are different, very different.

At home, Pat is well known for her thick skin and for the general reluctance of any insect, either airborne or terrestrial, to attack it. She very rarely gets bitten by anything, so that's not something that she has to give too much attention to.

In Australia, it was a different story.

She was bitten and bitten badly. These ferocious creatures took a malicious liking to her skin and attacked it with unbridled enthusiasm with devastating effect. It was so unpleasant and uncomfortable for her, due to the swelling that followed these mozzie attacks, that she was very reluctant to do anything that involved leaving the building for the outdoors.

For me it was great to go to work. Tim had bought an old banger for his personal use, so that I could use his Subaru to get to work and do the sightseeing. I also had a bank account into which my earnings were paid so life was pretty good especially as the practice was airconditioned. The staff were lovely and the patients wonderful. Roseville Chase was a quiet suburb, with many retired professionals and English ex-patriots. They had been warned of my arrival so much of my surgery time was taken up by chatting! I must say that the influence of American dentistry and materials was quite surprising, so there was a bit of a learning curve for me in getting used to Tim's methods and materials which were not common in the British NHS.

Tim went off on holiday and on Christmas eve, I was running two surgeries and was quite busy. I'd put an emergency patient in the back surgery and whilst the local anaesthetic was working, I got chatting to him. He asked me where I came from and so I facetiously replied (all Australians like an honest approach!) that if I told him, it was unlikely that he would know. 'Try me' he said.

'OK, I come from Suffolk', I told him.

'I know Suffolk quite well' came the reply. 'I did my National Service there'.

We've got a couple of army bases and several RAF ones, so I asked which one he served in. 'Neither I was in the Royal Navy'.

That came as a bit of a surprise as there are no Naval bases in Suffolk and during the era of National Service, the reserve fleet was based off Parkstone Quay which is in Essex. If and when required, the sailors would come ashore at Shotley, and this would then account for a 'Suffolk' address.

When I mentioned this, he replied that yes, he had been in the headquarters ship of the Reserve Fleet, HMS Woolwich. The hairs on the back of my neck began to rise. I hadn't been prepared for this sort of conversation.

He didn't know my name and when I asked him who the First Lieutenant of HMS Woolwich was, he thought a minute or two before answering 'Lieutenant Commander Barter'.

The next question came out before I had even considered it 'What was he like' I asked him.

When he had given me a description of a very nice and well-liked officer who was keen on discipline and everything being done to a high standard, but who was very fair in dealing with the ratings misdemeanours, I felt as though someone had opened a door to my past.

I then explained to my patient that I never really got to know my father and to hear this testimonial from someone on the other side of the world was nothing short of remarkable.

Several days later I received a letter from the patient, thanking me for the treatment, and then telling me much more about his time in HMS Woolwich with more stories about my father. I was so pleased to receive this letter and when I sent it off to my brother he too, was delighted to hear so many nice things about our dad.

Tim came back from holiday and asked me if I would extend my stay so that I could cover another surgery up the coast so that his friend could go back to England for a visit. I said that I would be happy to do this, and a meeting was arranged with the owner of the other practice. I had to go to Sydney Airport to meet him when he flew in in his Cessna, did a quick turn-around and then flew north to Kempsey. I told him that I had done flying training before becoming a dentist, so he graciously allowed me to take the controls and fly to Crescent Head, where he lived. He took over for the landing for which I was very grateful. It was just a clearing in the rain forest and with only just enough runway to get the thing to stop.

We agreed the start time for the locum and he said that we could stay in his house which was a beautiful house built on top of a promontory jutting out into the Pacific Ocean.

We flew back to Sydney where I heard that we had been invited to Brisbane for New Year. Brisbane doesn't look far from Sydney on a map of Australia if you do not consider the scale, so we packed our bags and headed North to visit Paul and Doreen who had lived there for several years. Paul had been in the Navy with me. He had also trained as a Helicopter Pilot and was going to specialise in Aviation Medicine but became

disillusioned with service life and resigned and went to Australia.

The view from Crescent Head

He had asked me to be Godfather to his daughter Emma but that is a duty in which I had failed miserably.

There's only one road North from Sydney to Brisbane and that's the Pacific Highway. It's a good road, single carriageway for most of the way but with frequent sections of dual carriageway for overtaking. It's a very pleasant drive but a long one. We broke the journey at Crescent Head to where we were to return after the holiday and live whilst I covered the practice in Kempsey. We had intended to stay overnight but when we opened the door, we could see that every surface was alive, crawling with ants, spiders and cockroaches. The owner had been gone for several days and hadn't bothered to take any preventative measures against infestation by the innumerable variety of undesirable insects who were waiting for this heaven-sent opportunity to colonise an empty house.

We had been advised that should we have any problems during our stay, we should contact a friend of the dentist, a neighbour, who happened to be a pharmacist.

We didn't think for one moment that we would need to get in touch with him so early in our stay – in fact it was well before our intended arrival, but he was very helpful and agreed to deal with the infestation. There was no way that we could overnight in this house, so we left it to him and went on our way in search of a B&B.

When we got back after our trip to Brisbane there were many insect bodies lying as evidence as to their late residency, but at least the smoke bomb that the pharmacist had detonated on our behalf had been successful.

We spent a Happy New Year with Paul and his family in Jimboomba, catching up on the previous few years of Christmas Card correspondence. On our return journey, we called in to see another Paul, but this time a dental friend from Bristol, who lived in Byron Bay on the Gold Coast, famed for the Hippy colony and lifestyle that prevailed in this most beautiful part of the Australian East Coast. It didn't take long to understand why the hippies came to Byron Bay for the road verges were thick with lush green cannabis plants, ready for the taking!

During our first night in Crescent Head, I was awakened by something running down my leg, inside my pyjamas. As a reflex action, I hit it as it ran over my foot and then went back to sleep. In the morning, I was keen to see what it was that had woken me and was somewhat startled to find the corpse of a cockroach, some 2.5 to 3.0 inches across at the foot of the bed.

The following day was a Sunday, and I was due to start work the next morning so in the afternoon we went to find the surgery so that at least I knew where to go the following morning. It was a single storey tin roofed building a few miles away in Kempsey. As one might expect, the outer door was locked so I peered through the letterbox and when my eyes had adjusted, I could see a long dark corridor, at the far end of which a shaft of light illuminated a patch of carpet on which several cockroaches were scampering around. Obviously, these animals were part of Australian life so the sooner I accepted that, the better.

One of the first patients was a double amputee who had served in the Vietnam war. Australia sent soldiers to help the Americans in that dreadful campaign.

In Australia, the majority of people take out Private Health Insurance which also covers a percentage of dental costs. However, if you are on benefit, like this patient was, and you want to access Dental Care you have to go to a nearby hospital where the 'community' dentist looks at their teeth and then awards them a 'voucher' of a certain value which they then take to a dentist of their choice, and he/she provides treatment to that value.

This chap had a voucher for fifty dollars-worth of treatment and when I examined him, I realised that he needed a lot more treatment than fifty dollars would buy. I was quite used to this scenario in England, so I told the patient that I wasn't worried about the voucher, I would complete his treatment for the 50 dollars. The words were still in the air when the nurse (who had once been the partner of the dentist for whom I was covering) sprang across to the chair and said in a very forceful manner

'Oh no you won't. That's not how it's done here. Mr So-and- so will just have to go back to the hospital when we've used up this voucher and get another one!'

The first patient the next morning was booked in as a 'surgical'. Out of habit, at the end of the day I always look at the list for the following day so that I don't get caught out and have big surprises waiting for me at the start of the next day. I saw this man's notes and it was for the surgical removal of a lower molar. No problem. I'd done hundreds of these.

Next morning, I saw the patient. He was of Aboriginal stock and big with it, and his teeth were not only larger than normal but set in a jaw of the size that I rarely see in England. After the initial chat whilst waiting for the local to work, we got down to work and the first thing I asked the nurse for was the 'surgical tray'. All I got was a blank look.

In my surgery at home, I always had two surgical trays laid up and sterilised so that, if during an extraction, a surgical approach had to be adopted, a nod to the nurse would be all that was needed. She could see that the tooth had refused to give itself up in a conventional approach (or it had broken off in the process) and it was necessary to carry out surgery to relieve that patient of the offending tooth or roots. There was never any need to even tell the patient that I wanted the 'surgical tray' as that would introduce more (and unnecessary) anxiety. The patient wouldn't know until it was all over.

Things were different in Australia.

Here I was, faced with a large tooth in a very large jaw belonging to a much larger Aboriginal and with no tools to get it out. It was quite possible of course that the dentist, now on holiday in England, whenever faced with the need to perform surgery on a patient, just sent them across the road to the hospital. As this patient had been booked in for me to treat, I assumed that I should get on and do it.

We managed to find a scalpel, and, with only the absolute minimum of instruments, I managed to do what was necessary to get the offending tooth out. I don't think it would be appropriate for me to describe the operation in this text, suffice to say that it was one of the most challenging examples of what should be a routine procedure, that I have ever had to participate in.

The two weeks passed very quickly, and I enjoyed the work immensely. The patients were very friendly and hugely appreciate and I made many friends. It was an experience that I shall never forget and the fact that I was breathalysed at 7.30 in the morning on the way to work was just another experience that contributed to the feeling that life in Australia was full of surprises and never dull.

We returned to Sydney briefly before jetting off to New Zealand. We concluded that as it was unlikely that we would ever get the chance to be in this part of the world again, and as I had earned enough money to fund it, we should do a tour of New Zealand whilst we were this close. We booked a coach tour of both Islands and set off after we'd made a quick visit to Pat's cousin Robbie, who has lived in Auckland most of his adult life.

We were on a coach with 30 or so Australians; mostly retired and from all walks of life and who we got to know very well during the two weeks we spent together. Pat and I were probably the youngest couple on the coach and certainly the fittest. Aches and pains were a common and unifying feature of our fellow travellers. Pat's interest in homoeopathy soon became well known around the coach and her advice and opinion was sought on a daily basis for all complaints and conditions that were being experienced or imagined by the passengers.

Pat goes nowhere without her electronic acupuncture tool. It's a pen shaped, battery driven gizmo that has the ability to send out pulses of varying intensity. When pulses are transmitted, there is an accompanying high -pitched squeal from the machine which adds nothing to the procedure other than drama. The application of this type of acupuncture, when applied to the right area and in the right conditions, undoubtedly have a beneficial effect, but there is no doubt in my mind, after observing the results obtained during our two-week trip around New Zealand, that the placebo effect is very prevalent.

As Pat's therapy sessions increased in popularity, before the coach was able to set off each morning for the next destination, Pat had to complete her 'clinic' at the front of the bus. Any attempt by the driver to get on the road before that last patient had received either one of Pat's homoeopathic remedies or a shot from her 'welding tool' was met with open hostility from the rest of the gang.

South Island was amazing. Well, North Island was too but the grandeur of the landscape through South Island was nothing short of spectacular. I wish that I had had more time to paint for South Island is a painter's paradise. I did improve my rapid sketching techniques as I burnt out a sketch book with very quick sketches of the passing landscape as the bus hurtled southwards. Fiord land at the Southernmost tip was exciting too as was the glaciers near Mount Cook and a trip in a small aircraft which landed high up the glacier was one that I couldn't miss.

Queenstown is the place of extreme sports and whilst I said no to bungee jumping or whitewater rafting, I did get a flight from a mountain top in a hang glider. It was a tandem machine which was assembled by the pilot and me after a 30-minute climb up a rough mountain track in his land rover. At about 3,000' on a very narrow finger of rock with vertical cliff edges on either side, we got out of the land-rover, unpacked the hang-glider and assembled it. Strapped in and briefed for take-off we were ready to go. Take-off involved nothing more than running down the short slope towards the cliff edge- probably no more than three paces- and then committing ourselves to the mercy of the wind and the Gods. Just as we were about to begin the run to the cliff edge, the wind changed direction and plan B was invoked.

With the hang glider still attached to us, we shuffled around the peak until, clear of all obstacles, we counted down to running at the cliff edge but in the opposite direction. It was at this moment in time that I felt that I'd made a big mistake.

It was too late. We were one our way. Two, three four, five steps and there we were. Hanging beneath this oversized kite looking down to the valley floor some three thousand feet below. No, they were not minuscule ants, but people going about their business completely oblivious of the fact that high above their heads, amongst the developing cumulus clouds, was a fragile piece of material, stretched out on a flimsy aluminium frame, beneath which were suspended two people; one of who was almost certifiably insane and the other, so stupid that he had actually paid good money to this lunatic to be subjected to what could have been a terminal and terrifying experience.

So much for our New Zealand adventure. We flew back to Sydney, spent a couple of days with Tim and family before heading home to England. Pat was very glad to be going home whilst I wanted to stay. Australian life suited me, and it reminded me that many years before, when both Sarah and Nick approached their 18th birthdays, I had offered them each a return ticket to Australia. In the end, neither of them took up the offer – they both went off to France, but I now believe that had either of them decided to have a look at Australia at the age of 18, it is likely that they would have stayed there and made Australia their home.

20
A new Practice in Norfolk

When I returned to the East from that disastrous experience in Cornwall, I started working with Bernie Mayston, who had been my trainee at Meadowside, and who had then bought the practice when I moved to Tattingstone. My practice in Eye had been totally NHS, but Bernie wasn't too keen to continue like this. With the large patient base that he had inherited, he was ideally placed to convert to a Private Practice. This is what he did. When I returned from Cornwall, Bernie was looking for someone to help out with his NHS Patients and this suited me nicely. I worked with Bernie for several months before we left for Sydney in December.

When I left to go off to Australia, Bernie, (or his wife, or his manager) sacked my nurse, Anita. They obviously did not want to pay her wages whilst I was away. Sadly, instead of just terminating her contract, they dismissed her for unprofessional conduct. This was complete fabrication as Anita was one of the most experienced, loyal and professional Dental Nurses that I had worked with. A few hours before we left, a very tearful Anita had told me that she had been sacked so I faxed a letter to Bernie advising him of the error in this this and I added that unless he re-instated her, if Anita went to an Industrial Tribunal, I would be forced to appear in court to support her.

Bernie would not reconsider his action and the job that I was to return to was removed as neither Bernie, Teresa nor his staff would speak with me.

Back in Britain, and without a job, I needed to work. I considered several offers of associateship but had to decline them but took a temporary position as a locum for a very busy practice in Lowestoft. Back in Diss, a small shop with six months left on the current lease (but with exorbitant rent), became available. It had planning consent for D4 use, which included a Dental Surgery, and this meant that I could use it straight away. I bought some good second- hand equipment, advertised for staff, put an advert in the Diss Express, and opened up an NHS surgery near the town centre.

This is called, in the Dental Profession 'Doing a Squat'.

One morning, after we had been open two days, I went into the surgery to find that all the windows at the back of the surgery had been broken. I never did find out who was responsible, but I hope that one day I shall have the opportunity to ask Bernie (or Teresa) if they know anything about it.

During the following six months, a bungalow would become available not far from the centre of town and which I thought might make a good Surgery. I bought it and converted into a Dental Practice with four treatment rooms. I recruited three associates from Sweden and in no time at all we had a flourishing four surgery practice.

Mahmoud and Sharpour came over together. I had advertised for an Associate in the Dental Journal and both of these young men turned up as they wanted to work together. They were Iranians who had trained in Sweden, and they were on a tour of the UK trying to find a suitable Practice for them to start life in England. When I said that I had enough work to take them both they agreed to start with me in Diss in a couple of weeks' time.

Pat and I had rented a small house for them near to the surgery. They arrived on the Saturday and settled into their new home, and I showed them around the surgery.

On the following evening the phone rang, and it was Mahmoud. Could I go to the surgery and help Sharpour?

I duly arrived to find that Sharpour had cut his hand very badly on a glass whilst doing the washing up. Obviously, the glass had been broken and the pieces hidden under the washing-up water... Putting his hands into the water caused a huge deep cut to Sharpour's hand which required suturing. My first task was to sew up the hand of my new associate – on the evening before he started work! The next morning, he was able put a surgical glove on to cover the wound so none of his patients were aware of the previous evening's mishap. What a start to a new job!

Later, Ali, came to join us. Ali was married to Mahmoud's sister Fahima so at one stage we had a Dental Surgery with me as the Boss and three Iranian Associates who had all trained together in Sweden and two of whom were related by marriage. A big and happy family.

It was a very interesting time for me and Pat as 'our boys' as we called them, frequently needed help with domestic matters as well as other things. Both Sharpour and Mahmoud wanted to get their intended wives from Iran to England and that was not as easy as it sounds. I had to write letters to the British Embassy to get the ladies out of Iran, firstly to Cyprus and then in to the UK.

Mahmoud and Sanaz settled in Ipswich and so did Ali and Fahima whilst Sharpour decided that he wanted to be nearer London so he and Shararey, his new wife, moved to Upminster in Essex. Mahmoud and Sanaz still live in Ipswich with their two sons; Ali and Fahima live nearby to Mahmoud but their two sons, being somewhat older, are still based in Sweden. Sharpour's wife Shararey, went to Art School in London and then trained as a dental Hygienist before giving birth to their first child.

As I approached the age of 60, my blood pressure decided to go up to dangerous levels and because of this, quite suddenly and without much warning, I started getting a very shaky hand. This is not good for a dental surgeon, especially when one built up a practice essentially based on being able to give an injection without the patient feeling it. A steady hand was essential in my practice.

I could no longer carry out surgery (and I was carrying out quite a lot of this) and I was losing confidence very quickly. I spoke with my GP who advised that retirement was the best option, and before I had to deal with litigation. I wasn't too upset by that suggestion for I realised that to continue would be foolish and, in any case, I had an insurance policy for just an eventuality as this. I had paid the premium for many years to cover the possibility of an accident or injury that would prevent me from earning a living from dentistry and the premiums were not cheap.

I took retirement and submitted a claim to the Insurance Company with an accompanying Doctor's Report. It was a bit of a shock to then learn that the company, to whom I had paid in to for many years, had folded a month before, and there was no money to pay my claim!

I advertised the Practice and had lots of interest, but Ali and Mahmoud decided to buy it. I was even offered several thousand pounds above the asking price by a colleague who came to look at the building with me before I bought it. On that occasion his advice was 'don't buy this – you'll never get it to work'. He was now offering several thousand pounds above the price I had agreed with Mahmoud and Ali, but as I had agreed to sell to them, I couldn't consider it.

And so, on my 60th birthday, I retired from clinical practice.

I was aware that many people who go from a busy life to one of pipe and slippers, don't see much of their retirement. A busy surgery is adrenaline fuelled and to suddenly be without this would be asking for trouble, so I decided to set up a consultancy to help young dentists set up their own surgeries.

Most dentists are impractical people. Give them a screwdriver and they don't know what it's for. As for creating their own surgery, which involves acquiring a suitable building, getting planning consent, organising tradesmen to do the work to conform with the regulations and to do it to a good standard and undertake all the host of things that are involved in getting a dental practice up and running, is beyond the ability of most of them.

I placed an advert in the British Dental Surgery, offering my help to anyone who wanted to have their own surgery.

I was expecting about 4 replies which would then take me nicely along the path to retirement with a gentle descent.

I received 78 replies.

Of course, I could not help them all, but over the next six years I have helped almost 30 young dentists to create their own surgeries. Life is too short for me to include the antics of the numerous people involved in these projects – dentists, builders, plumbers, electricians, planners, landlords, neighbours, printers, carpet fitters, clinical and administrative staff, newspapers reporters, not to mention friends and relatives of the dentist, but one doesn't complete this huge number of new dental surgeries without rubbing shoulders with numerous characters in all trades and professions that, by necessity, one comes into contact with.

With possibly two exceptions, all the new surgeries were created for Iranians, most of whom had been trained in Sweden. They are wonderful people. Well educated, well mannered, polite, humorous, generous, and ambitious. They all have the most frightening tales to tell of the hardships and difficulties that they have endured in order to get to this stage in their lives. They are all amazing people, and my life has been enriched enormously by working with them and I feel honoured and privileged to have been able to work alongside them.

It was a very simple exercise. The 'client' for want of a better word, would tell me where they wanted a surgery and after checking out a few essential bits of information I would find a building, get Planning Consent; negotiate a purchase price or terms of a lease; design the surgery; put it out to tender, select the tradesmen; oversee the project and installation of the equipment; recruit and train the staff and advertise the Practice and enrol the patients.

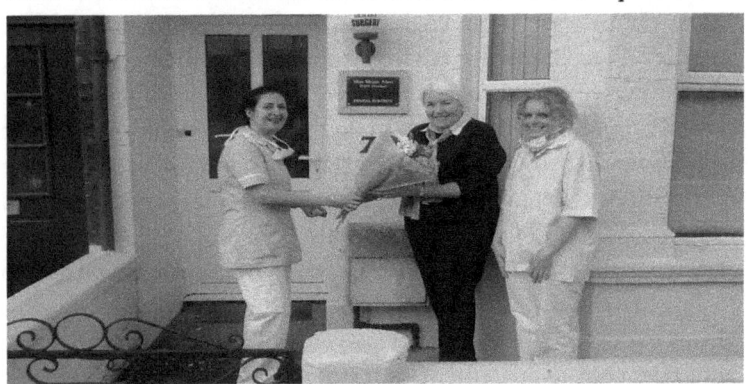

Megan Alavi at the opening of her surgery in Worthing

The first one I completed, for a lady in West Sussex, was just like this. She handed her notice in, went on holiday and when she returned, I showed her her new practice, introduced her to the staff, showed her how to operate the equipment and left the surgery as the first patient came through the door. As I write this, twenty years later, she is still at that surgery, and it is a very good business.

At sixty-five I had had enough.

Travelling was getting to be nothing short of a nightmare. Five years earlier I could get from home to the south coast in three and a half hours. Now it was taking much longer as the volume of traffic increased so I decided to call it a day. Instead of doing all the legwork myself, I decided that I would write a book to help the young dentist along this journey. I published the book online, and it has been a great success. It was a bit more than a 'self- help' book, it was more in line with a cookery manual. If they started at the beginning, followed my instructions, they would come out the other end with a surgery. It was very successful especially as each copy brought in £100! I also ran courses in London, and they too were very well received.

Shortly after I had completed the last one, and on the day after my 65th birthday, I was contacted by the Primary Care Trust in Ipswich and asked if I would help them set up a surgery to provide NHS dental treatment in Stowmarket.

It appeared that many of the Stowmarket dentists had opted to leave the NHS. (this sounded familiar). The town was one of the fastest growing in Europe and the Green Party Councillors had handed a petition to the PCT demanding access to NHS Dental Treatment. It was a triumph for 'people power' and brilliant that the 'Greens' had taken up the challenge and seen it through.

I agreed to help them and six months later a new NHS surgery was created in Stowmarket.

Some months before we opened, an article appeared in the Daily Mail accompanied by a photograph, taken in Scunthorpe, of a huge queue of people snaking around the neighbouring buildings, waiting their turn to sign on as patients in this new NHS practice. It was reminiscent of a third world country.

This was bad press for the NHS and the Department of Health warned the Suffolk PCT that if this was repeated in the press when we opened in Stowmarket, they, the Suffolk PCT would be fined heavily. To avoid this, I placed an advert in the local paper saying that we would be opening soon and if anyone wanted to become a patient, they should put their contact details on a piece of paper and put it through the door and they would be contacted by us when we were ready to offer them an appointment. We had 1,000 envelopes in the first week. But the troubling aspect of this was that there were many from further afield – from Bury St Edmunds and Hadleigh. When I told the PCT of this situation, they said, 'please could you help us create surgeries there too' and once the Stowmarket Surgery was up and running, I concentrated on Bury St Edmunds and Hadleigh.

Anyway, I set about the process of acquiring an appropriate building in these two towns and started the refurbishment. We were halfway into the project, if not more, when the PC T informed me that they had run out of money and sorry, there wasn't going to be an NHS contract for these surgeries.

This was a serious problem. The lease had been signed and I was paying the rent. What could we do? The neighbouring surgeries were either NHS (all full) or Private (very expensive) so we decided to make our surgeries 'Independent' (another way of saying Private) but our fees would be the same as, or as close as possible to, NHS fees.

The local MP for Bury St Edmunds – David Roughly, was no lover of the PCT and so took great delight in supporting our campaign from the standpoint that the PCT had let us down (which they had) and that we were doing this to make dental treatment more accessible to the community. The local media were very supportive too and we had a lot of very positive exposure in the papers, on local radio and on TV.

We created an amazing surgery. It was a large building, so we were able to put in four treatment rooms, an X-ray scanner an OPG for full mouth X-rays, a dental laboratory and an office as well as a superb reception area with seating. Each treatment room had state of the art equipment which included an intra oral camera and digital X-rays. It was a very modern, 'state of the art' Dental Practice and the wonderful thing was that all this was available to the public at fees which were the same as the NHS.

We had an opening party with much publicity. The father of Nick's best friend, who happened to have been my Squadron Commanding Officer at Culdrose, when I was grounded from flying was invited to the opening. It was great to see Captain Casdagli again and he really enjoyed his day.

The local press was there as well as the regional TV and we opened with a blaze of publicity and on that day, we had over 500 patients booked in for treatment.

This was amazing for what was essentially a Private Practice.

21
Yacht deliveries

During the days of Shotley Sailing School, when I had the idea of teaching people to sail in catamarans, a window opened for us to deliver yachts for their wealthy owners. Busy yacht owners who wanted to enjoy their new-found hobby in a warmer and less taxing environment would often ask for it to be moved to the new location during the winter months or in any case before their holidays, so that they could travel to their chosen location to find their boat ready to accommodate them for the duration of their stay. Often this meant that we brought the boat home again after the holiday. We didn't mind – we were paid to do it!

In addition to that, we were frequently called upon to just take a boat from one location to another, and for any number of reasons which we were not always party to. One particular trip comes to mind when I had to take a wooden boat from Levington to Calais for an experienced sailor who was the part owner of a marine Electronics Business. The boat was wooden and had a petrol inboard engine. Consumption was one third of a gallon an hour, or so we were informed, and we therefore had enough fuel on board to motor all the way to Calais, if need be, and we would have some to spare.

Tony Thipthorpe was my crew. Tony and I had joined the Navy together and Tony had subsequently trained as a Solicitor and had a successful practice in Southend. He could never resist the opportunity to come sailing.

We left Levington at 8o'clock on the Sunday morning under a cloudless blue sky and no wind. The tide was with us as we motored across the Thames estuary and through the Dover Strait. We crossed the busy shipping separation lanes and approached the French Coast as the sun was setting, the tide was now against us. As so frequently happens, the weather suddenly deteriorated.

From a beautiful calm day without a cloud in the sky, as darkness fell clouds began to build and the wind quickly rose to gale force within the space of half an hour. The swell increased and the boat began to slam into the waves and then the engine stopped. The first thing we checked showed quite clearly the problem. We had run out of fuel. No problem with that, we set the sails and continued on our way to Calais. As the wind increased and the seas became steeper, the poor old wooden boat slammed into every wave as though she were hitting a wall. And each time she slammed, she shuddered before seeming to pick herself up again and got ready for the next one. I was on the helm and Tony went below and as his eyes got accustomed to the subdued light in the cabin, he let out a shriek. 'We're sinking' he yelled. There was about 12 inches of free water swilling around in the cabin below and as we slammed into the heavy sea we could see where it was coming in. She was a wooden boat and unless kept moist the wooden timbers shrink and the space created needs to be filled with caulk. This had not been done.

As we slammed into each wave a plume of water squirted up between the planks at the bow and contributed to that which was already creating problems for us. We took it in turns to bale, using a bucket that we found in the locker on deck.

Fifteen-minute spells – one on the helm and one below with a bucket, baling. After about an hour we had reduced the water level and had it under control. I was baling and at the end of my shift I came up to take over the helm and was startled to see two very bright lights alarmingly close. I grabbed the helm and took drastic and immediate avoiding action as the bow of the French trawler passed within a hundred feet from us. I slipped into very nautical language and asked Tony whatever was he thinking about allowing us to come into such a dangerous situation without altering course, or even telling me. 'Well' he said 'I thought that steam gives way to sail'.

'You idiot', I replied, 'That does not apply to French Trawlers'

That was a very lucky escape. Another few minutes and we would have been run down by that trawler and it would have been our fault.

The next problem we had to deal with was the Port Authority

for Calais. As it's a very bust commercial port, ships are only allowed to enter under power, so we had to call them up and ask for permission to enter under sail as we had an engine failure. I dare not tell them we had run out of fuel. All they needed to know was that engine didn't work so that's all that I told them.

We were given permission and fortunately made it to our berth, under sail without a problem. Once alongside and secured I discovered that all the lockers in the cabin were locked and had we been boarded by Customs Officials this might have proved problematic. But we were left alone. Some years later, I heard that the chap for whom we had delivered the boat, had done a runner from his Electronics business and taken much of the stock with him. Obviously, although I am unable to prove it, but I suspect that inside those locked cupboards of the boat that we had taken over to Calais, lay the answer to the question as to where the stolen stock had been taken.

I bought a Catamaran in Shetland. I flew up there to look her over, decided she was just right for the sailing school and agreed a price. As I was unable to come up and collect her for some time (as I had a delivery from France booked in), the owner kindly offered to deliver his steel catamaran to me in Suffolk.

I went off to Bordeaux (with Tony again) to collect the Sadler 32 and bring it back to Portsmouth.

We decided to break our journey in La Rochelle. The harbour is in the centre of the old town with a fort standing guard at the entrance and the harbour walls edging the central part of the town square. The tide was low as we entered so high above us, we could see many faces of holidaymakers watching yet another boat come in to the small marina in the centre of town.

As we approached our berth, smoke started pouring out of the cabin and in a short space of time it was obvious that we were seriously on fire. Tony grabbed a fire extinguisher whilst I tried to manoeuvre the boat away from that marina and the other boats and into the channel. Fortunately, the Fire Extinguisher was operational, and Tony soon got the fire under control whilst I headed for a marina outside the city walls and where we managed to secure a berth.

One of the first tasks was to inform the owner that sadly, his boat would not be in Portsmouth at the end of the week but was stuck in La Rochelle where it would probably remain for a considerable time whilst we got it repaired. When we explained to him about the fire his response was 'Oh, Sorry, I should have warned you about the engine overheating'.

Christophe and Tony in La Rochelle.

Fortunately for us, Christophe was based in La Rochelle (that is why we decided to stop over) and was able to help us get the repairs to the boat sorted out and fortunately for me, this trip had been organised by Tony, so he took the responsibility for her repair and onward passage to the UK at a much later date.

Whilst this was all happening, in the Bay of Biscay, the owners of my recent acquisition had set off from Shetland and were heading for Suffolk and were now off the Northeast Coast of Scotland. They had insisted on delivering my new boat from Shetland to Suffolk whilst I was occupied in France. When I had returned home, I had expected to see the new catamaran, but it was some time before I received word that the boat would not be arriving. They were hit by a gale and a pretty strong one at that. Both rudders were torn off, they had to send out a 'Mayday' call and were taken in tow by the Inverness lifeboat.

They were an honourable couple. Not only did they return my deposit, but they also sent me my airfare to Shetland!

Time does not permit the inclusion of all the 'delivery stories', as there are so many, and I quickly came to the conclusion that people only asked for their boats to be delivered because there was a strong possibility that the said boat wasn't really up to the journey that was being asked of it.

On reflection, and from a perspective that is wiser and now more cautious, I will say that 'Boat Deliveries were a lot of fun – but I'm very lucky to have survived unscathed'.

22
Our French Son

In 1982 a group of boys from a school in Modane, in the French Alps, were visiting Suffolk on an exchange which had been arranged through Nick and Sarah's school, Thomas Mills High School in Framlingham. They should have been staying elsewhere but as that fell through, they were in effect without accommodation, so we put them up and they were delightful. We all so enjoyed their stay.

Four years later, just after we had moved to Tattingstone, Christophe came back to stay for a few days. He was at university and not too happy. This was not surprising as he had been expelled from two of his previous schools and he couldn't settle at his university.

During his visit, I took him sailing.

I think it might have been a 'Eureka' moment for him. When we got back home, he simply stated, 'This is what I want to do'.

All that I could do was to offer him a chance to learn to sail if he wanted so I said that if he were serious, and came to stay with us, I would teach him to sail and take it from there. The Sailing School was working well so he could fit into that without too much disruption.

His arrival was delayed for reasons which I have forgotten, and he eventually turned up in November – not exactly the preferred time of year for starting a sailing course. Anyway, on most days he and I sailed the Prout Sirocco Catamaran, 'Chiquita' and when we couldn't sail, Christophe helped me in the nursery, with the flowers.

He made remarkable progress. Everything that I showed him he seemed to understand, and he was a model student. I gave him homework and he wanted more.

In early January, I stood on the dock at Shotley Point Marina and watched Christophe take my beloved Chiquita across the Stour Estuary and back, single handed. It was similar to a trainee pilot going solo for the first time and he had passed with flying colours.

From then he went from strength to strength. Chart-work, navigation, rule of the road, boat maintenance, - in fact anything to do with sailing, Christophe could never have enough.

The highest qualification for the small boat sailor is the Royal Yachting Association 'Yacht Master' certificate which most people achieve after many years' experience. Evening classes are necessary to cover the syllabus and pass through the various stages of the exam – competent crew: day skipper: coastal skipper as well as courses for navigation and for a VHF Certificate. Christophe bypassed all of these.

After only four months of being around boats, this amazing boy from the Alps, who had never sailed before, passed the 'Yacht master' exam shortly after Easter with the second highest marks in the UK.

I had come to the end of what I could teach him, so I asked my friend, a sailmaker, if Christophe could join him for a few months to learn a bit about sails. Christophe's attitude to this was just as enthusiastic as it had been to sailing.

Within three months, he had graduated from repairing sails to designing them. In that short space of time, he was now an important member of the Sail-making team and in all probability would have been able to set up a business as a sailmaker.

At that time, an advertisement appeared in the 'Practical Boat Owner' magazine. Southampton University was asking suitably qualified candidates to apply to join a new course that they were introducing, in 'Small Boat and Yacht Design' leading to a bachelor's degree.

I telephoned the course organiser and gave him an outline of the career to date of this young Frenchman from the Alps who was a natural sailor and asked him if Christophe could come on his course.

Christophe started in Southampton three months later and after three years of study was awarded a BA degree with Honours.

Christophe is now a senior designer with Fountaine-Pajot the foremost builder of catamarans in France with an international reputation, but in the meantime, he has taken boats across the Atlantic, crewed on a delivery of a boat from Australia, competed in the Round Britain race as a member of the French crew, sailed a dinghy across the North Sea in appalling conditions and many more startling feats of seamanship.

He is a natural sailor, as fearless as he is skilled, and it was rather lovely to have been invited to his 50th Birthday in la Rochelle and once more meet up with him and the friends who came with him to England on that exchange visit all those years ago.

I have always felt privileged to have met Christophe and to have been so closely involved in the development of his sailing career. Many people never have the opportunity to help someone achieve so much, and I will feel forever blessed that I was in a position, at the right time, to be able to offer Christophe a chance to realise his dream.

But it was not just one sided. I got a huge amount of pleasure and joy out of our relationship and that enriched not only my life, but that of my family, enormously.

23
In search of the Irish in me

Twelve years ago, I was invited to an art exhibition at The Petley Gallery in London. I had known Roy Petley many years before, through Alfred Saunders, the Painter, in Harleston. In those days, Roy was a struggling artist, knocking out East Anglian scenes in the style of Edward Seago and he was very good. He expanded his repertoire and soon became a very successful artist with Prince Charles and the Queen Mother purchasing examples of his work.

Pat and I went off to Bond Street to Roy's swanky gallery. The exhibition featured two painters – Desmond and Patricia Turner, father and daughter and they were fantastic. These were painting that I could relate to and admired. If only I could paint like this!

Talking to Desmond and his wife at the end of the show and before we came home, I discovered that Desmond ran courses in Ireland and there were some places left on the next one. I immediately signed up for a two-week course later in the year.

Pat and I went to Achill Island, County Mayo and stayed in a holiday bungalow where she relaxed as much as she could whilst I painted.

It was a life changing week.

For the first time in my life I could get up early and paint; paint all day and then paint well into the night. The other members on the course were long standing followers of Desmond and many had attended every course that Desmond had run over the last fifteen years. They were a very friendly lot, and they accepted this bloke from England without reservation. Under Desmond's watchful eye, we painted a different subject each day, chosen by him, then in the afternoon we retired to the classroom where we would have the opportunity to look at and comment on, each piece of work that we had all created that day.

It was an enjoyable and productive two- week holiday.

I felt very much at home in Ireland and with the Irish – so much so that I felt that I belonged there. It was a very strange sensation. I just FELT Irish! I knew that my grandfather had graduated from Trinity College Dublin with a degree in Pharmacy, so I quite reasonably expected to have some Irish ancestry and to that end I got involved with tracing my ancestry through the internet and the many websites that encourage this research. But I was to be disappointed.

I discovered that my dear old grandfather – my father's father-had been working in Southampton (as a Chemist) and sadly dispensed the incorrect medicine for a patient.

In many instances this would just have been a serious mistake and would have been rectified before too much damage could be caused.

But in this case, the patient died, and Granddad was charged with manslaughter, was struck off the Pharmacist's Register and sent to Prison. Some years earlier, his wife had died so when our grandfather went to gaol, his children had to be taken into care.

My Dad finished up as a Barnardo's Boy and when he came of age to leave the Children's home, he joined HMS Arethusa and then Royal Navy. My Dad had been Christened Herbert Edward Tresidder Barter and I was intrigued by the Tresidder bit as that is a common Celtic name, frequently found in Cornwall. This was just another fragment in my family history that encouraged me in the belief that I had Celtic (or even Irish), roots. Why should my dad be given this 'Cornish' name if there was no link to the county? Why also did my dad include the 'Tresidder' on Leonard's birth Certificate, and not on mine? The more questions I asked the more convinced I became that there was some Irish connection that lay hidden, waiting for me to uncover it.

Sadly, I was to be disappointed. At the time of writing anyway, I have still been unable to uncover any Irish connection as my great, great, grandfather was a Vicar in Essex. He had a very chequered history, and he too had a run-in with the law! but this is not the place to talk about that!!

Maybe in the future, I will continue the search and go deeper into our family history but at this moment in time, although I felt a strong emotional bond to Ireland, and to the Irish people, there appears that there is no greater foundation to this other than 'wishful thinking'.

24
SPAIN and the Spanish Experience

When Sarah fell pregnant with Bean she and Javi decided to come back to Norfolk and have the baby in England. It just so happened that the workshop/ barn adjacent to Algar's Barn had once been used to accommodate the father of the people who bought the barn from the neighbours, Tony and Betty so that he could live in what we called the Annex whilst he was carrying out the refurbishment. It was equipped with a small kitchen, bathroom and two bedrooms with a small sitting room downstairs.

It was perfect for Sarah and Javi. Javi got various jobs working as a chef before starting an access course in Norwich which would enable him to apply for a place at university. Bean was born in the Norfolk & Norwich Hospital and spent his first seven months shuttling between the Annex and Algar's Barn. Javi got a place to study Medical Illustration at Derby University and to make things easier for them both I bought a house on the edge of the city so that they could all be together. Because of his previous experience as a professional photographer, Javi was allowed to complete the course in two years instead of three and at the end of that second year Sarah decided that she had had enough. It transpired that

Javi was not the man behind the façade that he presented to us. He was prone to violent outburst and his very intimidating presence when he was in that sort of mood made Sarah very frightened. Before Javi graduated, Sarah came home, and Javi went back to Spain for a while. Sarah needed to work and her previous job, working on 'Hello' magazine in Madrid was still open to her. We all agreed that if Sarah wanted to continue with this job she would fly down to Madrid on a Wednesday, work on the magazine, and when it had been passed to the printers, she would fly home on the Saturday or Sunday. Whilst she was away, Bean would live with us in The Barn where he and Pat and I enjoyed this arrangement immensely.

After several months of this – in fact Bean must have been three years old, Sarah decided to get a place of her own in Madrid and once that had been sorted, we had the emotionally difficult task of taking Bean to Spain where he would join his Mum and then go to school. It was a very painful journey which I still remember very clearly.

We were heading south to Gatwick. Bean knew that he was going to Spain to live but was probably unaware of significance of this journey. As we drove down the A140, only 5 miles from home, there was a large conspicuous house adjacent to the road, nearing completion and it obviously had, (to me anyway) some Mediterranean influence in its' design.

Beannie looked at the house as we drove past and turned to me and said,

'Ayah, why can't you buy that house, and we can all live in it for a hundred years'.

Obviously 'a hundred years' was, for him, 'forever'.

Each time I pass that house I am reminded of that time, and I still feel a pull of emotion and we still call it 'the hundred-year house'.

After leaving him with his Mum in Alcala, we returned home to an empty house. We missed Bean terribly and this made us think about our lives and the future, and we came to conclusion that we should possibly get somewhere small in Spain so that we could fly down and see Sarah and Bean on a regular basis. Bean had occupied such a huge place in our lives, it was very difficult getting used to life without him. He and I spent a lot of time together and

I missed him more than I was prepared to admit.

Agars Barn was a beautiful house with the field behind but if we were to spend half of each year in Spain then the best thing that we could do was downsize. The perfect solution was to convert the Annex, where Sarah had lived, into a small manageable cottage, suitable for us and easy to run and maintain, so that when we were not in Spain we could be there and when in Spain it would take very little maintenance.

So this is what we did.

The only problem was a covenant on the cottage, placed by Tony and Betty when they sold it, which stipulates that the cottage could only be used by the family of the owners of the Barn. This was fine when we lived there (as it was for the previous owners) but not if we sold the Barn. Tony wanted good money to release the covenants and to give his position a bit of weight, he sought the opinion of the Planning Department regarding the possibility of obtaining planning consent for use of the annex as a separate dwelling. The advice that came back was that no, there's no chance of that. I offered Tony £5,000 to release the covenants and he was reluctant to agree so one Monday I saw him walking his dogs and I said that my offer of £5K for the covenants would expire on Friday. The planners have said no to the idea of a separate dwelling, so he ought to consider my offer as a generous one. On the Thursday he agreed to release the covenants for that price and the deal was done.

My next move was to apply for planning consent. Fortunately I got it and started the conversion.

Chris Garrod, who I thought was a friend of mine organised the project. It was my design. I paid for the materials and at the end of each week I would pay the labour. The cost of materials included VAT at 17.5% and at the end of the project Chris claimed this VAT back as a new build/conversion was zero rated. When he presented me with the final bill Chris stated quite incorrectly that we had agreed a figure of £70,000 for the refurbishment. Chris wouldn't engage me in discussion about the bill, blaming his accountant for arriving at the final figure. I was very disappointed in that he had effectively cheated me out of at least £15K, especially as I now believe that a significant amount of various building materials that had been paid for by me, went towards a project at his own house where he was converting outhouses to holiday lets. All this is water under the bridge now, but it is difficult for me to forget about it as I had known Chris for a long time and considered him to be a friend. He's no longer on the Christmas card list.

Soon after Bean had moved in with his mummy in Alcala, on the outskirts of Madrid, we decided to fly down and have a look at a number of mobile homes in Andalusia as Sarah said that she would eventually move to Grenada. A few hours before we set off for Luton Airport, we had a visitor. It was Bruce, Pat's half-brother who arrived not alone, but with a friend. This was typical Bruce. We'd had no communication from him for months then suddenly he appears with a strange looking bloke who, Bruce assured us, was a talented builder who would be happy to do any jobs that we wanted done!

We didn't have any jobs that needed doing (maybe we did, but not by him) and we were certainly unhappy about giving them the run of the house whilst we were away, so we said they could stay in the Annex. The only problem was that the oil for the boiler to the Annex had run out so off I went, two hours before leaving for Luton, down to Diss with 25 litre cans to buy heating oil for Bruce. When full these cans are quite heavy and pouring the oil into the top of the tank whilst perching on a ladder was not easy. I was on the third and final trip and must have been a bit tired. Anyway, I slipped from the top of the ladder and hurt my leg. It swelled up immediately, so I asked Pat to bandage it as we left for Luton. She was insistent that it was broken but as our flight was in a few hours we had no choice but to go to the airport and fly to Spain. We hired a car in Malaga and went to view these caravans. One was in the Sierra Nevada and so high up that before we reached the site the general consensus was that this was totally impractical. So we never actually viewed the site. As we drove through Granada, we passed an orthopaedic hospital. My leg, by this time was beginning to become very painful. The previous evening I'd taken Beannie for a swim in the sea and my leg behaved as though it had an extra joint below the knee, so I knew that something wasn't as it should be.

The hospital was immaculate. All the staff were beautifully

turned out in pristine uniforms – it was though they were waiting for a high-powered dignitary to inspect them. With Sarah's help, I was quickly attended to. Within the space of 30 minutes, I had been X rayed, had a pain killing injection, seen the consultant (who called in several colleagues to have a look at this idiot from England who had been walking around with a broken leg for three days) and then been plastered up. Incredible efficiency. They were amused too, when they found out that I was a Dentist who, in their opinion, ought to have known better!

We continued our search for a mobile home and found a nice site in Mollina, just north of Antequera. It was in the grounds of a large hotel which had been built specifically for the Barcelona Olympics and the Olympic sized swimming pool was still in use. The manager was a English lady and the hotel owner, Fernando was a lovely Argentinian who ran a very tight ship and everything was done well.

I think we paid well over the odds for our caravan, but it suited us. It was on a secure site, with beautiful facilities, and within walking distance of the neighbouring village of Mollina and a short drive to the larger town of Antequera whilst still only an hour from the airport at Malaga and the same distance to the one in Granada.

Over the years that we owned it, we had several modifications and additions to the caravan – paving of the patio and a covered veranda where we could sit out all year and enjoy our meals.

We spent a lot of time in Mollina. It was a most relaxing bolt hole. We often arrived late in the evening and after a meal went to bed with the shutters drawn and in complete darkness. Without the morning sun to awaken us we frequently slept through until the following afternoon, completely oblivious of the passage of time. It was very peaceful. Across the road lay the hills and mountains beyond the olive groves and a quarry. Every day I would pack my rucksack with sandwiches, water, painting gear and set off into the hills. I walked miles and miles and painted many pictures too. When Beannie came to stay, he and I used to go off for hours in the hills and woods and he too, although only 4 years old, walked miles with his grandfather.

Antequera is famous for many reasons, but no visitor can go away from this lovely town without admiring the 'face' mountain in whose shadow the town sits. The silhouette of the mountain gives it the name and there are several stories in the folklore of Antequera which describe the mountain as the place where two lovers leapt to their deaths. As soon as I first saw the mountain, I wanted to climb it. I would have loved to have taken Beannie with me, but he was just too young. I went with a friend from the Caravan site who assured me of his love of climbing and his fitness to do it. I managed to get to the top with John in tow, but it soon became apparent that he wasn't as fit as either of us had assumed. I was very glad to get him back to his caravan as I had wondered during the descent if he was ever going to make it.

We visited Antequera often as well as Malaga, Grenada and the Alhambra and other places of interest. Our main interest however was not on sightseeing but for rest and recuperation. With the hotel at our disposal and the swimming pool behind the caravan; beautiful countryside a few minutes away, lots of friends on site, there was little more that we required to make our stay relaxing and happy.

They say that you should never follow your children and I know that there's a lot of sense in that. As soon as we had settled to this comfortable lifestyle – six months in the UK and six in Spain, Sarah and Javi got back together and decided to return to England. They bought a house in Spixworth shortly before the twins arrived then moved to Diss before Lucia arrived.

Soon after the arrival of Emily and Lorca, Sarah and Javi decided to get married and thought it would be good to have the twins Christened at the wedding ceremony. This was all to be carried out in Spain and they asked Leonard if he would officiate. Leonard had to get special dispensation from the Bishop of Truro in order to carry out these duties in another country, but he obtained permission and Christened Emily and Lorca at the same ceremony as blessing the marriage of their parents.

Sarah and Javi had been through a Civil ceremony in Diss in advance of the jamboree in Spain, where they hired a holiday complex consisting of several converted outbuildings around a central swimming pool and patio with barbecue and terrace. It was a great occasion with many of Javi's relatives and their friends enjoying a couple of days partying in the sun. Pat and I, together with Leonard and Joyce, stayed in a quieter location a few miles away. When the partying had died down, we went off to Mollina where we hired another caravan for Leonard and Joyce and we spent a few days on the site before heading home to England. Before we came home, Leonard and I went to Granada and spent the day at the Alhambra Palace which was an amazing experience.

Sarah and Javi at their wedding with Leonard holding Lorca and Emily

A BULLFIGHT

I have always had a fascination for the Bullfight. For so many young people the writings of Hemingway and others had fired my imagination with the romance of the spectacle and the traditions that surround it. I've read and re-read 'The Bulls of Parral' so many times that in theory, I am an 'Aficionado'.

But I hadn't actually seen a Bullfight. I needed to witness one.

Antequera, like so many towns right across Spain, has a large Bullring in the centre and I was particularly excited when I saw that the start of the Bullfighting season was being marked in Antequera with a fiesta at which three- or four-star matadors would be appearing.

I bought my ticket and sat in my seat in the sun anxiously awaiting the start.

It was all very disappointing.

I had expected the ring to be full on such a special and prestigious fiesta with the packed crowds contributing to and creating an unforgettable atmosphere. Only half the seats were taken, and the atmosphere was no better than a village football match in Suffolk.

The pageantry of the opening procession was amazing, and the band was playing just as I had imagined the music of the bullfight to be (after all I have had a record of Bullfight music for nearly 60 years which I still play infrequently when I want to immerse myself in the romance of Hemingway).

There were four bulls killed that afternoon before I left. There might have been more later, but I didn't stay to see them.

By the time the fourth bull had been sacrificed I had come the conclusion that this was indeed what many writers and critics had suggested.

It was a barbaric attempt to create a romantic art form out of a sadistic ritual at which the central participant, the bull, is at a massive disadvantage.

They talk of the 'bravery' of the bull; its 'nobility'; of the 'artistry' of the matador and his bravery. Undoubtedly, to be a matador you do have to be brave and you do put your life on the line when you face those horns and it's something that I shouldn't care to do.

However, before the matador confronts the animal, the bull has usually had a good going over by other people. Firstly, he arrives in the ring fired up and frightened and after an initial gallop around chasing anything that moves or attracts him, the picadors on heavily padded horses, wade in to place the 'pics' (very sharp spears) in the bull's withers and in the muscles of his neck. Frequently, as this is happening, the bull attacks the picador's horse (hence the padding) but if he gets his horns underneath the protective armour, the horse will take a goring and have to be put down.

Once the picadors have done their work the bull is bleeding badly from these lacerations on his neck. The anxiety, and the expending of so much nervous energy in such a short time, together with the heavy loss of blood, helps to tire the poor animal out.

The next part of the spectacle is also not nice. The weakened bull is further irritated by the second-rate matadors who cape the bull whilst the main man watches to see how this damaged animal behaves and the line he takes when he runs at the cape. When he's satisfied that not only does he understand how the bull behaves when being caped, but the bull is sufficiently weakened for him to take over, the Matador then capes the bull and plays with him to entertain the crowd, getting the bull to follow the cape as close to his body as he can without taking a hit with the horn.

After this bit of stylish entertainment, the matador places the darts. He capes the bull and controls him until he is stationery whereupon the matador places the darts in the neck of the bull. The net result of this is that the muscles in the bull's neck are further traumatised and often so damaged that the bull now has difficulty in raising his head whilst at the same time the bull loses massive amounts of blood. The matador then may decide to play with animal with the cape for the benefit of the crowd before lining the exhausted animal up for the kill. He takes the sword from a helper and with the bull mesmerised and exhausted and usually with a lowered head, the matador thrusts the sword into the bull behind the head, severing the spinal column.

The bull collapses on to the sand and dies instantaneously in a pool of blood that has been flowing from him constantly over the preceding minutes. The matador is awarded an ear, or two ears by the President depending upon how his performance (and that of the bull) has been judged by the reaction of the crowd.

It is a barbaric spectacle and one that ought to be banned. All the odds are stacked against the bull and its fate is predetermined. Any preconceived idea that I might have had as to the romantic and artistic justification of this cruel, medieval and barbaric activity have been totally eradicated from my mind. I shall not go again.

As a result of the economic recession and the credit crunch and all the financial difficulties that we suddenly found ourselves in, we had to sell our lovely van. The timing couldn't have been worse as this coincided with the collapse of the Spanish property market. We had to sell and got less than a third of what we had spent on it. I still miss those trips to Spain and the freedom of walking the hills and mountains and the joy of the pure tranquillity of being in the mountains of Andalusia.

25
On Art and Painting

As the country began to rebuild itself after the Second World War, my mother took me and Leonard to the recently reopened Norwich Castle Museum. Although I still remember the visit, only one part of it remains firmly embedded in my memory.

In the Art Gallery, alongside the many beautiful paintings of the East Anglian Landscape was a small painting of a horse. I suppose it could be described as a 'Horse Portrait' as the animal was dominant on the canvas. No, it wasn't a huge picture, I suppose it might have been no bigger than 15" across and 12" deep but I couldn't stop looking at it. From close up it was a mess (at least it was to my seven- year old eyes) just a jumble of browns and reds and greens and greys, all of which had been applied to the canvas like butter – so that the 'lumps of colour' had a strange physical quality whilst at the same time meaning very little to me visually.

What I found mesmerising was that as I moved away from this unintelligent mess of colours, an image gradually emerged and at a distance (predetermined by the artist, I can only imagine) this beautiful painting of a horse emerged and the gloss on its coat was almost stroke able.

I remember being transfixed by this painting by Alfred Munnings from Mendham and that image has been with me for the last seventy years – always there, always in the background like a visual rendering of music by a favourite composer. Because of this one trip to the Norwich Museum and a chance exposure to this small painting, I have spent my life in awe of people who could paint whilst concealing an ambition of my own to be a painter.

Now that I've run out of time and there's no chance that I'll be able to realise that ambition at least I can confess that I've always harboured the idea. If my grandchildren were to say to me that they had an ambition to be something or other, I would encourage them and say 'Go for it', but I didn't do it myself.

And the reason why I didn't take the advice that I would willingly give to my grandchildren is one of confidence. I simply didn't believe that I could do it; I didn't believe that I had the talent and of course I did not think that being an artist was a viable career, especially at a time in post war Britain when young people were encouraged to aim for a 'proper job with a life time career'.

Art was not offered at school, so I had no opportunity to develop any latent talent that might have been deep beneath the surface. Any talent that I might have possessed remained buried there until I first took up a brush whilst at HMS Temeraire. One of the more onerous of the weekly tasks at Temeraire was the handing in on Monday mornings of our 'Journal'. We had to complete four pages of writing on a topical subject of our choice. If, however, we chose to illustrate the article we need only produce three pages of text and this opportunity was too attractive to be overlooked. I bought a pack of poster paints (the fore runner of acrylics) and either drew a sketch, painted a picture or created a cartoon, all of which I found more agreeable than a page of writing.

Visits to the galleries in Edinburgh, provided food for the ghost of an artist sitting on my shoulder, but life continued to get in the way of any artistic leanings and that genie was put back into the box along with the brushes and paints. After Temeraire they didn't see light of day for another seven years.

I had been admitted to the Royal Naval Hospital in Haslar with a mysterious illness. The sickness manifested itself a week or so after Pat and I had been looking after Tregolls farm whilst Leonard and Joyce went on holiday. As well as milking the cows, we consumed the milk straight from the churn – prior to pasteurisation. That illness has never been given a diagnosis but my research whilst working at the Bristol Royal Infirmary as part of my course at the Dental School, led me to believe that I had been suffering from Brucellosis, an infection from cows.

But I digress. After a two week stay in Haslar I was well enough to get out of bed but because I still had an unexplained temperature, I wasn't allowed home or back to my ship. I was bored. I bought some paints and a few brushes and started painting again and when I was discharged and went home, I completed a few more pictures and felt that my technique was improving.

Over the years I have come to the conclusion that whenever one has a plan that deviates from the usual hum drum business of domestic activity, life gets in the way, and in regard to my ambition to develop my painting, life really did get in the way.

It was several years after my enthusiastic dabbling whilst in Hospital, that I was able to take up the brushes again.

Sarah arrived during my last two years in the Navy and we had several moves to enjoy – Helston; Belfast; Weymouth (sharing with John and Mary); Portland (Mobile home!) then Exeter whilst I was training at St Luke's; then Holbrook whilst teaching at RHS; then Bristol. The next stop after Bristol was Eye, and Sarah and Nick were growing up.

As she approached her 'A' Levels which included Art, Sarah demonstrated an amazing talent for painting. She could paint, and paint well and paint quickly.

Frequently it was necessary for me to be the hard father and say to Sarah that she couldn't go out with her mates until she had completed a picture. In rebellious mood, she would respond by painting just what was in front of her, without moving from the spot where she sat. Consequently, she was able to create amazing pictures from the most mundane of subjects – the corner of the room; a violin on a chair; a couple of dustbins.

I felt that Sarah had a talent and ought to be exposed to the commercial side of art.

Many of my patients were painters of varying aptitude and ability, so I was well placed for organising an exhibition which would include some of Sarah's work and this is what I did.

I hired a local building which used to be a game warehouse -(as in pheasants, partridges, hares etc and was the one used by Reg Bailey during his 'Black Market' activities during the war.). This was a great space for an exhibition, and centrally placed in Eye, so I invited all these artists to exhibit with us.

These exhibitions were a great success and Sarah was soon selling her paintings. This encouraged me to get the brushes out again and I also managed to sell a few and from then on, I used to paint whenever I had a spare moment.

When I converted the garage at Meadowside to create the surgery, there was room for a small studio in the loft and that is where I used to paint, although gaining access to that space was such a challenge that I used it only when desperate!

I also had the surgery in Debenham where I hung several of my better paintings on the walls for decoration. During a particularly bleak and cold winter, when deep snow prevented many patients attending the surgery, I made more money selling paintings from the surgery walls than I did from Dentistry.

For one of our exhibitions in Eye, I was very fortunate to persuade Margaret Glass, a local painter in Pastels, to exhibit with us. Margaret went on to be the President of the Pastel Society and is Internationally respected as a very fine artist. Somewhat naturally, Margaret's painting are quite expensive and these high prices topped the bill at out exhibition.

The artists brought their painting in on the Thursday morning and we hung the exhibition in the afternoon. Burning the midnight oil, I compiled the catalogue, and printed it out ready for the scrum that would occur the following evening at the Private View.

At nine o'clock on the Friday morning I unlocked the 'gallery'. The paintings on the wall immediately opposite the door, and the first ones to be seen as you entered the gallery, were our star exhibits.

As the lights came on I could not believe my eyes. All of Margaret's painting were damaged. And this damage had occurred overnight. And I had no insurance.

Pastel painters often use 'glass paper' on which to paint, just as oil painters use canvas. The glass paper provides the 'key' on to which the pigment attaches and because of this, a pastel painting is often so realistic in tone and colour.

Unfortunately, glass paper comprises a layer of fine sand which is stuck on to the paper with glue. This glue absorbs moisture, so it is vital that when glass paper is used for pastel painting, the picture is kept in a very dry environment.

The walls of our 'Gallery' (which had been a game warehouse) were constructed from clay lump and no damp proof course. This wasn't a problem when storing game as the damp kept the temperature quite low, but as a support for a pastel painting it couldn't have been worse. Although it was nicely decorated and looked perfect for a place to hang paintings, it could not have been worse.

The sandpaper had absorbed moisture (of which there was plenty) through the back of the picture against the walls and this resulted in the paper buckling and losing its 'flatness'.

As it buckled, and came into contact with the glass, the pastel pigment stuck to the glass and effectively destroyed the painting.

My heart was sinking as I saw what had happened over night. My heart raced as my mind tried to think of a solution.

I opened the 'Yellow Pages' and phoned every Painting restorer listed in the East of England. I carefully explained the predicament that I was in. No one wanted to get involved. Some suggested a hair dryer to get rid of the moisture, so I tried that. Yes, the paper did 'straighten' a bit, but in doing so it left a nasty smear of pastel on the inside of the glass.

There was no alternative. I had to phone Margaret and confess.

Margaret's Husband was her manager. He did all the admin and the commercial side while she painted. He answered the phone.

I was most apologetic and offered to pay for the damage (knowing that if he had demanded that it would take a month or more to earn that sort of money).

I remember his response to this day.

'Do not worry, old chap, I'll bring some replacements over straight away. Funny that, we were experimenting with a new kind of glass paper and hadn't used it before. We will go back to our old supplier!' I could have hugged him!

Not only did those exhibitions introduce Sarah to the commercial side of Painting, it introduced me to another aspect of being an 'Exhibition Curator' which I wasn't keen to repeat!

Those exhibitions, however, were great fun, and when Sarah went to Art College (having spent a year at Art School in France) she certainly had some experience in exhibiting her work.

As mentioned earlier, Life often 'gets in the way' and so it was for me, for it was not for another twenty years that I was able to indulge my secret passion.

Pat and I had been invited to an exhibition in a swanky London gallery which was now owned and run by Roy Petley who I had met through a great friend and painter Alfred Saunders. The exhibition was showing the work of two painters, Desmond and Patricia Turner – father and daughter from Ireland. It was amazing.

I met up with Desmond who said that he ran annual courses in Ireland and he had a place on the next one coming up a month later. I signed up.

Pat and I went over to Ireland and stayed in a rented cottage, complete with Peat fire and I did nothing other than paint – all day and every day, from very early in the morning until late at night. For the first time in my life I had no distraction and I could paint. It was the most wonderful two weeks of my life and when we returned home I was really fired up to become a painter and immediately started building a studio on the field at the back of the house.

The difficult bit was that the field lies in an area of outstanding natural beauty and with the increasing use of satellites to spy on people like me, the Planning Department can keep tabs on unauthorised developments.

The challenge was to create a studio that looked like a shed so as not to attract the attention of under employed council workers.

And that is exactly what I did. With a digger, I excavated a hole six feet deep, poured ready mixed concrete to form the floor and foundations and I built a largish studio. I have always enjoyed building. It seems to satisfy a primitive need in me to create something of a permanent nature – a bit like painting I suppose, and over the years I've done my share of construction. In the early years in Cornwall Leonard and I built the pig's houses, the dairy and other buildings; in Bristol I added two bedrooms, a porch and a utility room to our bungalow; at Meadowside I built greenhouses out of bricks and blocks as well as walls and sheds; in Tattingstone I built an extension and at Algar's Barn once again I built sheds, workshops and a micro-propagation house so the construction of my studio didn't present me with too great a challenge.

Once at ground level I continued upwards and finished it with a flat roof. Once I had cladded the outside with feather edge board it certainly looked no different from an allotment-standard garden shed. But if you cared to open the door you were immediately on a landing from which a staircase took you down to tiled floor of the studio. Heated by a wood burning 'Pot Bellied' Stove and full lighting was provided from a petrol generator to enhance the natural light from the north-facing windows.

It was a very sad time when, having moved to Eye, a serious accident meant that I could no longer do the work necessary to keep the field and because of the economic situation that I found myself in, I sold the field and polytunnel and, of course, the lovely studio.

And now, as I quickly approach the octogenarian state, I paint as much as I can and I have just agreed to rent a studio into which I can disappear and spend a day painting when I am moved to do so. Despite the advancing years, I am still trying to learn to paint, improve my techniques and make up for all those years in which I just lacked the courage to 'follow my dream'. Maybe next time I'll do it differently.

26
THE SHOTLEY PENINSULAR

If I am going to leave a record of what I've done during my lifetime, then it would be wrong not to include something about the Shotley Peninsular.

That lovely part of Suffolk – which thankfully is still a very well-kept secret - has been very much a part of my life from the age of 11 and continues to be so today. Not only do I continue to make the journey along the A140 and A14, then under the Orwell Bridge to Freston and beyond, in order to visit my grandchildren at school, but I go to the banks of the Orwell and Stour to paint. I go to Alton Water for Caspian to attend sailing courses and we frequently walk around to Pin Mill and finish with a pint or a meal. Until recently I kept my boat in Shotley and have sailed the two rivers more times than I care to remember, from Ipswich to Mistley. During the exciting times of the Shotley sailing School, the two rivers, one lying east /west and the other north/south, meant that no matter what direction the wind was coming from, nor how hard it blew, we could always find somewhere sheltered to teach our students to sail.

Right in the middle of the Shotley Peninsular, is The Royal Hospital School, which has been a very important part of my life for a number of reasons which I am sure I've mentioned before in different sections of this book. Now, I would just like to bring them all together in one short chapter.

My Dad didn't have much influence on or involvement in the upbringing of Leonard and me, simply because he was in the Royal Navy and his duties took him far from home, especially when we were growing up. Leonard had a rough deal. Because he was being bullied and not doing too well in the local primary school and all the signs were that he would not be passing the 'Eleven Plus' he went to live with friends of Mum in Bromley in Kent and went to the local school. It must have been a very traumatic time for him, for he hardly knew the family and Bromley was quite different to Eye. But the poor little chap just got on with it and did his best, but it must have been very hard for him.

Despite the upheaval and change of schools he didn't pass the 11+ and came home to the Secondary Modern which was essentially the same environment that he had suffered under, a year or so earlier at the primary school.

Dad knew of Holbrook. It was a charity school set up principally for the sons of seafarers when it was established in Greenwich many years ago. It transferred to the banks of the Stour and reopened there in 1933 continuing to provide an education for sons of naval personnel and Dad thought it would be a good idea if Leonard and I went there. I don't think Mum was terribly happy about it but obviously agreed after considering the alternatives. So Dad made all the arrangements.

Once again, Leonard drew the short straw. He was eighteen months older than me, so he was the ice breaker and endured it for a year or so before I started. He did have a little support in that our cousin Bruce, whose father had lost his life in HMS Exmouth, joined RHS too and entered Anson house a couple of terms after Leonard started, so when it was my turn I had both Bruce and Leonard to show me the ropes.

I became a Petty Officer Boy – a House prefect -and was put into the upper stream and by a quirk of fate, as my birthday was in February I joined the school in May and at the time was the youngest in the school. The only advantage to this, that I can remember is that I was chosen to present a Bouquet of flowers to Lady Jellicoe when she came to open the new woodwork and metalwork block.

I appeared to progress through the years quite well, always in the top three of the class and even picked up a prize for Poetry (something that my Mum was very proud of and reminded me frequently of how I had never lived up to the promise shown!)

The difficulty for me was my Housemaster. For some reason, probably quite justified, he appeared not to like me very much (but having said that, why did he make me a House Prefect?) Although there was an opportunity for me to stay on to Sixth form and try for University, I chose to leave the school at 15 and 4 months and try my luck in the Navy. My grandparents and my Mum were very disappointed at this decision but to alleviate their worry I promised to get to Dartmouth from the Lower Deck – which I did, and I achieved that whilst my grandfather was alive! I don't often 'name drop' simply because I don't rub shoulders with famous people but through my school days at RHS I have great chance to change that. My academic journey was very short but as we progressed from Upper 1 to Upper 5 (when I left the school), the person with who I always competed with for the top place in the form was no less that John Studd, who stayed on into the sixth form and then studied medicine, becoming the World Expert on Hormone Replacement Therapy with many Books, Studies and Academic Papers to his name. For a brief moment in my life I was in a position where I had great potential – never to be repeated and never achieved! Now I know why my Mum was so upset when I told her that I was joining the Navy. At times, on reflection, I look back with regret at this decision, but then when I consider the bigger picture, my grandmother was, from the time I was old enough to understand the need for a job, constantly telling me that I was 'just like your father' and that 'you will join the Navy just like him'. My grandmother was not overly keen on my Dad so her assessment of me, my ability and character and the fact that I was 'your father's son', was not the greatest compliment that she could have given me. But the seeds were sown, and it should not have come as a great surprise to anyone that I fulfilled the promise and became a sailor.

HMS Ganges, just around the bend in the river from RHS was the next stop and despite it being similar in many ways to a Borstal Institution (a Corrective Training Establishment or 'Boot camp') I found it quite easy. As I completed my training I collected an arm full of prizes and when my contemporaries left for further training and then their first ship, I was transferred to the Annex – the satellite establishment to Ganges where the New Recruits arrive and are 'broken in' to naval life. I was to be an 'Instructor Boy' effectively a poorly paid member of staff.

When I next returned to Shotley some twenty five years later it was to create the Shotley Sailing School in a marina that once had been the Lower Playing Field where we had competed in track and field athletics; learnt how to dismantle a field gun, heave it over a wall and over a chasm; reassemble it and run with it for 100 yards before firing a couple of rounds. Now it was a posh marina with a lock which gave access to the River Stour at all states of the tide.

The sailing school came at a time when I'd had a rest from dentistry and moved to Tattingstone but Holbrook had loomed large in our lives well before that.

On being released from the Navy

I became a teacher and RHS provided me with my first job, which I have recorded in another chapter. This was a wonderful couple of years and looking back, it seemed like a never-ending childhood when the weather was always sunny. My memory of that two years teaching is one of cloudless skies and long walks to the beaches at Harkstead. I'm sure it wasn't all like this, but it certainly seems like it! The children went to Holbrook Primary and it was a very happy time.

After the Sailing School came the Dental Job at RHS and the very bad decision to go to Cornwall. In the months following my departure from the Dental Surgery at RHS I had many letters from the children at RHS who I had treated, saying how sorry that they were that I was no longer there which was very touching and only compounded the feeling of sadness that I had when I realised the move had been for nothing.

I am now unable to sail so I've sold my last boat – a heavenly Twins catamaran called 'Sassi'. It is fitting that I handed her over to her new owner In Shotley Marina and my last sail was with

Bean and Lorca and we sailed up the Stour into Holbrook Bay from where, from the river we could see RHS in all its glory.

But Holbrook still plays an important part in my life.

Bean is now in the Sixth form; Lorca has started in Blake House and is Captain of the Under 12 rugby team and Lucia has passed her entrance exam and will be starting there in September 2017. There are very few weekends when I'm not at RHS for some reason or another – either to pick Bean up for a driving lesson or to bring him home; to attend divisions and chapel, the school play, a concert or to watch Lorcs in a Rugby match and to take a bag full of tuck to replenish his stocks. His rugby team mates look forward to me being there I think, as they always hang around after the match in the hope that my pockets are stuffed with sweets and other goodies to help with energy levels after a hard-fought match.

In theory I shall now have more time to paint and my next exhibition is to feature paintings of the Orwell and Stour for it is to these two rivers and their marine environment which will continue to inspire my paintings for many years to come.

Two paintings from my 'Orwell' Series.

27
The Making of an Unusual Film

As a mature student at Bristol, with two young children, I was determined that I would not fail any of my exams (I just could not afford to!) so I got involved in as much activity at the Dental Hospital as I possible could, simply to broaden my experience.

The Prosthetic Department, not yet into Dental Implants, as they had yet to be developed for general use, were leaders in their field and heavily into research, despite the fact that theirs was the most unglamorous area of Dentistry. Research included dental materials, methods of construction of dental prostheses, and design and construction of crowns and bridges and in this case, film making.

One of the great mysteries of full dentures was why some patients adapted so quickly to them and others would never be able to tolerate them. Full dentures, one would hope, were a thing of the past, especially in a progressive and educated society. Sadly, this was not so, and multiple extraction of teeth followed by the insertion of a full set of plastic knashers was still a very common treatment option. In fact, I met several people who had been subjected to this procedure and fitted up with a full upper and lower denture on attaining their 21st birthday!

The two professors at the Head of the Prosthetics department were ex-servicemen. The main man, Prof David Berry was a Flight Lieutenant Flying Instructor in the RAF until he went to Bristol to read dentistry at the end of the War. His side kick was a Surgeon Rear Admiral and I got on very well with both of them. So when I asked if I could assist in the research that they were about to begin, they were delighted, as not many students actively volunteered for such extra-curricular activity.

A high proportion of Denture wearers have problems of some

kind, but mostly with either stability or retention. Stability, (or lack of it) is frequently exacerbated by poor design, such that during speech and mastication the muscles and soft tissues dislodge the denture. A small amount of disturbance can often be dealt with by the wearer, but when it is severe is may result in complete ejection from the mouth! If, however, the retention of the denture is good, instability is usually not an issue. They are inextricably linked.

At least, that is the theory. In practice it can be quite different, and one frequently comes up against a situation where everything that is humanly possible to do to improve retention has been done and yet the patient is far from happy. Some patients return to the surgery time after time after time, and the dentist finds it increasingly difficult to think of anything to do that might alleviate the problem or indeed make the patient happy. Sometimes one's only escape route is to tell the patient to keep the denture whilst refunding their money and advising them of the address of another dentist nearby! Passing the problem on to your unsuspecting colleague is often the only way out.

Some dentists refuse to provide dentures, and certainly not on the NHS as the 'hassle factor' is so high. If a Private Fee is charged that is so exorbitant many would be patients are excluded by the price and when the offer is taken up, at least there is room within the fee to employ the best laboratory for their manufacture, thereby increasing the chances of success, especially if the patient is made aware of the high end technical skills that have been involved in sorting out their teeth.

That is just one side of the story. Other patients have their teeth removed one day and dentures inserted on the same day and never have a problem. They eat what they like, never take them out, chew sweets and steak with no difficulty whatsoever. Some have sore spots that look really painful but evidently are no cause for concern whilst others would protest in the loudest and most hostile way even when the mouth ulcer was miniscule.

Professor Berry wanted to investigate the relationship between the fit of a denture and the degree of satisfaction as recorded by the patient. He wanted to try and assess if the retention and fit of the denture and movement during mastication – the overall stability - were related to the 'satisfaction level' of the patient. The only way to do this was on film. But not an ordinary film, it had to be an X-ray film which captured the movement of the dentures during mastication so that each patient could be scored according the observed stability of the denture. If this score was then matched to the patient's opinion of the 'success' of the denture, (and satisfaction level) the results may throw some light on why some people were always complaining about their dentures, whilst others never did.

A number of patients were chosen from the regulars who attended the Bristol Dental Hospital, where, it must be admitted, the treatment was free and therefore that aspect of the equation could be eliminated. (A high fee might heighten some patients' expectations, whilst it may have a reverse effect on others.)

Dentures for our 'film stars' were carefully constructed to a standard criteria using a barium salt in the Acrylic Base material so that they could be seen on X-ray. They were given a few days to get used to the new dentures and any sore spots were eased so that when we started filming, to all intents and purposes, the patient had been discharged from the clinic with a perfectly good and functional set of full dentures (at least from a clinical perspective1

Come the day of filming, a fruit bun, with once again a small amount of Barium Salt included in the ingredients was provided for each patient and the X-ray camera and screen set up so that the patient, wearing the new dentures would be viewed in profile and filmed whilst eating the bun. I must add at this stage, Barium Salts are used frequently in medical procedures and cause no harm to the patient.

The filming process was interesting – as you might imagine, considering the actors were all Bristolians of varying backgrounds, all beyond middle age and representing the full range of the social spectrum. But it got completed. And that was no mean feat since X-Ray cinematic photography was not generally available and as an artistic genre, was in its infancy!

The films were made and at the end of each filming, each patient was given a very comprehensive questionnaire to complete so that there was no doubt as to what the wearer thought of their dentures.

When the film was developed, it was very amusing, especially as this was the first showing of anything in this genre. This was the first time X-rays had been used to create such a film as this in the name of scientific research. On the screen we could see the patient's skull in profile, with the mandible and the maxilla (lower and upper jaws respectively) showing clearly with the dense outline and shape of the full upper and lower denture. At the start of the sequence, the teeth were together ('in occlusion') with full contact between the upper and the lower plates.

As we watched, a skeleton hand came up from the lower left and in between the thumb and fingers was an object which turned out to be the 'Barium Bun'. As the BB approached, the jaws parted, the outline of the lips opened and the false teeth took hold of the nearest bit of Barium Bun. For the next minute or so, we witnessed the massacre of the BB and once it had disintegrated, it disappeared down the throat of the subject. The common feature of all the films was the skeleton hand bringing the bun to the mouth and the first bite being taken. From then on, everyone was different.

Some dentures hardly moved during the process and exhibited high stability whilst in other cases it looked as though there was a battle royal being waged, with dentures, bun and tongue all fighting for position until the pulverised bun pieces had vanished down the throat and the dentures returned to their 'resting positions'.

From what we had witnessed, we could see quite clearly that in some patients the dentures were stable and retentive for they hardly moved during the process of eating. At the other end of the spectrum it was quite, quite different – the dentures were anything but stable and retentive, for they moved around by a surprising degree during the filming and I think that surprised us more than anything - that in some patients, there was no semblance of stability and the dentures appeared to have a mind of their own.

It was so obvious that some patients really did have a problem with interference of the dentures whilst eating whilst others had little to complain about. It looked as though the conclusion to this experiment would be as predicted from our observations. That was until we had analysed the data from the questionnaires and compared it to the film.

The results were stunning - the opposite to what we had

postulated. The data showed quite clearly that many patients who had the less stable and less retentive dentures, were happiest with them, and those who generally had stable dentures, complained the most.

The outcome of this research suggested that those patients who were able to quickly learn the art of keeping a denture in place (with tongue and soft tissue) and then submit this learning to the sub conscious, were the ones whose lives would be unaffected by wearing a denture. But for those who were unable to push 'denture wearing' into the subconscious, would be the ones who always had a problem. And for some, their lives would be made miserable because of this.

I don't think the film was ever put on general release, but it was a most interesting experiment to have been involved in as a student.

28
On Busking

I've always liked the idea of busking. Of course, if one embarks upon such an activity, it usually means that a musical instrument is involved, together with a certain proficiency in its use. I have none of these. But having said that, some time ago, when I still owned the field at the back of Algar's Barn, I frequently headed off in the direction of one of my sheds with a clarinet under my arm, where, away from distraction and beyond the hearing range of most humans, I set about teaching myself to play it.

Self- praise is worthless but at the risk of being considered impossibly conceited, I must say that after six months of daily toil, I thought that I was doing well, and I was quite pleased with myself. In fact, my ambition to play the instrument well enough to busk for a few minutes was almost reaching fruition. Sadly, life got in the way – we moved, then moved again, we looked after Bean whilst Sarah was working in Spain then the business collapsed. Clarinet playing got pushed further and further down the list and it was such a long time before I started up again, that when I did, I found to my horror, that I had really forgotten much of what I had learned. I was a beginner again. The expression that 'if you don't use it, you lose it' was painfully accurate. I would just like to add that the older one gets, the greater the need for daily practice, for without continual reinforcement the brain soon ejects that which has been recently learned.

It was therefore so wonderful to have two grandchildren who appear to enjoy music. Bean started with the violin whilst at Diss High School, and after only three months tuition appeared solo at an evening Concert in Diss. Sadly it didn't last, although there were times when it looked as though he might progress to better things. When he started at RHS he had music lessons and during one particular lesson his violin teacher asked for a volunteer to play the Viola. Bean volunteered, so I bought one on eBay and took it over to Woodbridge Violins for checking over and new strings if necessary.

Whilst waiting for the owner of the shop to deal with my request, the lady on the desk asked me about the instrument and when I told her it was for my grandson who was a pupil at RHS. 'What a co-incidence' she said. 'My friend teaches the violin at that school and she told me the other day that she had taken on a new pupil to play the viola. She was very excited about this because, she said, 'he's a natural'".

When I heard this, the hairs stood up on the back of my neck. She was talking about my grandson.

Anyway, it didn't last. He asked to drop the music lessons as he had too many other things to do and not least of all, he had to catch up with his GCSEs. He had only just started at that school so had been on another syllabus for GCSEs at his previous school, so I could understand his concerns. That was the end of his musical career.

Next came Lorca. Lorcs said that he would like to play the flute. Being a bit cautious after the Beannie experience, I said to Lorcs that if he could demonstrate to me that he had the ability to learn to play an instrument (the recorder) and that he could cope with practising regularly, I would buy him a flute.

We started in September and within two months he was quite proficient, and I was amazed at how quickly he had picked it up and at his inherent musicality. Because he had done so well, I bought him a flute in December, together with a guide book and he was very soon playing a few notes. Biddy Channon who lives next door but one, agreed to teach him and under her tuition Lorcs made good progress. He missed Grade one, took Grade 2 at Easter then Grade 3 three months later. He was especially fired up because he wanted to join the Band at RHS and thought that he would be able to do so as soon as he started there.

Sadly, that didn't happen despite me writing to the Bandmaster asking if Lorca could join, and for a couple of terms he didn't make much progress. On the next term I enrolled him for music lessons and since then has performed in several concerts and 'Notes and

Nibbles' on a Monday lunch time when students perform in front of the general Public.

That summer he was due to go to France for a trip with his school so wanted to find a way of earning some money to cover the cost.

Busking. That was an idea that he seemed prepared to consider, so, during the summer holidays he learned a selection of tunes and melodies and I bought a battery driven amplifier and microphone, and off we went. I'd painted a board saying 'Hello, my name is Lorca, I am 12 years old and am trying to raise some money to pay for a school trip. Thank you.' And placed it at the foot of his music stand as he set up his gear in Mere Street, Diss.

Not unnaturally, he was quite nervous on the first day. We put all the gear outside the 'Grape Tree' Health Food shop in Diss purely because it was centrally placed along Mere Street and, more to the point it had an overhang above which might keep a bit of the rain off. He fiddled a lot with the music stand, with the microphone, with the amplifier, with the music until he had nothing more to fiddle with, and he started to play. On the way to Diss, we had discussed the subject of what he might take during the afternoon. We thought that he might be lucky to get £40 but if the crowds were not too generous, then he'd have to accept less. In any case, this was a Thursday and we were going to busk for no more than an hour and a half, just so that we knew what to do the following morning which was Market Day.

It went well. His playing seemed to have been well received although he didn't count his takings, he put them in a bag ready for tomorrow, but from the look at the coins in the old violin case it was a promising start.

The next day, Diss was heaving. Other buskers were about and were vying for the best pitch. One had taken Lorca's spot by the Grape Tree, so we had no choice but to take up a pitch closer to the market. This was nerve-racking for Lorcs. There was no shelter from the crowds, or the elements and he was right in the middle of the market. It must have been very intimidating for him. But he played well, and the punters liked him and after a couple of hours his violin case was bursting.

A constant stream of people came to put money in to the case. Many asked him about his trip to France, many wanted to know about his school. Many asked about his name as 'Lorca' is not a common name in Diss! He spent almost as much time talking to 'his public' as he did playing his flute.

It was humbling to see so many elderly people, obviously on limited income, stop and rummage in their purse for some change. But it wasn't only the elderly, many youngsters too, made a contribution to his pile of cash and a ten-pound note was not an uncommon sight. One gentleman stood in front of Lorcs and listened to him play whilst reading the board in front. He carefully took out of his pocket a ten-pound note and a business card. He handed the money to Lorca, congratulating him of his initiative at such a young age, and added, pointing to the board 'And, if you don't raise enough money to pay for the trip, call me and I'll make up the difference'.

It was an emotional day, and he was quite tired when we got home but he was not too exhausted to count his haul. There was no way that we could have been prepared for that, but on the final count, over the two days – one hour on Thursday and double that on the Friday, Lorca had collected £450.

Opposite his pitch in the Market, there was a collector for The Salvation Army and when Lorca had worked out his costs for the trip to France, he had almost £50 over so he donated that to the Salvation Army. An amazing gesture from one so young.

That was last year and now the goal posts have moved. The next school trip is with the Band, in 2020 to Dubai, The Emirates and Shri Lanka and the cost is high. He's got to find over £2k (well, someone has to!) so the more that he can earn the better.

He's been on half term and think that that has inhibited him somewhat. He was a bit concerned about a lot of other children of his age, lurking around the streets of Diss whilst he was playing. Teenage sensitivity I suppose. Anyway, on the Thursday of the second week we set our gear up outside the Grape Tree as usual and spent an hour and a half playing to the half term shoppers. And they loved it too. One lady handed over £30 and several gave five-pound notes. Gathering around the Kebab shop a hundred yards away, were twenty or so teenage lads from the local High Schools several from well-known families in the area! In any other town they would have been intimidating but this was Diss. As they passed, the sky went dark as the sun was excluded by their mass. And as the 'swarm' passed by Lorcs, it slowed, whilst hands were put into pockets to rummage for spare cash and as they placed the change in Lorca's muttered 'well done bro' or 'Cool, bro'.

I can think of no better compliment for Lorcs from his peers than 'Cool, Bro'. And I'm sure he took it on board too. His haul today was £145, which, for 90 minutes work, was, by any standard, pretty amazing.

As before, that hour on the Thursday was just a rehearsal for the following day. We turned up at ten-thirty to claim our pitch only to find it occupied by a disabled lady, in a largish disability scooter, slugging back a 'Costa Coffee' and she showed no signs of being in a hurry to move so we set up in the adjacent bay, outside the Grape Tree. The wind was whistling down Mere Street and it was a cold one too, and our new pitch was rather exposed and at irregular intervals the odd sheet of music took flight and I had to leg it in its wake until it came down to earth. The board, being considerably heavier, didn't lift off but was blown over several times so from my ringside seat on the terraces of 'Costa Coffee' opposite Lorca, I was kept busy retrieving the misbehaving musical scores and board. At one stage, I even tied the music stand to Lorca's body to stop that being pushed over by the wind. But patience and perseverance prevailed. We stuck it out for 90 minutes and he was well rewarded, although not with the blessing of everybody. The chap on the adjacent pitch, selling 'The Big Issue' was not happy at the perceived intrusion in to his space, but I pretended not to hear him and helped Lorcs set up his stand.

The busker from the next pitch came to have a word with Lorcs. He had been playing a complicated musical construction consisting of drums, cymbals and guitar with backing tape whilst singing Country and Western. I suppose you would describe him as a musical multi-tasker. He came over to give Lorcs a bit of advice on the delicate subject of intrusion into another busker's space. I'm sure that he had a point. Mere Street is not very big and the only spaces for busking are along the pedestrian bit. There were two other buskers when we arrived, and we set up mid- way between them – in what we consider to be 'our' pitch so together with the Big Issue seller, there was a lot of demand for shoppers' money – and that was in addition to the shopping list in their bags.

There's been a lot of bad publicity in the local press regarding Buskers, caused mostly by the high volume coming from a local chap who, whilst not really appreciating that he's not very musical, insisted on playing the same old stuff whist shouting in a most un-musical way for a period of three hours. The shop keepers felt that his presence was detrimental to the commercial survival of the shop behind him, so it was made clear that in future, Buskers should get permission from the shopkeeper before they set up their pitch. We have always done that and without exception Lorca has always been made to feel very supported and welcome.

The busker from next door came to advise Lorcs, in the nicest possible way that in the etiquette of buskers, it wasn't a good thing to encroach on another busker's pitch. He had no issue with it, but others might, and he thought that Lorcs ought to know about it. He was very friendly and talked to Lorcs about the trip he was earning money for and then offered to buy him a coffee.

After 90 minutes of wind and cold, we decided to call it a day and packed up and went home. Even as we were closing the pitch down, people were still coming to give him money. His playing was better today, and he's learned a new song 'Danny Boy'. It was very interesting watching the punters respond to this piece. When he played it first he got seven people moved to put money in his case – like bees attracted to a flower.

His takings for the day were £126 so over the two days he took about £270.

And all for a total of two and a half hours work. Who said there was no future in Busking.

Lucia plays the Clarinet and joined Lorca for a session of busking. Lucia's instrument has a most beautiful tone and together they make a lovely sound. Now that Lorcs has got Grade 5 and Lucia Grade 2, they could be on their way to a musical duo and I am looking forward to being with them when they busk in Diss during the warmer weather. The big problem that we face is how to divide the takings!

EPILOGUE

Epilogue. ... An epilogue or epilog (from Greek ἐπίλογος epílogos, "conclusion" from ἐπί epi, "in addition" and λόγος logos, "word") is a piece of writing at the end of a work of literature, usually used to bring closure to the work.

The Epilogue, or conclusion, to this piece of writing, almost occurred six years ago.

Had that happened, it would have been a little inconvenient in that the conclusion occurred before the story had been written, as I penned most of this whilst recovering from that accident. Had I not recovered (and the odds weren't in my favour) it would have been like the Final Curtain at a Theatre Production coming down before the play had started!

We were living in Eye – at 48 Church Street. It was a sunny day and I set off to collect Bean from Diss High School. He could easily have walked home, (to Walcot Green) but I wasn't doing anything else and I just wanted to keep an eye on him as he had suffered a bit of bullying from the lads in his year. Walking home would give them another opportunity to continue with this unpleasant activity, but not if I were there.

I still find it amazing that despite all that happened subsequently, and the time that has lapsed since that day, I can still remember as clearly as though it were yesterday, everything that happened up to the point where I was rendered unconscious.

I came up to the 'T' junction at Brome and as I looked left there was the empty road and I thought to myself how unusual that was, at this time of day. It was a very sunny day and no cars on the A140 heading north! I indicated that I wanted to turn right.

As I looked to the right, I saw an HGV. Not the usual type, but one that was taller than average. It was white and had no livery markings on the front – also somewhat unusual. Anyway, it was about 100 meters distant, was slowing down and indicating left. It obviously intended to travel down the road that I was on. Another look to the left confirmed that the road was clear and I was safe to cross and head north along the A140.

My next recollection was waking up, in the dark, surrounded by people I didn't know. I was lying on the edge of the road and my back was very painful. A doctor then explained to me that I had been involved in an accident and that I would soon be taken to the Norfolk and Norwich Hospital where my injuries could be attended to. He was from the Air Ambulance and had it not been for another call out, I would have been taken to hospital by air but there had been another severe accident in Thetford and, as I was now conscious, they had to leave me to go to the Norfolk and Norwich Hospital by road.

The Para-medics were amazing and once in the ambulance they phoned Pat with my mobile and told her to come to the N&N. Once inside A&E they started assessing my injuries and after a few X-rays, they decided that I had broken my skull, my shoulder, and seven ribs and my liver was torn, and my kidney crushed, and my right lung had collapsed. It wasn't until three weeks later that they found that my leg had been broken too (and the senior Radiographic Consultant apologised profusely that they had missed it!) The biggest problem was in the rib-cage. Although seven were broken, they were not simple fractures and amongst it all I had what they call a 'flail chest'. This is where a section of the rib cage is completely detached and 'free floating' so what when I breathed in, as the rib cage expanded and the pressure inside dropped, the free-floating bit of rib moved inwards, and the ends of the broken ribs caressed each other as they passed. It was very painful. The Consultant in charge of me was brutal in getting me to cough a number of times during every one of his visits, which I began to dread. He was so concerned about me getting pneumonia on the ward that he agreed to let me go home in to Pat's care as soon as I was able to 'Zimmer' around the ward.

Leonard and Helen came up from Cornwall to see me and father Andrew came to give me what he considered 'the last Rights'.

The day before I was discharged it snowed heavily and there were still a few inches on the ground when they sent me home. It was good to be back in Eye and luckily our downstairs bedroom with the en-suit shower and toilet made life so much easier. I was unable to do anything for myself, but I had no need for concern as Pat was such an expert in looking after people in my condition and I know that I made much better progress under her care.

I hadn't been home more than a couple of days before we had a visit from a Policeman who, it transpires, was the traffic cop assigned to deal with the accident in which I was involved the week before at Brome Crossroads.

He was very officious and interviewed me 'under caution'. He admitted to me, early on in the interview that he was determined to charge me, 'if for other reason that being the cause of the A140 being closed for 5 hours'.

'If', he said 'you plead guilty to causing this accident, we will not press for charges as long as you surrender your licence'.

Of course I refused to agree to this as I knew full well that I was not responsible for this accident. David, my neighbour was very supportive and went out of his way to try and prove my innocence. Although his help was invaluable, I had to get a lawyer involved to stop the ludicrous quest by the traffic cop to get me done for dangerous driving.

Lawyers are not cheap and at £250 per hour plus expenses he was engaged to help me clear my name. The Suffolk Police hadn't done much of a job investigating this accident. The chap who hit me refused to make a statement: the person behind him, (we think a friend from Bedford who was to give him a lift back home after delivering his car to Humphries, just up the road) stated that I had pulled out in front of the Audi and that he didn't have a chance to avoid me. Suffolk Police had made up their mind – I was guilty of dangerous driving and they wanted me to go to court.

My solicitor put our case to the Crown Prosecution Service saying that the damage to the vehicles was not consistent with me pulling out in front of the other vehicle. If this was how it happened the damage to my car would have been on the side. In fact it was from the off-side front which could only have occurred if my car was heading north on the other carriageway.

The damage to the Audi was centred on the 'off-side' too, and the only place where the two cars with this damage would fit together is on the opposite carriageway.

My solicitor suggested to the CPS that I crossed the carriageway ahead on the HGV that was turning in to the road which I was leaving. The Audi, seeing the Lorry indicating left, overtook it only to find that there were two bollards opposite the turn. He then went the other side of the bollards and hit me on the far carriageway as I completed the right turn.

The CPS, obviously not happy with Suffolk Police's findings, referred the case to another Force for further investigation. A week later it came back saying that there no grounds for prosecuting me and all charges should be dropped. Whilst that was very welcome news it still left many questions unanswered and in particular why the Suffolk Police were just not interested in investigating the 'science' of the accident further.

My insurance company were quite dismissive too – they just said that the vehicle joining the main road from a minor road is responsible if an accident occurs, which means that irrespective of how the vehicle on the main carriageway behaves the responsibility will always be with the car coming from the minor road. I was advised that if I got a Forensic Team involved (at my expense), they would probably come to the same conclusion that was obvious to me, when they considered the only position in which the damaged vehicles could fit together. Pat convinced me that I should not go down this route. Her opinion was that I was lucky to be alive and I should be content with that. Chasing the driver of the other car, in order to establish his responsibility for this accident, would be stressful, expensive and may not deliver the result that I was hoping for.

'Let it go' was her advice and, difficult though it has been, that's what I have done.

During my recovery period, when I was unable to do very much, I thought that one way of filling in the time usefully was to record the story of my life which might be of interest to my grandchildren's children. Because I had regretted not having any record of the lives of my parents or grandparents, I thought that this might be a suitable project to occupy my brain whilst getting back to full health and mobility.

This 'Epilogue' is therefore just that.

It brings to a conclusion the story of my life despite the fact that I continue to live and enjoy life. This 'epilogue' could easily have been so different in that it could really have brought about the end of my time on earth. The extent of my injuries and the circumstances of that accident were such that not many would have given me much of a chance to survive. But survive I did, and that is due to Pat's love and professional care during my recovery, the power of prayer and to luck.

As my story reveals, throughout my life I have been the beneficiary of a lot of luck, perhaps more than I deserve, and it now appears that that is holding, right to the end!

But the story continues...........

29
Dentistry

Having been involved in Dentistry for the best part of my adult life, once I had retired, that interest didn't go away and every time dentistry was in the headlines, my ears pricked up. And my goodness, the profession appears always be in the news, mostly about the difficulty that some patients, in some areas have in accessing Dental Treatment under the NHS.

Shortly after I retired, the Government decided that Dental treatment was now costing far too much, so they commissioned a handful of academics to create a 'New Contract' for the Dental Profession which would deliver dentistry at much less cost. And therein lies the error. Those tasked to create this contract were academics and not 'wet-fingered dentists'. The contract they came up with was unworkable and totally unacceptable to the hard-working profession.

I'll just explain the basics of that contract.

Dentists cannot cherry-pick. If a patient comes to you for treatment and requires six fillings, you, the dentist have to complete all the fillings so when you sign off at the end of treatment that the patient is 'dentally fit', he or she, in your eyes does not require any further treatment and that patient really is 'Dentally fit'.

Here comes the small print. When the dentist has to do one filling he will get paid a fee for exam, 2 X-rays; scale and polish and one filling, let us say £26.00

If that patient requires a further 6 fillings, you, the dentist have to complete those as well, in order to get the patient 'dentally fit' and for that you would still get the same remuneration - £26.99

If you had a well established practice, where all of your 5000 patients had been cared for over the years by you, then when these patients came for their check-up, they were unlikely to require loads of fillings to get them 'dentally fit', so under those circumstances it was a workable arrangement.

One can see why established practices refused to take on new patients (for fear of them requiring a mouth-full of fillings .It appears that no-one in the NHS Dental Hierarchy can see this!

And now, as I write this, 80%of people cannot access NHS Dental treatment and have to go Private. This has spawned numerous Private Practices, many of which are run and owned by Dentists who really don't have the experience you would expect for a 'Private' Practice. The Government in their wisdom announced a generous 'golden hello' for anyone committing to work in the NHS. This is all very well but the problem remains the same. The contract is unworkable and those bright-eyed young things who commit to the NHS now will soon find that the contract works against them.

NHS dentistry should be looked at from a different standpoint. At the moment, the perceived responsibility for keeping the teeth in good order is the dentist, whereas it ought to be the patient. The Patient should take full responsibility for their own teeth and act accordingly.

Dentistry, like any other branch of medicine, is evolving constantly. New materials are developed; new equipment becomes available so the range of treatment available expands monthly, but you cannot expect the patient to fund these new changes.

I suggest that each patient is allowed to have a certain value of NHS treatment every year and this 'allowance' will include treatment to correct much of what resulted from 'wear and tear'. An idea to start might be: 2 fillings; scale and polish; 1 extraction. One partial denture; 2 x-rays. Plus a full oral examination. Any treatment beyond this would be applied for and, if approved would be charged out privately.

This routine would pass the responsibility to the patient and if they cleaned their teeth, they would be able to access NHS Dental Treatment.'

At the same time as this was coming into effect, Dental Students whilst at University, would have their tuition fees discounted by say 10% each year and in return, for a period of 5 years post qualifying, they would work in an NHS Practice under the watchful eye of a 'Registered Trainer'.

If this idea was taken up, dental students would benefit by a 10 per cent fee reduction; the demand for NHS treatment would return, there would be no need for the silly contract; and NHS treatment would once again be available.

30
Kidney Dialysis

For the past 20 years or so, I have been attending the Norfolk and Norwich University Hospital Renal Department as my kidneys have been failing. High Blood pressure has a very destructive effect on the kidneys and I suspect that this was in some way responsible for my renal failure. Another contributing factor was the use of sprays for control of aphids and the like in the greenhouses at the Nursery. I had a petrol driven power spray and I ought to have worn professional protective clothing. But I didn't and I'm now suffering for it.

Twenty years ago, the kidney consultant announce that my kidneys had 20 years of life left in them. To that I replied that I could deal with that, not realising for one moment that 20 years would pass in a flash. I was admitted to hospital as an emergency when the kidneys had finally given in, a line was placed into my neck and through this, I was dialysed several times to get me back to health. I was asked if I had a preference and I elected for home dialysis or peritoneal dialysis so this is what I started with.

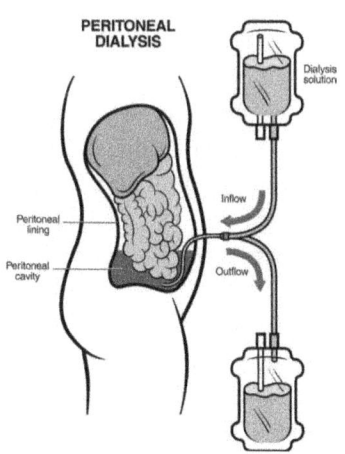

The catheter was to be inserted into by stomach at the same time as a hernia was repaired and because of the latter, the whole procedure was to be carried out by a General Surgeon. He came to see me post-operatively, saying that he hoped that he didn't have to replace it.

Why was that I asked.

'Well', he said 'the cathers are usually put in by kidney surgeons but as a hernia had to be repaired, I was ordered to do both'.

From that moment I realised that he hadn't put it in correctly so I checked it up on U Tube and asked the consultant if we could have another x-ray. He was very reluctant to, but agreed eventually to this, but when the film came back to reveal a 'kink, he said that it was OK really and the catheter would eventually gravitate to the correct position. The direction the catheter should follow ought to be a gentle curve passing beneath the belly-button and ending up at the lower extremities of the stomach in the pubic region. With my finger I could trace my catheter and I soon discovered a sharpish bend in it in the region of the bowel.

Six months later I had to go to A and E in the middle of the night with acute abdominal pain. A scan showed that the bend in the catheter was, because of its close proximity to the bowel, was causing erosion of the bowel. It was a late Saturday, early Sunday and the duty surgeon arrived and set himself the task of sorting the problem out. When I asked him how he was going to do that, he just said that he wanted the catheter OUT.

I then said 'I hope you are going to give me a GA for that'.

Without further discussion he grabbed the catheter, gave it a hefty tug and it was almost out.

The pain had taken me by surprise. 'You bastard' I shouted at him. 'At the kidney centre, when the staff want to take me blood pressure or my temperature, they ask my permission. You have assaulted me!'

He ignored my comments but just said 'I've got to do that once more and it will be all over'.

He then proceeded to give it another robust tug and it broke away from my stomach. I can still feel a short length of catheter under the skin of my stomach which I'm sure ought not to be there.

So that was the end of my time on Peritoneal dialysis and I

very sorry to finish with it for I had built my life around it and it appeared to work well with me. Essentially it was the body using the principle of Osmosis to get rid of the toxins. The catheter was used to introduce a bag of glucose (2litres) into the peritoneal space where it sat for 4 hours. The blood supply to the wall of the peritoneum was generous so any toxins in the blood would move over into the glucose by osmosis thus cleansing the blood as it passed through. After four hours, I drained the glucose and replaced it with a fresh bag. All of this was carried out at home and once a month we had a delivery of 60 boxes of glucose and all the other paraphernalia associated with this type of dialysis.

Once the catheter was out, I had only one option and that was haemodialysis but before this could be started, I had to have a minor operation where a very skilled surgeon spliced together a vein and an artery in my arm to create what is known as a 'fistula'.

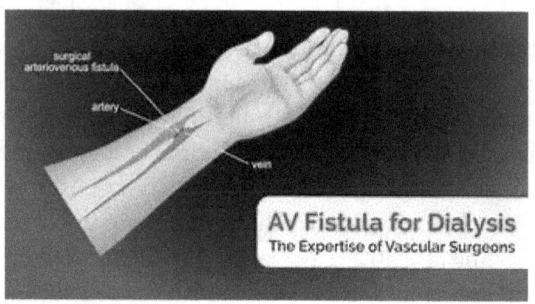

When the operation was finished, I had about a month's worth of exercises to get the fistula 'mature' before it is ready to accept needles. And now, it feels like a part-time job. On Mondays, Wednesdays and Fridays, I get picked up at 10 am, go and pick up Barry, then off to Stoke Holy Cross where Mervyn joins us and off we go to the Kidney centre. We each do roughly four hours on the machine, then home again, arriving home at approximately 6.30 – a long day. But............it keeps me alive! Without dialysis it would all be over.

For a long period, dialysis was purgatory. Every time I went of the machine I either started itching or had cramp, and neither was better than the other. Frequently the cramp was so bad that when the muscle contracted it actually pulled itself off the bone or tendon and it started to bleed within the limb. So dialysis became purgatory and after a couple of years like this I asked to see the Palliative Care Doctor when dialysis is stopped, the patient booked into a Hospice and the end arrives in a dignified manner. The PC Doctor spent over an hour with me and when he left he said 'Before I book you into the Hospice, I am going to speak with all the Consultants who are involved in your treatment, and ask them if there is any last thing they might be able to do for you.

The first thing to change was the medication. I was then put on Quinine and from that moment, my cramps vanished and for the first time, a session of dialysis was fairly comfortable. The Palliative Care Doctor had literally turned my life around. I've not had cramp to that degree since I started taking Quinine.

The staff who run the Kidney Centre are amazing and deserve a mention. The Kidney centre is located on an industrial estate four miles from the main hospital and has two parts. Home dialysis occupies about one third of the floorspace and Haemodialysis the reset and the home dialysis is exactly what it says it is , in that it trains the patients in that first step in peritoneal dialysis. Many patients don't bother with home dialysis but go straight to haemodialysis but I'm glad I did the home bit first. I'd still be on it had the surgeon put the catheter in the correct position.

The kidney centre work on a three shift per day, six days a week routine, starting at 7.30 am and going n to 10.00 at night so service about 80 patients at a time and the staff are dedicated to their job. In my case I have been attended to by some fabulous nurses whose main task when I arrive is to get the needles into my arm and then hook up to a machine where I remain for up to 4 hours. Teresa, Abbi, Melon, Rachel are but a few of the outstanding staff that look after me, but one in particular deserves a mention. Uma is Nepalese, born in Brunei and came to England when he dad, a Ghurka was, like all the Ghurkas, allowed to remain in this country after they had retired from active service. Uma went to University in London then additional training at Hammersmith Hospital, where Pat trained all those years ago. Uma was in charge of my bay when I was going through s difficult time with dialysis. Every session was purgatory but after the palliative care Doctor had helped my cause, Uma took over to ensure that I was getting the best possible dialysis whilst on the machine. She basically 'tuned' the machine and the treatment to suit me and as a result I went through a period where I had felt better than at any time over the previous four years. Uma was amazing and when I went for dialysis, I knew that Uma would ensure that I was receiving the best possible treatment. Sadly she has now been moved to another part of the Dialysis unit, so I now see her only occasionally. I would like to think that the quality of the treatment will be the same.

31
Dahlias

As you will have read, when we lived at Meadowside, we had an acre of land which I used to cultivate and from the sale of Dahlias, Nick was able to go skiing every year.

I took over the Alstromeria Nursery and sold my Dental Practice in 1986. Very quickly I had increased the number of polytunnels, increased the varieties of Alstromeria and had increased the range of flowers that we grew for the 'cut-flower' market.

Sarah lived in Gissing and her neighbour was a very hard-working lady called Gabbi. Gabbi had a spare tunnel, so I gave her enough Alstros to fill it and that part of her cut flower business was established.

Fast -forward the clock some forty years and Gabbi had rented a piece of land from thew council; had turned it into a productive little unit. Then her husband dies.

Gabbi came to see me to ask my advice about ways of increasing her cash-flow. I thought about it and came up with a solution. But I wanted to test the theory of this solution for viability, so I did a mail-shot down one side only of Church Street Eye.

It was a simple idea. I would buy in some attractive dahlias, bring them on early, harvest the shoots and grow those cuttings until they were big enough to plant out. I would then sell 'collections of Dahlia Cuttings similar to the 'collection' shown here,

At the end of the first year, I had proved beyond doubt that it was a workable idea especially if Gabbi used her extensive mailing list from 'Gabbi's garden'.

So I then gave Gabbi, all my tubers and detailed instructions on how to market this as a business.

My first-year trial was so successful that all my customers placed order for this year without me owning a Dahlia tuber!

I've sold about £400 worth of rooted cuttings this year, but my main focus this year is to cross- pollinate the best dahlias to see if I can grow a new one!. Watch this space!

I wonder if Sinatra would mind if I now quote part of a song that he has made so spectacularly famous as I just feel that it sums up my life (like it does for so many other people).

Have you got a minute?

And now, the end is near
And so I face the final curtain
My friend, I'll say it clear
I'll state my case, of which I'm certain
I've lived a life that's full
I travelled each and every highway
And more, much more than this
I did it my way
Regrets, I've had a few
But then again, too few to mention
I did what I had to do
And saw it through without exemption
I planned each charted course
Each careful step along the byway
And more, much more than this
I did it my way.

www.ingramcontent.com/pod-product-compliance
Lightning Source LLC
Chambersburg PA
CBHW050104170426
43198CB00014B/2459